Enhancing E-Learning with Media-Rich Content and Interactions

Richard Caladine
University of Wollongong, Australia

 Information Science Publishing

Hershey • New York

Acquisition Editor:	Kristin Klinger
Senior Managing Editor:	Jennifer Neidig
Managing Editor:	Jamie Snavely
Assistant Managing Editor:	Carole Coulson
Development Editor:	Kristin Roth
Assistant Development Editor:	Meg Stocking
Editorial Assistant:	Deborah Yahnke
Copy Editor:	Holly Powell
Typesetter:	Elizabeth Duke
Cover Design:	Lisa Tosheff
Printed at:	Yurchak Printing Inc.

Published in the United States of America by
      Information Science Publishing (an imprint of IGI Global)
      701 E. Chocolate Avenue
      Hershey PA 17033
      Tel: 717-533-8845
      Fax: 717-533-8661
      E-mail: cust@igi-global.com
      Web site: http://www.igi-global.com

and in the United Kingdom by
      Information Science Publishing (an imprint of IGI Global)
      3 Henrietta Street
      Covent Garden
      London WC2E 8LU
      Tel: 44 20 7240 0856
      Fax: 44 20 7379 3313
      Web site: http://www.eurospanbookstore.com

Library of Congress Cataloging-in-Publication Data

Caladine, Richard.
  Enhancing e-learning with media-rich content and interactions / Richard Caladine.
    p. cm.
  Summary: "This book presents instructional designers, educators, scholars, and researchers with the necessary foundational elements, theoretical underpinnings, and practical guidance to aid in the technology selection and design of effective online learning experiences by integrating media-rich interactions and content"--Provided by publisher.
  Includes bibliographical references and index.
  ISBN 978-1-59904-732-4 (hardcover) -- ISBN 978-1-59904-734-8 (e-book)
  1. Education--Computer network resources. 2. Web-based instruction. 3. Internet in education. 4. Multimedia systems. I. Title.
  LB1044.87C35 2008
  371.33467'8--dc22
                   2007039598

British Cataloguing in Publication Data
A Cataloguing in Publication record for this book is available from the British Library.

All work contributed to this book is new, previously-unpublished material. The views expressed in this book are those of the authors, but not necessarily of the publisher.

Enhancing E-Learning with Media-Rich Content and Interactions

Table of Contents

Foreword

"Tradition!" In the opening scene of *Fiddler on the Roof*, Tevye poses the first of many questions: "How do we keep our balance?" His answer: "Tradition!" While tradition for Tevye was the force that maintained social balance in his village, modern society has found that change, not tradition, is inevitable.

Academic tradition is closely linked to the print medium, and writing has perpetuated the academic tradition since the first text was introduced into the classroom. Academics have always written books, chapters, and papers, and the development of the printing press only strengthened that tradition through an affordable, distributable medium.

Ever since Al Gore invented the Internet (just kidding!), universities and colleges have recognized the value of the World Wide Web for teaching and learning. In many cases, the Web has become an indispensable partner in the classroom. For many, technology has provided a wealth of new instructional tools and become the foundation for an entirely new delivery system called distance education.

Change and technology are nearly synonymous terms; certainly, they are interchangeable terms. In the last two decades, we have witnessed an evolution of distance-based education from its initial roots in the form of printed correspondence-by-mail programs to the astounding current growth rate in the sales and implementation of learning management systems.

The functionality of technology-based systems over their hard copy ancestors has far exceeded the imagination of even the most late-20th-century educators. Student assessments are delivered online, grades are recorded in digital grade books, and class standings are sent to students and their parents instantly. Students create electronic portfolios that chronicle their learning experiences. They collaborate with their teachers and peers using a set of communication tools embedded in their curriculum and provided by expert learning management systems. Instructors deliver content face-to-face or electronically with equal effectiveness. Still, even with the plethora of technology-based applications, the majority of online learning remains grounded in text. The contemporary text-rich environment of online learning is further evidence that the tradition of teaching and learning, as well as reading and writing, remains central to the academic rigor of the 21st century learner.

Surely the print or text-rich rituals of learning are at odds with the online experiences of the majority of students entering colleges and universities. Today, students who graduate high school have been raised in an environment of Nintendo, Apple computers, and digital media. They are not strangers to technology that records and plays back pictures and sounds. They capture video on cameras and phones. Further, they share videos, images, and sound bytes on sites such as Flickr, YouTube, and Apple Podcasts. They embrace a range of social activities online that is cultivated by rich digital media.

In 2007, it was estimated that as many as nine million people communicate simultaneously with Skype with over one hundred million registered users. Today high school graduates deftly use video communications, text messaging, and learning management systems without wavering. Surely, the sheer scope of online users is testimony to the need to change the way online learning is designed and offered. Media-rich applications scream out a need to move away from the confines of text-rich content and text-based interactions. Learning must increase the amount of its media-rich content and expand its opportunities for integrating media-rich communications into online learning. The nature and scope of these changes are significant and provide challenges to those who design and deliver distance education.

As online learning has matured, so have those who design these distance-based courses. Originally, it was primarily early adopters and instructional designers who picked up the gauntlet of online learning. The ongoing debate of the times was whether it was easier to train an educator in technology or to educate a technologist in instruction. Fortunately for the industry and the student, the educator seems to have won out, due, not exclusively, to the fact that learning management systems have evolved quickly and effectively into user-friendly development environments. Online learning is becoming predictable venue for all educators—traditional and innovators. Today, the challenge to design effective online learning is further amplified by the need to integrate media-rich content and interactions.

Caladine's book chronicles many of the successes of the University of Wollongong, which has won many of the most prestigious awards for excellence in preparing their graduates for life in the e-world of the 21st century, including the 2006

Commonwealth University of the Year. In 2007, they were recognized by Good Universities Guide with five stars in the seven categories: (1) positive graduate outcomes, (2) getting a job, (3) graduate starting salary, (4) educational experience: overall satisfaction, (5) educational experience: generic skills, (6) educational experience: overall experience, and (7) staff qualifications. The author has worked at the university for over 20 years, researching educational technologies, supervising postgraduate studies, managing audio visual, and mastering a host of technology-based applications as well as helping faculty to use learning technologies in effective and efficient ways.

Enhancing E-Learning with Media-Rich Content and Interactions provides the necessary background information, theoretical frameworks, and practical guidance to help design truly effective online learning experiences by integrating media-rich interactions and content.

For those of us committed to providing high quality instruction and effective online learning strategies, this book may become the most useful ready guide in your library of desktop reference materials. I invite you to reflect conscientiously on the content and models proposed as you create your own new traditions for teaching and learning.

Lawrence A. Tomei, Ed.D

Robert Morris University

Moon Town PA

May, 2007

Lawrence A. Tomei is the associate vice president for Academic Affairs and Associate Professor of Education, Robert Morris University. Born in Akron, Ohio, he earned a BSBA from the University of Akron (1972) and completed his masters' degrees in public administration and education at the University of Oklahoma (1975, 1978) and his doctorate in education from USC (1983). His articles and books on instructional technology include: Online and Distance Learning (2008); Integrating ICT Into the Classroom (2007); Taxonomy for the Technology Domain (2005); Challenges of Teaching with Technology Across the Curriculum (2003); Technology Facade (2002); Teaching Digitally: Integrating Technology Into the Classroom (2001); and Professional Portfolios for Teachers (1999).

Preface

This book is about the future of online learning. It argues that online courses that include significant amounts of video and audio should replace many of the current text-rich courses. Video and audio will not be used only as elements of content but also as replacements for many of the interactions that are currently hosted by text-based technologies. The history of e-learning is relatively short and perhaps the examples that we see today reflect the tradition that came before e-learning. The traditions of face-to-face and correspondence courses are both traditions in which printed text plays a large role. In face-to-face learning presenters have for years used written notes to guide what they say. They have, on occasion, handed out printed materials to students. They have asked students to read books, articles, and papers. They have written book articles, papers, and theses. In correspondence courses students received printed materials from their instructors they would then read these and create further written materials, which were in turn sent back to the instructor for assessment. Clearly the printed word is central to traditional learning.

The history of the World Wide Web is also short. However, it has evolved from a collection of text-rich pages into a place where pages employ a suite of media-rich resources to provide users with sound, color, and movement. The Web is also now highly interactive with users writing to the Web almost as often as they read from it. Many users use the Web as their primary networking device. Portfolios are created online, which users can present to prospective employers. Online social spaces abound with places to meet possible friends and future partners. With video sharing sites like YouTube, simulations like Second Life, and video communications services like Skype—enjoying huge usage levels—it can reasonably be assumed that rich online media are here to stay. Further, if the trend of increasing levels of bandwidth continues, bigger and clearer video images and higher fidelity audio will be available in the near future.

Students' expectations of their online learning experience will no doubt be flavored by their experiences of their other uses of the Web. Clearly their expectations will not be ones of text-rich resources but rather ones of media and interaction. The challenge then for designers of e-learning is to develop courses that make use of media and interactions in pedagogically sound ways. It is to these people that this book is primarily directed, whether they work for a college, university, government department, private organization, or other. Of course there is a place for text in e-learning and it is suggested that part of the challenge is to find the right mix of text and rich media.

Much has been written about the use of computers and the Internet in learning. Articles, chapters, and monographs of case studies of online learning are available online and in hard copy. While these abound, little has been written that takes the case studies and builds theoretical underpinnings. Such theories are needed to guide the design of e-learning.

This book draws on the literature from several fields to provide an appropriate context. Of course the field of distance education strongly features the development of online learning, flexible learning, and e-learning. Many of the techniques and technologies used in e-learning are adaptations of distance education practices. However, literature from other areas also has contextual value for the appropriate use of rich media in e-learning. Many attempts to guide educational designers in the appropriate use of technology and media are reported in the literature of instructional design. Also, technology has been used in training and the literature of human resource development and organizational communications provides interesting insights and comparisons to the literature from the other fields and additionally provides a theoretical basis on which one of the theoretical models in this book is based.

The aim of this book is to meet the challenge of selecting technologies, both media rich and text rich, for e-learning events and to ensure that they are used in ways that are appropriate for the students, the learning objectives, the context, and the budget. In this way e-learning events will be created that effectively and efficiently meet the learning objectives. New theoretical tools are presented that will assist in the selection of learning technologies. Two theoretical models and a practical method are described and exemplified—they are, The learning activities model, the learning technologies model, and the technology selection method.

Who This Book is For

The research behind this book has been drawn from a number of disciplines. The tools that are put forward later in the book bring together elements of:

- Distance education theory and practice.
- Educational theory and practice.
- The concept of media richness and trait theories from the area of organizational communications.
- Information and communications technology studies.

Just as the approach taken has been interdisciplinary so too is the intended audience. Many teachers in many different fields are asked to design online learning as part of their academic duties. This book is for:

- Teachers at universities and colleges who are designers.
- Trainers in business, industry, and government who are designers.
- Instructional designers.
- Researchers in the area of instructional design or training design.
- Students of instructional design or human resource development.

Organization of the Book

This book is in three sections. The first section, including this introduction, sets the scene for the future of online learning and argues that media-rich content and interactions will have a greatly increased role. It sets out reasons for the argument that video and audio will play significant roles in online learning of the future or e-learning 2.0. The first section also poses a challenge to all designers of online learning, that to be effective and efficient online learning of the future must not just include, but incorporate appropriately, the rich media of video and audio.

Chapter I introduces the future of online learning by considering some possible future approaches to the Web. In particular Web 2.0 and the Semantic Web are discussed regarding the impact they might have on e-learning and the concept of e-learning 2.0 is described. The changes in learning technology that have resulted in e-learning (both 1.0 and 2.0) have been sufficiently far reaching to be considered paradigm shifts. As with many paradigm shifts new terms are introduced to assist in the description of its new elements. In the early 1990s the term *flexible delivery* was coined to describe some of the aspects of e-learning. Since then other terms have been used to describe many of the variations of online, flexible, or e-learning. Chapter I concludes with a word of warning. The concern is one of equity between students with different levels of access to the Internet. If some students have cheap, high-speed connections and other have slow or no connections, a further challenge is presented to the designers of e-learning—that is, the challenge to avoid creating a second digital divide between the bandwidth rich and the bandwidth poor.

The first section of the book goes on to consider the literature from several disciplines to provide a historical perspective and thus provide a better understanding of the future of rich media in e-learning. The reviews of the literature also provide the basis of the theoretical frameworks that are developed in later chapters.

Chapter II investigates the literature of open and distance education to provide a historical background of learning technologies. The chapter includes a discussion of the context and background to generational changes in learning technologies, their role in learning, and the ways in which they have been conceptualized. Understanding the changes in learning technologies in the past and the forces that shaped these changes helps not only in the understanding of their contemporary role in learning but provides direction to their future. Two key, early commentators in the literature of distance education suggest generations of distance education that reflect the paradigm shifts in teacher and student experiences as different families of technology were added. The first generation is based on the technology of print called the correspondence model. The names of subsequent generations reflect the predominant technology and are called: the multimedia model, the telelearning model, the flexible learning model, and the intelligent flexible learning model. The chapter compares the latest generation of distance education as described in the literature with the move to Web 2.0 and the Semantic Web. The chapter concludes by reporting on the changing role of technology in teaching and learning—changing from adjuncts to a face-to-face process to a role of centrality in the provision of e-learning.

Chapter III discusses key attempts that have been made to develop theoretical frameworks of learning technologies in the fields of higher education, human resource development, and instructional design. In many cases the theoretical frameworks are intended to guide the selection of learning technologies but often the conceptualizations have not kept pace with technological changes. A review of the literature of these fields helps to evaluate the suitability of conceptualizations of learning technologies to their selection in the process of designing learning events. The chapter provides a perspective on the sometimes difficult transition from an educational model centered on face-to-face experiences to one centered on face-to-technology. The chapter also considers the difference between classification and categorization and the value of these organizational systems to those who design e-learning experiences. The chapter concludes that the attempts in the literature to organize technologies in ways to help designers use them appropriately are not as helpful as they could be. Many have just not kept pace with changing technologies and others, while valuable in large institutions where e-learning is designed by teams, are far too complex for individual designers.

In **Chapter IV**, existing approaches to the selection of learning technologies are reviewed. As the methods suggested in the literature of instructional design are limited and are generally applied to human resource development and higher education, the reviews of them have been combined. Another area in which methods of technology selection are investigated is *organizational communications*. As the efficiency of communications between managers and other members of an organization has clear links to profits, a sturdy body of literature that conceptualizes and theorizes the selection of technologies for communications has developed. The chapter draws some basic conclusions as generalities from the literature. In particular there is some commonality of the criteria used in the selection of technologies for e-learning. These are the costs, the nature of the subject, and the implications for learners. The chapter concludes with the finding that the technology selection methods reviewed are not completely appropriate for designers who work individually and are seeking simple yet robust tools to guide the selection of appropriate technologies for e-learning.

Chapter V sums up the previous four chapters by arguing that generic tools are needed to assist designers of online learning. Shortcomings in existing models of learning activities, learning technologies, and methods of technology selection are discussed and the conceptions or key elements of the literature are described. The chapter concludes by foreshadowing the next section of the book in which the new theoretical frameworks are introduced.

The central section of the book introduces two theoretical frameworks and a practical method. These tools have been developed to assist in the development of online or e-learning programs that make appropriate use of the technology and in particular use media-rich content and interactions.

Chapter VI introduces the first theoretical model, the learning activities model (LAM). This model is the first of two theoretical frameworks described in this book. The model is intended to assist designers of learning events and is based on the thesis that categories of activities, which are subdivisions of the learning process, can be matched to techniques, technologies, and methods as part of the design process. The LAM categorizes the activities of students and teachers in the process of learning into the five categories: (1) provision of materials, (2) interactions with materials, (3) interactions with the facilitator of learning, (4) interactions between learners, and (5) intra-action. The last category is included in the model for the sake of completion and contains activities that probably form the heart and soul of learning, things that learners generally undertake and control themselves; these include, but are not limited to, structured and unstructured reflection, refinement of opinion, critical thinking, and the comparison of new experiences and information with older ones.

Chapter VII introduces the second theoretical model, the learning technologies model (LTM). Learning technologies have increased in number and diversity to such an extent that a theoretical framework is needed to help teachers and designers understand the nature of different technologies and hence apply them appropriately.

The LTM is made up of two primary components. The first consists of the categories of the LAM to which the technology is suited. The second component further describes the technology by the criteria; synchronous or asynchronous; one-way or two-way; and the type of communication channels available. The communications channels are divided into three levels where the most basic level is text alone. The next level is voice/audio which is considered as text plus the non-verbal attributes and the final level combines pictures and sounds which is considered as text plus non-verbal attributes plus non-vocal attributes such as body language. The chapter contains examples of 10 different technologies as interpreted by the LTM.

Chapter VIII brings together the theoretical models from the previous two chapters and combines them to form the technology selection method (TSM). The TSM is a robust tool for the selection of appropriate learning technologies. It assumes no specialist knowledge in the field of instructional design and provides users with an understanding of the technologies as well as the selection process. The TSM considers a number of criteria in three areas. They are:

- Mechanics of the subject, or institutional factors
- Implications for learners and facilitators
- Costs.

The mechanics of the subject refer to any technology requirements that are essential for the efficient and effective attainment of the learning objectives. These can include answers to questions like:

- Is text necessary or desirable?
- Are black and white graphics necessary or desirable?
- Are color graphics necessary or desirable?
- Is audio necessary or desirable?
- Is animation necessary or desirable?
- Are moving pictures (movie/video) necessary or desirable?

The LAM is then revisited and categories of it are matched to broad categories of the LTM and a step by step method for selecting technologies is presented. The chapter concludes with a number of examples of the TSM and with placing the method into the course design context.

The third section of the book applies the theoretical models and the method by describing a number of learning technologies and describing their appropriate use in teaching and learning. The learning technologies covered are:

- Video
- Recording lectures
- Streaming
- Downloading, podcasting, vodcasting, and Webcasting
- Real time communications technologies such as videoconference, video chat, and the Access Grid

In **Chapter IX**, the traditional role of video in education is revisited briefly as a basis for the exploration of new and different uses of this technology in e-learning. The chapter provides some basic technical background information and introduces a production method that is appropriate for those new to the technology. Film theory is touched on briefly as it forms the basis of the *language* of the technology. The educational use of video is explored and examples of new and different uses of video are provided. The chapter concludes with a review of how video camera and editing costs have changed in recent years and that these are now accessible to many. This, and changes to the ways in which video can be shared, have driven the production of domestic video to higher levels. This has increased the ways in which video can be used in e-learning.

Chapter X covers the related technologies of streaming, downloading, podcasting, vodcasting, and Webcasting, which can be used to record and distribute lectures or presentations. As many of these technologies are new they need to be clearly defined before they can be applied to the process of teaching and learning. A short historical case study of an Australian university's implementation of these technologies provides insights into the way in which lectures can be recorded and distributed as well as the ways in which they are used in teaching and learning. Details are provided on what can be recorded other than lectures and on the layout, installation, and equipment required to facilitate institution-wide recording. The LTM is used to describe the technologies and the chapter concludes by hinting at the articulation of these technologies into m-learning or mobile learning.

Chapter XI provides an introduction to the three chapters that follow it. The chapter provides a theoretical approach to the design of teaching and learning with real time communications technologies (RTCs). The LTM and the LAM are revisited in the context of RTCs in teaching and learning. From these a continuum of learning activities is proposed. The continuum has poles of completely one-way activities and completely two-way activities and between the poles varying degrees of one- and two-way activities. The chapter argues that somewhere on the continuum there exists a threshold of effective teaching and learning. A number of criteria are suggested as affecting the position of the threshold and model is suggested as a guide to designing appropriate learning events that use RTCs.

Chapter XII introduces three RTCs: videoconference, audioconference, and video chat. The technologies are defined and technical aspects of compression and quality, point-to-point and multipoint, continuous presence, and codecs are discussed.

The chapter also describes large and small videoconference installations, standards, and room layouts. A case study of an Australian university provides an insight into the advantages of Internet-hosted videoconferences over integrated services digital network (ISDN). The chapter concludes with a look to the future and the potential of video chat technology to displace appliance-based videoconference.

Chapter XIII takes the technological description of videoconference and video chat of the previous chapter, describes the use of these technologies, and recommends practices for teaching and learning. The technologies are analyzed in terms of the LTM and the relationship between technical quality, interactivity, and learning outcomes is presented. The chapter covers the elements of planning for teaching with videoconference and argues that successful educational videoconferences generally stem from sound planning. The chapter describes a number of teaching and learning activities and how they can work with videoconference.

Chapter XIV investigates a related RTC, Access Grid. The technology of the Access Grid is described and directions to the open source software are provided. Details of different levels of implementations are provided and the Access Grid experience is described and compared to that of videoconference and video chat. The technology and plans for equipping teaching and learning spaces for Access Grid are presented. The chapter also covers teaching and learning with Access Grid by analyzing the Access Grid in terms of the LTM and a case study of the use of Access Grid to host inter-institutional teaching and learning is presented. The chapter concludes with an analysis of the costs and benefits of this technology in e-learning.

In **Chapter XV** the future of RTCs in higher education is addressed and future directions for each of them are summarized. A comparison of the functionality, costs, and support requirements is also provided. The chapter concludes by arguing that in the medium term it is likely that institutions and organizations will use a mixture of RTCs and that they will need to be used in ways that facilitate easy interactions and thus render the technology transparent.

The book concludes with a look to the future of online learning and rich media. It argues the benefits for integrating rich media communication technologies with learning management systems and the benefits of sharing rich media resources through repositories such as content management systems.

Two appendices are included. The first is a glossary of terms used in the book and the second is a short introduction to the measurement of computer memory and bandwidth.

Conclusion

Unfortunately one of the problems with writing about technology is the rate of change of the technology. If the evolutionary trajectory is not considered when writing about a technology, there is a good chance that the written material will be out of date soon after it is published. For this reason care has been taken in this book to consider where rich media technologies are heading and to plan for their particular trajectories. From the title of this book, it can clearly be seen that the emphasis is on rich media. It is the belief of the author that those who offer e-learning opportunities that are rich in media stand to enjoy the creation of learning activities in which students achieve the objectives with greater efficiencies and effectiveness.

Chapter I

The Future of Online Learning

Introduction

To write about technology is to write about change. In the first decade of the 21st century the rate of change of technology is greater than ever before. At a recent meeting of human resource developers using online learning, an executive of a local, national broadcaster mentioned that a year ago his organization did not know what podcasting was and that today they have managers of it. Change in technology has been recognized by almost all who live in developed countries, and it is clear to most that the only certainty about technology is that, for the foreseeable future at least, it will continue to change. Yet a conundrum appears to exist as fundamentally, little has changed about online learning or e-learning in higher education and human resource development for the past 10 or so years. Content is still predominantly text-based and the communications tools are generally limited to text. This contrasts markedly with the trend in other online experiences to include audio, video animation as well as text and graphics. This book argues that it is high time for e-learning to change. The book puts forward theoretical models designed to assist trainers, teachers, and instructional designers to create e-learning where rich media are used for content as well as interactions.

Just as many terms have entered our language with the introduction of computers and the Internet, so too have terms been coined to describe the use of these technologies in learning. Online learning clearly refers to learning that uses the Internet. Today distance learning often also uses the Internet and blended learning is used to refer to learning that blends online and face-to-face. In this book the term *e-learning* is used to describe online learning, whether distance or blended. Throughout the book the terms e-learning and online learning are used interchangeably as both terms are used in the parlance common to teachers, trainers, students, and instructional designers. These terms and others are described in greater detail in the following section.

Definitions

The information society has been defined in many places and most definitions concur that in an information society, information is critical to the success of organizations and individuals (Doku, 2007; Mobileman Glossary, 2007; World Summit on the Information Society, 2003). In an information society, information becomes a commodity or essential to the production, distribution, and use of other products. A central tool in the creation, use, and manipulation of information is information technology and a central tool in the distribution and diffusion is communication technology. In the past 20 years the impact of information and communications technologies has been felt in almost all aspects of life in developed countries as they become information societies. It has had an impact on all sectors of education from kindergarten to further, technical and higher education. Many new words have entered our lexicon to describe the hardware and software that make up the technologies, so too have new words been created to describe the many aspects of the application of technology. Education is no stranger to technology. For many years technologies have been used in the classroom as adjuncts to face-to-face teaching and learning. They have also been used to deliver education to students in distant locations or who were unable to attend classes through limitations of time or mobility. In the field of distance education the technologies used have evolved and the concept of generations of distance education features in the literature (Nipper, 1989; Taylor, 1995, 2001). It is to the most recent generation that this book is addressed.

As mentioned earlier, many terms have been used to describe the current application of information and communications technologies to education. Online learning, flexible learning, open learning, e-learning, and blended learning to name a few and these have been defined in the Glossary in Appendix One. In this book many of these terms are used in a generally interchangeable way to refer to intentional learning that is fully, or has a large component that is accessible via the Internet.

Originally online learning consisted of a limited number of technologies, all of which were text-based. These were generally communications technologies such as e-mail, listservers, bulletin boards, and other computer mediated communications or CMCs. The advent of the World Wide Web in the early 1990s added an easy way to display text and graphical content. Today online learning refers to a mixture of technologies that are often encapsulated within an environment or management system. Early online or virtual learning environments allowed students to interact with content, fellow students, and faculty within the one Web site. Today these environments have grown to include other functions such as student tracking, grade management, and interoperation with databases of resources and records. In addition, students can create content within the virtual environment. These are now referred to as learning management systems (LMS), virtual learning environments, or course management systems (CMS). In this book the term *learning management system* or LMS is preferred to differentiate it from CMS, which can also refer to content management system.

For the purposes of designing education an LMS is best considered not as a single technology but rather as a collection of technological elements, as these elements have different roles in teaching and learning. The commercially available LMS with the largest market share at the time of writing lists the technological elements on their Web site. Rather than describe each element they list the activities students and faculty can undertake with individual elements. The list includes (Blackboard, 2007):

- *Create powerful learning content using a variety of Web-based tools*
- *Develop custom learning paths for individual students or groups*
- *Facilitate student participation, communication, and collaboration, evaluate students' work using a rich set of assessment capabilities*
- *Bring top publisher content into e-Learning* (Blackboard, 2007)

It is suggested that as new uses of the Web gain popularity they will be added to LMSs as new technological elements, and the advent of the second generation of the Web, or Web 2.0 is characterized by a number of example of new uses.

Web 2.0

Web 2.0 is a term used to describe the second generation of the World Wide Web. However, unlike most generations the transition from Web 1.0 to 2.0 has been characterized by gradual, multiple, and ongoing changes. The first generation of the

Web was focused primarily on information posted by agencies, experts, teachers, or vendors and read by the general public or specific users, and to the public, the Web pages appeared reasonably static. There was often color but little movement. There is some debate (Madden & Fox, 2006; O'Reilly, 2005) as to who came up with the term Web 2.0 but the literature concurs that in 2004 the term was coined to describe a raft of new uses or technological elements of the Web.

There are a number of characteristics that differentiate Web 2.0 from Web 1.0. One is the posting of information by members of the public. Sites like Amazon.com now actively seek feedback from customers on items they have recently purchased. The feedback is then added to the Web pages, linked to the items, and developed into a user-generated commentary as well as an online shopping site. In this way the Amazon.com site has moved from a site in which users read and purchase, to one on which they read, purchase, and may write comments. Downes (2004) suggests that the original vision of Web 2.0 is "read-write."

...that the Web itself was being transformed from what was called "the Read Web" to the "Read-Write Web," in accordance with Tim Berners-Lee's original vision. Proponents of this new, evolving Web began calling it Web 2.0 and in short order the trend became a movement.

However, Web 2.0 is more than Web applications that allow feedback from users. Web 2.0 can be thought of as an umbrella term for a number of applications that while they all allow writing to the Web they also have expanded functionality. Social software is one area of this expanded functionality. In the past few years a great number of applications have been launched that allow users for low or no cost to post personal information to the Web. Examples abound and include the following: MySpace and FaceBook are free services that allow users to create online personal profiles consisting of pictures, text, blogs, other media formats, e-mails, Web forums, and other tools. Del.icio.us is a site dedicated to sharing of Web bookmarks. Users upload their bookmarks to the site for public viewing. Some refer to the lists of published bookmarks as link blogs. Flickr is a site to which users can post digital photographs. The Flickr site argues that it is the "best way to store, search, sort and share your photographs." Wikipedia is a wiki that is an encyclopedia. Wikis allow users to add, edit, and remove content and Wikipedia is hence created and edited by users. Thus Wikipedia is a good example of how Web 2.0 facilitates collaboration through writing to the Web. Another force that has the potential to change the way the Web operates and is used is the idea of the Semantic Web. The Semantic Web is based on the concepts that data can be machine readable, that searching the Web will become automated, and that communications in audio and video will be created, stored, analyzed, and otherwise processed.

Semantic Web

The Semantic Web is called *semantic* as information on it is machine readable and hence has meaning to the technology. The Semantic Web is also a project of the World Wide Web Consortium (W3C) and has as a goal the provision of "a common framework that allows data to be shared and reused across applications, enterprise and community boundaries" (W3C, 2007). The Semantic Web is about connecting data from different places. One example provided on the W3C Semantic Web, Web page is that of connecting photographs, bank statements, and a calendar. This would allow a person to see what purchases were made with credit or debit cards on the same day as a photograph was taken. Those who write about the Semantic Web promise the development of powerful applications but as yet little has been delivered. Today we are not sure of when or if the Semantic Web will be used to improve online learning but the literature indicates that the potential is high as the educational Semantic Web will have more effective and efficient means to store, sort, filter, and manage information. It will use agents to work in the background augmenting the learning processes and enhancing communications. To some futurists the combination of the Semantic Web and Web 2.0 has been dubbed Web 3.0. In the meantime the application of the Semantic Web and Web 2.0 to online learning is one facet of an emerging body of literature based around the next generation of online learning or e-learning, which has been called e-learning 2.0.

E-Learning 2.0

E-learning has been around for almost as long as the Web and some would say that a second generation of it is overdue. In this age of online-rich media it seems archaic and not always appropriate to have educational content predominantly delivered as text. The majority of discussion forums in LMSs are still in text, which appears to be at odds with the rise in the popularity of video, instant messaging, and other rich-media communications.

There is an emerging body of literature that looks to the future of online learning and suggests that the most significant change will be away from monolithic LMSs to personal learning environments (PLEs). PLEs will take advantage of the high usage rate of the newer applications of the Web, in particular the social software applications that have been described as elements of Web 2.0. In this way e-learning 1.0, based on Web 1.0 will be make way for e-learning 2.0. PLEs will enable students to connect the Web 2.0 content they have developed previously or for personal purposes to an institutional virtual environment. This connection will then result in a larger environment and allow students to link files in one application to another and so on.

This will mean that interoperability will be the key to permitting the easy linking of files. Wilson et al. (2006) corroborate this notion and suggest that PLEs will link elements from the educational institution, with elements from students. The student elements could contain: photos (e.g., Fickr), bookmarks (e.g., del.icio.us), personal hosting (e.g., MySpace), blogs, wikis, and other applications. Of course the files on the social and sharing applications mentioned previously are generally available to the general public so opportunities abound for interaction with the public and of course the interactions are in the domain of the PLE thus providing opportunities for experiential and authentic learning. The following example from Downes (2004) illustrates how this can enhance authenticity and experiential learning.

Educators began to notice something different happening when they began to use tools like wikis and blogs in the classroom a couple of years ago. All of a sudden, instead of discussing pre-assigned topics with their classmates, students found themselves discussing a wide range of topics with peers worldwide. Imagine the astonishment, for example, when, after writing a review of a circus she had viewed, a Grade 5 student received a response from one of the performers.

As well as Web 2.0, it has been suggested that the Semantic Web will enhance education. In 2004 Anderson and Whitelock edited a special issue of the *Journal of Interactive Multimedia in Education* that was devoted to the educational Semantic Web. They suggest that the Semantic Web will enhance education as it is based on three "fundamental affordances" (Anderson & Whitelock, 2004). These are:

- *Better ways of storing and retrieving information.*
- *Non-human agents that will enhance learning through taking on some of the information processing in learning.*
- *Increase the capabilities of the Internet to support communications between humans in many formats across time and location constraints.*

The Semantic Web represents a major change to the way humans place information on the Internet. For the Semantic Web to work, information needs to be tagged with metadata. The metadata, being machine readable, will enable retrieval and organization of the information by non-human agents. It has been argued that this is the greatest barrier to the uptake of the Semantic Web (Doctorow, 2001) as it is an immense challenge and will not necessarily be performed to a standard or group of standards or by staff with online librarian skills. Thus it appears that while the Semantic Web has a great deal to offer education it is still some way off whereas Web 2.0 is here.

No matter whether designers of online learning are designing for Web 1.0, Web 2.0 or the Semantic Web, they must always design for a particular cohort of learners.

Alternatively, they must at least have an understanding of the skills and resources available to the learners they design for. In the next few years this challenge will be deepened as late baby boomers and members of generation X design online learning for the *net generation*.

The Changing Audience for Education

Often changes in technology are reflected in changes in society and vice versa. There has been much written about the changes in online technology and there is a growing body of literature on the changing nature of the learners for whom we are designing online learning experiences. Students who leave school and enter college and universities in the first decade of the second millennium are generally the children of baby boomers and have grown up with digital technology. An 18-year-old in 2008, was born into a world in which rich media were readily accessible to the general public in developed nations. In 2008, DVD players and video cameras were common in households as well as televisions and audio systems and video cassette recorders were being replaced slowly but surely by other recordable media. Personal computing was well established in homes as well as schools, colleges, and businesses. In North America in 1999 the net generation outnumbered its baby boomer parents 88 million to 85 million and there are similar sized proportions in most other developed countries (Tapscott, 1999). These net generation children are growing up surrounded with digital media and use digital media in all aspects of their lives. Tapscott argues that the net generation constitutes a force for social change.

And it is through their use of the digital media that N-Gen will develop and superimpose its culture on the rest of society. Boomers stand back. Already these kids are learning, playing, communicating, working, and creating communities very differently than their parents. They are a force for social transformation.

As anyone who lives in the same house as them can attest, members of the net generation use technologies in ways that are very different. To baby boomers like the author, often their use of several digital technologies at the same time appears to border on the impossible. To this baby boomer it would be impossible to watch television, send text messages on a cell phone, surf the Web, and listen to music at the same time, but many members of the net generation appear to see this technological multitasking as the way in which the technology should naturally be used. It is probably safe to assume that they will approach online learning in the same way, but what does this mean for designers? The challenge is not just to design for members of the net generation, but to design for the entire range of students. Of course this includes mature-aged students (many of whom are baby boomers themselves) as well as the growing number of workers entering or returning to higher education as part of life long learning. In the human resource development arena, online learning is growing rapidly as businesses and government departments are keen to take advantage of the efficiencies it offers. The majority of students in this area can be of any age, members of the net generation, baby boomers, or beyond.

The variety of technological literacy and ways in which students use technology certainly impacts the design of online learning, and those charged with the task of designing it need tools to guide the selection and implementation of technology. These tools and guides need to be sufficiently robust to provide designers with online learning programs that make appropriate use of the technology and do so within the designer's approach to, or philosophy of, learning.

Philosophies of Learning and Teaching

For many years academics in the field of education have deliberated on an appropriate philosophy or approach to intentional learning. In the mid-20th century the approach favored by most trainers, teachers in schools, and faculty in higher education was one in which students were provided with the teacher's conceptions as truth. Of course some enlightened teachers encouraged students to discover things for themselves but these were in the minority. This approach, and underlying philosophy of education, was characterized by instruction of students by the teacher and hence has been labeled *instructivism*. It assumes students absorb knowledge that is passed on to them from the teacher or other sources.

Later in the 20th century this dominant paradigm of learning was challenged. It can be argued that the change was driven by the findings from educational psychology and the changes in the popular views of epistemology especially towards the individual and social construction of knowledge. However, it is beyond the scope and outside of the purpose of this book to develop this discussion further. The new paradigm was labeled *constructivism* as it was based on the notion that students construct their own knowledge by building on their own experience and that of others.

Today constructivism is touted by most in higher education as the preferred educational philosophy. However, it appears that instructivism is still in use particularly for training in human resource development. It is suggested that the next educational philosophy could be a mixture of instructivism, constructivism, and other approaches that perhaps will be called *postconstructivism*. The teacher or designer could then vary the approach depending on the material, the students, the budget, the culture, and other constraints.

Many educational technologies can be seen as outside of educational philosophies as they can be applied in a range of ways. Therefore tools that assist designers in the selection of technologies that are appropriate to the students, objectives, and budget must be applicable within a number of educational philosophies. Further, it is known that students have preferred learning styles, and that if learning is to be effective and efficient these need to be designed for.

Approaches to Learning Styles

For many years designers have considered the ways in which learners learn. Obviously if designers have clear ideas of the preferred ways in which students learn they will be able to design for these and hence create learning events that are more efficient and effective. One of the more basic approaches is termed neuro linguistic programming (Grinder, 1989), and divides students into three categories depending on their preference for learning through the visual, auditory, or kinesthetic senses. Other approaches are based on the concept of Jungian psychological types. For example the Myers-Briggs Type Indicator is a test used in many institutions and it categorizes students according to a number of dichotomies such as extrovert/introvert, sensing/intuition, thinking/feeling, and judging/perceiving. There are a number of approaches to the classification of learning styles but it is beyond the scope of this book to discuss the advantages and shortcomings of the various approaches to learning styles. However, any tool that assists designers of learning to select technologies that are appropriate to the students, objectives, and the budget must be able to operate within the designer's choice of designing for students' learning preferences.

Rich Media and E-Learning 2.0

Learning styles, educational philosophies, and the changing audience for education all have impacts on the process of designing educational experiences. This book argues that rich media will be a central component of many learning experiences in the near future and that rich media impacts on the design of learning as well. Among the number of reasons for the increase in rich media are increased access to production, postproduction, and sharing technologies.

Video production has changed markedly in the past 20 years as we have moved from analogue recording with its inherent degraded or poor quality pictures to digital ones that can be copied with no loss. We have seen editing move from linear copying from tape to tape to non-linear manipulation of video files on computers. In the past few years the costs of the equipment needed to produce video of high technical quality have dropped by a number of orders of magnitude. Today we can create pictures with a $500 camera that are superior in technical quality than those produced by $50,000 cameras 20 years ago. Lower quality video capture is becoming ubiquitous and is possible in many new portable technologies such as mobile telephones and personal digital assistants (PDAs).

Also, more sophisticated editing can be done on a $1,500 computer today than could be performed on a $100,000 linear edit suite 20 years ago. The digital effects that cost tens of thousands of dollars 20 years ago, today are part of free video editing software that is often supplied with a computer's operating system.

The change from analogue to digital is probably the basis of the most significant rise in quality due to the predictability of a digital signal. A digital signal is a stream of ones and zeros. If the stream arrives at its destination with values that are slightly less than one, then the technology, as it was only expecting a one or a zero, can easily interpret the slightly lower value as a one. This is a rather reductionist interpretation of forward error correction but it serves to illustrate the copying of digital images, video, and audio with no loss. In this way, edited programs of high technical quality can be produced.

Video production and postproduction changes are not the only things that are influencing the popularity of this rich medium. Due to its immense popularity, sharing video on the Internet is now big business. There are further reasons that indicate that video will become common and an important part of online learning. Commercial Web sites aimed at users in their late teens and early 20s are rich in audio, animation, and video. It seems reasonable to expect students who enjoy rich media experiences in their online socializing and leisure will expect the same in their online learning.

Still further developments add to the argument for rich media in online learning. Commercially available applications and tools such as Annodex and Vquence allow makers of video to mark up video with annotations that can be used to assist designers in assessing the suitability of the video to the subject they are designing. Further these kinds of tools can add to the learning experience through the provision of further navigational options. These tools allow students to advance, no only to the next chapter mark in a media file but to select which chapter they wish to advance to by reading or viewing the annotation. In a way this technology can be conceptualized as an expansion of the scene selection options in DVD menus.

Video is not the only rich medium with a role to play in online learning. In recent years, new ways to distribute audio have given this rich medium impetus to be central in online learning of the future. In the early years of this decade Apple released the iPod technology. Today there are many millions of iPods and other MP3 players in the world. So pervasive is the impact of MP3 players that some countries have changed their copyright laws so that popular practice of copying music CDs to

MP3 players is now legal. MP3 files are compressed and hence more easily trans-ferred across the Internet. This has opened the door to Internet radio stations and to podcasting. Podcasting (a contraction of iPod and broadcasting) is a system of automated downloading of audio files. A user simply copies a Web address into their podcasting software, and then whenever they connect to the Internet the computer connects to the Web site of the podcast program and automatically downloads any new ones. Audio is also gaining ground in some of the social software applications such as audio blogging and of course voice over Internet is big business. There are also trends towards video telephony that use the Internet rather than dedicated telecommunications lines, and videoconference over the Internet is fast becoming the standard for business communications.

The trend towards rich media in the provision of content and the hosting of inter-actions is clear and expected to continue. There is no reason to expect that these trends will not impact online learning and hence designers of online learning will need tools to assist in the design process.

Designing Learning Events for E-Learning 2.0

If online learning follows the trend of the Internet towards more rich media, those who design online learning will need tools to help them do so. Many of the online learning programs offered to date have been text-rich. This should come as no sur-prise as the academics that created the courses have a deep history entrenched in the written word. They write theses, lecture notes, papers, articles, and books and, for hundreds of years, text has been the primary medium of academic communica-tion. In many institutions individual teachers have the responsibility of designing online learning programs. In other institutions there may be specialist instructional designers, but no matter who designs the online learning, they will need tools to assist in designs that include rich media.

Trainers, faculty, or designers will need tools to help them design media-rich, online learning experiences that are appropriate to the students, the learning objectives, the context, and the budget. The tools will need to be sufficiently robust to cope with a range of technologies, disciplines, and student learning styles. They will also need to be simple enough to be used with a minimum of instruction and to produce results in a wide range of discipline areas while ensuring that students are not disadvantaged by their learning style, the philosophy of education, or by lack of access to technology.

Avoiding a Second Digital Divide

When technology is used in education, it is possible to introduce issues of equity if there are different levels of access to the technology. When students with different bandwidth connections access online learning, it is possible to create a second digital divide, between the access rich and the access poor. This problem could be exacerbated by the use of rich media as the following example indicates.

Students in the same online course could access the same rich-media material from networked computers in a range of locations and situations. It is possible that students with access to high speed Internet (such as T1 or LAN) at their place of work could enjoy fast access for little or no cost. Other students in the same class might access the material through a slow modem and pay an ISP for the service, while a third group with no personal access or computer might be relegated to joining a queue at the campus computer lab.

It is quite possible that broadband could create another digital divide through creating a gulf between the bandwidth rich and poor. It is conceivable that some students may chose to use broadband while others, for reasons of affordability or access, might be constrained to a dial-up modem for access to their course. Of course where students live in regional or remote areas their options for high speed connections to the Internet are often limited to satellite. These connections are generally more expansive that terrestrial connections and often are highly asymmetric as the connections is download only from the satellite.

One way to address, in part, the digital divide between the bandwidth rich and the bandwidth poor would be to supply students with access options for the course materials. Students with broadband could conveniently download or stream media-rich content from the institution's server, while students with a narrowband connection could be supplied the media-rich content via distributed media.

In the past there have been ambitious plans to provide the world with ubiquitous broadband wireless Internet—for example, Teledesic, Iridium, and Globalstar. However, for a number of reasons each of these projects has stalled or failed. For the foreseeable future it appears that users of online learning will be connecting from a range of different bandwidth connections. This in turn means that designers of online learning, especially when designing courses that use rich media for content and interactions, need to be aware of their students connections and to design online learning in ways that avoid or at least minimize a second digital divide.

Conclusion

If the development of online learning follows the development of the Web, we can look forward to a future in which video and audio are the default media for online communications. We can also look forward to online learning in which students and teachers create video and audio content. We can further look forward to maximizing the return on the time and energy invested in the creation of these resources, through their placement in repositories that facilitate the sharing of them. This book is a guide for those who are charged with the task of designing online learning or e-learning and is in three parts. The first part provides a historical overview of the field and considers the literature that has informed it. The second section presents three theoretical models that have been designed to assist designers in the selection and use of appropriate learning technologies. The third section of the book contains a collection of practical examples, explanations of the technologies, and concludes with a brief look to the future of rich media in e-learning.

References

Anderson, T., & Whitelock, D. (2004). The educational Semantic Web: Visioning and practicing the future of education. *Journal of Interactive Multimedia in Education,* (1). Retrieved March 21, 2007, from http://www-jime.open. ac.uk/2004/1

Blackboard. (2007). *Instruction. Communication. Assessment.* Retrieved March 20, 2007, from http://www.blackboard.com/products/Academic_Suite/Learning_System/index.htm

Doctorow, C. (2001) *Metacrap: Putting the torch to the straw-men of the meta-utopia.* Retrieved March 21, 2007, from http://www.well.com/~doctorow/metacrap. htm

Doku, I. (2007). Reconsidering information literacy. *Academic Exchange Quarterly, 11.1, 143*(6). Retrieved July 31, 2007, from http://find.galegroup.com. ezproxy.uow.edu.au:2048/itx/infomark.do?&contentSet=IAC-Documents&type=retrieve&tabID=T002&prodId=EAIM&docId=A165912659&source=gale&userGroupName=uow&version=1.0

Downes, S. (2004). *E-learning 2.0.* Retrieved March 20, 2007, from http://www. elearnmag.org/subpage.cfm?section=articles&article=29-1

Grinder, M. (1989). *Righting the educational conveyor belt.* Portland, OR: Metamorphous Press.

Madden, M., & Fox, S. (2006). *Riding the waves of "Web 2.0."* Retrieved March 20, 2007, from http://www.pewinternet.org/PPF/r/189/report_display.asp

Mobileman Glossary. (2007). *Terms used.* Retrieved August 1, 2007, from http://mobileman.projects.supsi.ch/glossary.html

Nipper, S. (1989). Third generation distance learning and computer conferencing. In R. Mason & A. Kaye (Eds.), *Mindweave: Communication, computers and distance education.* Oxford, UK: Pergamon.

O'Reilly, T. (2005). *What is Web 2.0: Design patterns and business models for the next generation of software.* Retrieved August 22, 2007, from http://www.oreillynet.com/pub/a/oreilly/tim/news/2005/09/30/what-is-web-20.html

Tapscott, D. (1999). *Growing up digital: The rise of the net generation.* New York: McGraw-Hill.

Taylor, J. (1995). Distance education technologies: The fourth generation. *Australian Journal of Educational Technology, 11*(2), 1-7.

Taylor, J. (2001). *Fifth generation distance education* (Higher Education Series, Report No. 40). Canberra, Australia: Department of Education, Training and Youth Affairs.

Wilson, S., Liber, O., Beauvoir, P., MIlligan, C., Johnson, M., & Sharples, P. (2006). *Personal learning environments: Challenging the dominant design of educational systems.* Retrieved March 21, 2007, from http://dspace.ou.nl/handle/1820/727

World Summit on the Information Society. (2003). *Declaration of principles: Building the information society: A global challenge in the new Millennium* (Document WSIS-03/GENEVA/DOC/4-E). Retrieved August 22, 2007, from http://www.itu.int/dms_pub/itu-s/md/03/wsis/doc/S03-WSIS-DOC-0004!!PDF-E.pdf

World Wide Web Consortium (W3C). (2007). *Semantic Web.* Retrieved March 20, 2007, from http://www.w3.org/2001/sw/

Chapter II

A Short History of Learning Technologies

For over 3000 years from Homer, Moses and Socrates onwards, the teacher in direct, personal contact with the learner, has been the primary means of communicating knowledge...until the fourteenth century, when the invention of the printing press allowed for the first time the large-scale dissemination of knowledge though books. (Bates, 1995)

Introduction

A brief history of learning technologies provides the context to the changes in the nature and use of learning technologies, their role in learning, and the ways in which they have been conceptualized. It has been said that an understanding of the past is essential in avoiding the repetition of past mistakes and understanding the present. However, understanding the changes in learning technologies in the past and the forces that shaped these changes will help, not only in the understanding of their role in contemporary learning, but also provide guidance for their future direction.

Recent History of Technology in Learning

Technological developments in the past 50 years have had a marked impact on the lifestyles of most people in industrialized countries and a growing number of developing countries. By the 1970s the technologies of television and telephony became more or less ubiquitous in developed countries. In this time the role of technology in learning changed as well. In the 1960s and 1970s teachers in schools and universities as well as trainers in commercial, industrial, and government organizations had opportunities to include technological *teaching aids* such as overhead projectors, filmstrips, movies, radio, and television broadcasts in the learning events they designed. In the 1960s large computers could be found at many universities but it was not until the advent of the personal computer in the 1980s that computers made an impact on teaching and learning in a majority of subject areas. In the late 1980s and early 1990s, the development of the Internet and its combination with personal computers could be argued as producing the most significant change, especially in the higher education and human resource development contexts, to the way technology was used in learning. Assuming that print is a technology, then in distance education, technology has always played a more central role to teaching and learning than in classroom, or face-to-face, teaching and learning. Due to the "separation of teacher and student" (Keegan, 1986), technology has often been used to mediate communications between teachers and students and for the encapsulation of materials. When mainstream higher education and human resource management started to use technology to mediate learning, it was to the literature of distance education that designers and managers turned to—to seek theoretical or conceptual frameworks. They sought frameworks that would allow them to generalize the techniques and technological approaches of distance education to their own contexts.

In the distance education literature, the changing technologies and their roles have been charted and divided into generations that clearly differentiate between the technologies used. As mentioned earlier, technology has always played a central role in distance education and it is obvious that transitional stages in distance education are clearly linked to the uptake of new technologies. There are limited historical interpretations of distance education in the literature, and the work of Nipper (1989) and Taylor (2001) stands out as a framework that provides an evolutionary description of technological changes in this field. In addition the work of Taylor, in the development of a conceptual framework of the generations of distance education, provides part of the conceptual basis for the models that are described in later chapters.

History of Learning Technology in Higher Education

In 1989 Nipper classified distance education into three "generations," which provided a succinct start to the historical description of technology in distance education. This classification is sufficiently broad to provide a relevant framework for a historical overview of the changed role of technology in learning in other contexts. It has been extended by Taylor (2001) to include the then new field of *flexible learning*. Taylor was commenting in 2001 when learning management systems (LMSs) were gaining wide scale acceptance in mainstream higher education as well as in distance education. Around this time, and probably due to the wide spread use of LMSs, the parlance changed from flexible learning to online learning or e-learning. This probably reflects the immense impact of LMSs on mainstream education. It is argued that the impact of LMSs is the greatest that any technology has had on higher education at least in breadth if not in depth.

Since Taylor's work in 2001 online technology has changed. We have seen an increase in the bandwidth available to many in developed countries. Usage and technology have taken advantage of the extra bandwidth with video and audio becoming increasingly popular ways to communicate online. Also, the Web is changing from a static repository of text and graphics to a dynamic medium for public input. Some refer to this as the change from Web 1.0 to Web 2.0. This was discussed fully in Chapter I. These changes to the use of the Web are sufficiently significant to warrant a generation of their own, even though we are yet to explore the full extent of Web 2.0 for education. Thus a sixth generation has been added to the five developed by Nipper (1989) and Taylor (2001).

Nipper (1989) describes the first generation of distance education as consisting of correspondence courses based on printed matter delivered by the postal service. He describes the second generation as comprising multimedia packages and the third as a combination of broadcast media and teleconferences. In the second and third generations a mixture of technologies was used. Examples of typical mixes of technology were, print and video in the second generation and print and videoconference in the third. However, it was not until the third generation that the separation between technologies used for the provision of materials and others for interactions between people becomes clear. The changes in learning technologies as described by the generations of distance education are reflected in changes in the use of learning technologies in instructional design (Reiser, 2002; Reiser & Dempsey, 2002; Romiszowski, 1988). Similar stages of development can also be found in the human resource development literature with the adoption of open, distance, and flexible learning techniques and technologies to provide some flexibility of the place and time of learning (Wilson, 1999).

Taylor (1995, 2001) continues and extends Nipper's (1989) work to include fourth and fifth generations of distance education in which the boundary between distance education and mainstream higher education and human resource management becomes blurred (see Table 2.1). The boundary becomes blurred as flexible learning is used in mainstream higher education and utilizes technologies and techniques that in earlier generations were confined to distance education. Taylor's fourth generation, titled the flexible learning model not only reinforces the connection between distance education and flexible learning but suggests that flexible learning has evolved logically from distance education as it takes the flexibility of time, place, and pace offered by distance education techniques and technologies and applies them to mainstream higher education and to human resource development. In the fifth generation Taylor suggests that the use of technology has been extended into institutional processes and that they as well as learning are predominantly online. Table 2.1, reproduced from Taylor (2001), provides a description of the generations.

The Sixth Generation of Learning Technologies

While the last chapter of this book is devoted to the future of online learning and contains an in-depth discussion of it, it is appropriate to touch on the future here in the context of the history of technology in education. The fourth generation marks the extension of the application of learning technologies from distance education courses alone to mainstream education with the advent of flexible learning. At about this time the generic term *online and distance learning* (ODL and sometimes referred to as *open and distance learning*) gained currency to describe the wider application of the technology. However, this change in terminology also describes the borrowing of traditional distance education methods for mainstream learning. The changes to the technology and to the approach to learning between the fifth and sixth generations are significant. Taylor's criteria, while adequate descriptors of the earlier generations fall short in the description of the sixth. For this reason a second table (Table 2.2) is presented in which the criterion *advanced interactive delivery* has been changed to *advanced interactive environment* to draw attention to a fundamental change between the fifth and sixth generations. The change in learning between these last two generations is predicated on the change between Web 1.0 and Web 2.0, and while the change is significant it is not a complete change in which the old is eschewed to be replaced by the new. Rather the old still exists in that resources will still need to be available to students but rather than them being *delivered* at a predetermined stage in the program they are made available or provided so that students can make incorporate them into their learning when appropriate. Also, the sixth generation is characterized by an increase in the materials created by students. The materials are likely to be shared among the students' peers and are likely to include video and audio as well as text. Like Web 2.0, the sixth generation is also characterized by higher levels of input from students using social software like blogs and wikis. Wilson et al. (2006) argue that the dominant

Table 2.1. Models of distance education: A conceptual framework (Taylor, 2001)

Models of Distance Education	Associated Delivery Technologies	Characteristics of Delivery Technologies			Highly Refined Materials	Advanced Interactive Delivery
		Flexibility				
		Time	Place	Pace		
First Generation—The Correspondence Model	• Print	Yes	Yes	Yes	Yes	No
Second Generation—The Multi-Media Model	• Print	Yes	Yes	Yes	Yes	No
	• Audiotape	Yes	Yes	Yes	Yes	No
	• Videotape	Yes	Yes	Yes	Yes	No
	• Computer-based learning (eg CML/CAL)	Yes	Yes	Yes	Yes	Yes
	• Interactive video (disk and tape)	Yes	Yes	Yes	Yes	Yes
Third Generation—The Telelearning Model	•Audio-teleconference • Videoconference	No	No	No	No	Yes
	• Audiographic Communication	No	No	No	No	Yes
		No	No	No	Yes	Yes
	• Broadcast TV/Radio, Audiotele-conference	No	No	No	Yes	Yes
Fourth Generation—The Flexible Learning Model	• Interactive multimedia	Yes	Yes	Yes	Yes	Yes
	• internet based access to www resources	Yes	Yes	Yes	Yes	Yes
	• computer mediated communications	Yes	Yes	Yes	No	Yes
Fifth Generation—The Intelligent Flexible Learning Model		Yes	Yes	Yes	Yes	Yes
	• interactive multimedia online	Yes	Yes	Yes	Yes	Yes
	• internet based access to WWW resources					
	• Computer-mediated communication, using automated response systems	Yes	Yes	Yes	Yes	Yes
	• Campus portal access to institutional processes and resources	Yes	Yes	Yes	Yes	Yes

design of educational systems needs to change from fifth generation style LMSs if they are to better serve the needs of learners. The changes are several and include changing to social software based personal environments in which students arrange their own access to their own resources as well as those provided by the institution and their peers. The changes are systemic and the new generation of learning has been referred to as eLearning 2.0 (Downes 2006). As mentioned earlier, the sixth generation is discussed in depth in the last chapter.

Taylor's (2001) framework (Table 2.1) and the sixth generation of online and distance learning indicate that a salient characteristic of the technologies of distance education, flexible learning, and online and distance learning is the differentiation between materials and interactivity which is an important first step in the categorization of learning technologies. The two right hand columns in Table 2.1 indicate that each generation and technology mentioned includes some level of materials provided to learners and/or interactivity.

In the first generation the technology was predominantly printed material and while Taylor's (2001) framework indicates that there was no *advanced interactive delivery* some limited interaction could be had through the comments of the assessor on the work of the learner. Of course, as the technology was limited to printed material, its role in this generation of distance education was both to provide materials to learners and to facilitate limited feedback from assessors. And obviously as the generation is characterized by one technology, selection of technologies was not required.

In the second generation of distance education, use was made of several technologies such as video and audiotapes, as well as early computer-based learning. In this generation, designers of learning events were faced with an additional task—that of selecting technology—and in many cases would have engaged specialized instructional designers who selected the technologies as part of the design of the learning events. The available technologies from which selections were made were predominantly one-way as they were for the provision of materials; hence interaction between learners and between learners and facilitators of learning was limited.

Taylor's (2001) framework, (Table 2.1), can be interpreted as implying that the technologies of an earlier generation are not used in later ones. However, it is generally known that technologies of previous generations were typically available and used

Table 2.2. A sixth generation of online and distance learning

Models of Distance Education	Associated Technologies	Characteristics of Delivery Technologies				
		Flexibility			Highly Refined Materials	Advanced Interactive Environment
		Time	Place	Pace		
Sixth generation— Web 2.0 e-learning 2.0	- Social software - Student creation of resources - Sharing of experiences and resources - Media rich	Yes	Yes	Yes	Yes	Yes

in subsequent ones. For example, while printed materials are only mentioned in the first and second generations, obviously they have been used, to varying degrees, in all generations to date. The technologies listed for each generation represent a change in focus and the new technologies that were introduced in each generation; so designers in the third generation could design learning events, selecting from the innovative, two-way technologies of the third generation, which provided increased interaction between the people involved, and the more familiar, one-way technologies of the earlier generations.

The fourth generation marks a watershed in the application of the techniques and technologies of distance education. In the 1980s and 1990s many institutions actively borrowed approaches that hitherto were practiced only by distance education and open learning institutions and applied them in various degrees to what were traditionally face-to-face learning events. Although it is beyond the scope of this book to theorize about the reasons for this change, it is generally known that the increase in demand for flexibility of place and time of learning came about for two reasons. One was to meet the demand of an increasingly employed and hence part-time student body and the other was in the pursuit of the efficiencies of increased student-to-staff ratios that distance education techniques appeared to offer. This new approach to teaching had many names and in the 1990s *flexible delivery* or *flexible learning* entered the popular parlance of higher education in Australia. Taylor (1996) suggests that there were many contexts to which flexible learning was suited. In particular he cited continuing and professional education as the students were predominantly in full-time employment and hence only available to learn part time. For this kind of learning teachers had to take on new roles. Rather than simply provide face-to-face presentations and interactions, they now were required to produce resources in print or media. These resources needed to be high in quality and allowed students to interact with them at times and places that were convenient to them. In this way there was flexibility of where and when. Taylor suggested that these technologies allowed the student to "turn the teacher on, or off, at will as lifestyle permits." He also saw the potential of the Internet as a means of delivery of resources and as a host for online interactions without sacrificing these flexibilities.

For mainstream higher education this represented marked changes in the process of learning, which of course necessitated changes in the design of learning events. Designers who had previously designed for the classroom, where technologies were used as adjuncts to the learning process, were now faced with designing for technologies that played a central role in the learning process, and in many cases designers did so with the support of guidelines and checklists developed by institutions in attempts to facilitate and conceptualize learning in this context of changing technology. The salient difference was that where technologies were previously selected to be adjuncts to learning events they were now being selected to play central roles, of facilitating or mediating learning events. During this generation the World Wide Web was accepted by many institutions as a central and systemic learning technology. Web learning environments or LMSs, such as Blackboard and WebCT, have enjoyed rapid and wide acceptance in higher education. Describing itself as "the world's leading provider of e-Learning solutions for higher education" (WebCT, 2001), WebCT claims that over 2,600 institutions in 84 countries are licensed to use its learning environment (WebCT, 2001a). This widespread use of Web-based learning environments has engendered new terms in the parlance of higher education, and Web-based learning is often referred to as *online learning* or *e-learning*.

The fifth generation as described by Taylor (2001) builds on the fourth generation, with the addition of "campus portal access to institutional processes and resources" and "automated response systems." Portals provide students with an efficient access point to learning materials and resources as well as records of their progress and host communications with the administrative and support units of the institution. However, they do not impact to any great degree on the selection of technology at the tactical level.

At the time of writing many organizations and institutions have a degree of online learning. In some cases learners may do all their learning online, in others the online elements serve to support to the face-to-face experience. The resources to assist designers of online learning are limited and many organizations and institutions do not have sufficient specialized learning event designers to design all of the online learning events they offer. As the design of most learning events in higher education is undertaken by facilitators there is a need for guidelines to assist them in this process. Such guidelines necessarily would include a method for the selection of technologies that leads to applications of learning technologies that are appropriate to the learners, the material, the context, and the budget.

The generations of distance education as described by Nipper (1989) and expanded into a framework by Taylor (2001) provide an evolutionary description of technological change in distance education and in the later generations describe the changed role of technology in higher education. However, these technological changes are not confined to these fields. In the field of human resource development, parallel, but sometimes delayed changes in the utilization of learning technologies permits the application of Taylor's conceptual framework to it.

History of Technology in Human Resource Development

The changing role of learning technology in higher education is reflected in changes in human resource development. Training in organizations has been happening for a long time and the master/apprentice model has been used for thousands of years.

While it can be argued that this model has stood the test of time it is no longer considered appropriate to meet all the learning needs of organizations, and other methods of providing training to employees have increased in the post World War II period (Smith, 1992). During the 20th century, with the development of the discipline of psychology to include learning theories and the development of economic theories that provided a link between training and profitability, other models of learning within organizations were developed. After the second world war, and perhaps as a reaction to the need for highly efficient training and retraining needs, the term *human resources* entered the parlance of management and in 1968 was extended to *human resources development* by Leonard Nadler (Sredl & Rothwell, 1986). Since then the study and practice of human resource development has grown into a discipline with a sturdy discourse.

As mentioned in Chapter I, human resource development has differentiated learning into three modes: training, education, and development. Where training refers to learning that applies to the current task in the organization, education is learning in educational institutions and development is learning for growth of the individual but not necessarily directly related to the current task (Wilson, 1999).

The approaches taken by human resource development to learning within organizations have been driven in large part by the potential to improve job performance and hence increase profitability (Nadler & Nadler, 1994). To organizations the importance of training their workforce lies in the bottom line. Performance of the organization can be improved through increases in individual performance and competitiveness brought about as results of training. Smith (1992) argues that the consensus is that training is a key part of an organization's success in a competitive context.

Organizations are generally quick to adopt new training methods if they are more efficient than the status quo (Commission on Technology and Adult Learning, 2001). For example, the increase in the use of videoconference in Australia in the early 1990s, while driven initially by an airline pilots' strike, did not decrease to pre-strike levels after the pilots went back to work. It is generally known that, as organizations counted the savings in travel time and expenses, videoconference was retained as a more cost effective learning technology. A similar increase in the use of videoconference occurred immediately after the September 11th terrorist attacks on the World Trade Center. At the time of writing the threat of death or illness due to Severe Acute Respiratory Syndrome (SARS) has caused managements of organizations to curtail employees travel to those regions affected. In many of these cases learning technologies are being used to remotely provide learning events. The University of Wollongong, which has teaching commitments in the SARS-affected regions of Singapore, Hong Kong, and China, provided learning materials to learners through audio and video recording and Internet streaming as an alternate way to meet its commitments.

Traditional classroom technologies such as overhead projectors, slides, movies, video, and audio recordings have been used in training at much the same time as they were used in higher education. However the training needs of organizations have different levels of scale, and are more disparate than the educational needs of students in higher education. While this, and possibly the required investment in infrastructure, has resulted in a slower rate of uptake of organization-wide flexible learning, some organizations are actively investigating and deploying learning technologies that play a central role in the training process. Many terms have been coined to describe these approaches, including: technology-based training (TBT), Web-based training (WBT), Internet-based training (IBT), and e-learning to name a few. In the development of these newer uses of technology in learning, human resource developers have drawn heavily on the discourse of open, distance and flexible learning (ODFL) (Wilson, 1999) and the technologies used are the same as those described by Taylor (2001) in the Fourth and fifth generations of Table 2.1.

Flexible approaches to training have benefits and costs to organizations. The benefits from flexibility of when training occurs mean that trainees can learn when it suits the task or the organization. For organizations that have branches or are geographically dispersed, the benefits of where include a reduction or the removal of travel time and expenses between the trainee's workplace and the training venue. The costs of flexible approaches to learning arise from the resources and infrastructure required to provide it. These can range from the production costs of printed materials, videotapes, or Web pages to the costs to set up in-house, or hire external, videoconference or media production facilities. Of course a relationship exists between the amount spent on the learning event, the number of trainees that can be trained with it, and the increase in profitability that will result. For example, investment levels in a learning resource with a long shelf-life that can be reused many times can generally afford to be higher than those for resources that are subject to rapid change.

History of Technology in Instructional Design

The process of instructional design is concerned with the planning, design, development, implementation, and evaluation of instructional activities or events that facilitate learning, and the purpose of the discipline of instructional design is to build knowledge about the steps for the development of instruction (Seels & Glasgow, 1990). While the history of instructional design is relatively young compared with higher education, there are parallels in each that concern the use of learning technologies. The most recent of which is also evident in human resource development and concerns the use of technology as central elements of the learning process.

There is some confusion in the literature as to the origins of instructional design. It has been suggested that it started at the turn of the 20th century. It has been reported that the origins of the field go back to the late 19th century. In 1899 John Dewey addressed the American Psychological Association and called for "the development of a linking science between learning theory and educational practice" (Reigeluth, 1983).

However, other commentators state that the field grew out of the special training needs of World War II and the solutions to them that were designed by educators and psychologists (Reiser & Dempsey, 2002). During the second half of the 20th century, instructional design grew to be recognized as a discipline with its own literature.

The field of instructional design does not limit its output to one area. In many instances the field is described as designing instruction for schools, higher education, technical education, business, industry, the military, health care, and others (Reiser & Dempsey, 2002; Gagné, Briggs, & Wager, 1992; Reigeluth, 1983).

In many ways the history of the use of technology in instructional design reflects the patterns noted in higher education and human resource development. Apart from the practice of distance education, technology in instructional design during the 1950s and 1960s was confined primarily to classroom technologies such as movies, slides, audio recordings, and printed resources, where their use was confined to adjuncts to teaching activities. This was also the general use that learning technologies were put to in higher education and human resource development during the same period and is reflected in the term *teaching aids* that was used to describe them. During the 1970s, with the proliferation of mass media and affordable technologies of encapsulation, the term teaching aids was replaced with *instructional media* and *educational technology* and the role of the technology was increased to provide some level of individual instruction. This changed role of technology caused the field to change its conceptualization of the role of technology and included in the process of instructional design was the new task of selecting technologies, often referred to as *media* that would play a significant role in the learning event being designed.

The development and proliferation of personal computers in the late 1980s and 1990s, together with the Internet and the World Wide Web in the mid-1990s, created the opportunity for the next major change of direction in the use of technology in learning. This change was felt in instructional design, and recent contributions to the discourse have reflected the heightened role of technology in learning to the extent that in one notable monograph (Reiser & Dempsey, 2002) the field is renamed *instructional design and technology*. The technologies used in this stage of the evolution of instructional design are the same as those described by Taylor (2001) in the fourth and fifth generations of Table 2.1.

While the fields of higher education, human resource development and instructional design all have slightly different approaches to, and uses of, learning technologies there are parallel trends in each field that reflect the fourth and fifth generations of distance education (Taylor 2001). While each field might use the same learning technologies in slightly different ways, Taylor's classification, in Table 2.1, in which they are categorized as providing *highly refined materials* or facilitating *advanced interactive delivery* is sufficiently broad to apply to each field and to provide a rudimentary conceptual differentiation of learning technologies in general.

A review of the literature of the fields of higher education, human resource development, and instructional design to evaluate the suitability of conceptualizations of learning technologies to technology selection reveals that as learning technologies and their use have changed, different theoretical approaches to their conceptualization have been reported. In many cases the aim has been assisting in the design of learning events that make use of learning technologies in appropriate ways.

Conclusion

Since World War II, learning technologies have changed in the role they play, their complexity, and their proliferation. At the turn of the 21st century, with the burgeoning adoption of the new Internet-based technologies and an accelerated rate of technological change, the role of learning technology is more entrenched in the institutions and organizations than ever before.

As higher education and human resource development adopt flexible approaches to learning, as described in Taylor's (2001) fourth and fifth generations of distance education (Table 2.1), the role of learning technologies has changed from one of being adjuncts to the learning process to one of centrality in which technologies are the prime mediators of communications between learner and materials, learner and facilitator, and between learners.

As learning technologies and their roles have changed, the terminology used to describe them has changed as well. In places the terms *media* and *technology* have been used interchangeably and the term *teaching aids* had currency when technologies were used as only adjuncts to learning. Today, new terms have entered the vernacular of higher education and human resource development to describe the breadth and depth of the impact of new Internet-based learning technologies; for example, *online learning* and *e-learning*.

Before the theoretical frameworks and technology selection method are developed, the literature concerned with the selection of learning technologies in the fields of higher education, human resource development, and instructional design is reviewed to evaluate current and past practice and to provide details of the context in which the theoretical frameworks of learning activities and learning technologies have been developed.

References

Bates, A. W. (1995). *Technology, open learning and distance education.* New York: Routledge.

Bates, A.W., & Downes, S. (2001). Commission on Technology and adult learning. *A vision of e-learning for America's workforce: Report of the Commission on technology and adult learning.* ASTD: Alexandria, Virginia.

Downes, S. (2006). *E-learning 2.0.* Retrieved October 12, 2006, from http://www.elearnmag.org/subpage.cfm?section=articles&article=29-1

Gagné, R., Briggs, L., & Wager, W. (1992). *Principles of instructional design.* Fort Worth, TX: Harcourt Brace Jovanovich.

Keegan, D. (1986). *The foundations of distance education.* London: Croom Helm.

Nadler, L., & Nadler, Z. (1994). *Designing training programs.* Houston, TX: Gulf.

Nipper, S. (1989). Third generation distance learning and computer conferencing. In R. Mason & A. Kaye (Eds.), *Mindweave: Communication, computers and distance education.* Oxford, UK: Pergamon.

Reigeluth, C. (Ed.). (1983). *Instructional-design theories and models: An overview of their current status.* NJ: Lawrence Erlbaum.

Reiser, R. (2002). What field did you say you were in? Defining and naming our field. In R. Reiser & J. Dempsey (Eds.), *Trends and issues in instructional design and technology.* Upper Saddle River, NJ: Merrill Prentice Hall.

Reiser, R., & Dempsey, J. (2002). *Trends and issues in instructional design and technology.* Upper Saddle River, NJ: Merrill Prentice Hall.

Romiszowski, A. (1988). *The selection and use of instructional media.* London: Kogan Page; New York: Nichols.

Seels, B., & Glasgow, Z. (1990). *Exercises in instructional design.* Columbus, OH: Merrill.

Smith, A. (1992). *Training and development in Australia.* Sydney, Australia: Butterworths.

Sredl, H., & Rothwell, W. (1986). *The ASTD reference guide to professional training roles and competencies.* Amhurst, MA: Human Resource Development Publishing.

Taylor, J. (1995). Distance education technologies: The fourth generation. *Australian Journal of Educational Technology, 11*(2), 1-7.

Taylor, J. (2001). *Fifth generation distance education* (Higher Education Series, Report No. 40). Canberra, Australia: Department of Education, Training and Youth Affairs.

WebCT. (2001). *About us.* Retrieved September 9, 2002, from http://www.webct.com/company

WebCT. (2001a). *Who uses WebCT?* Retrieved September 9, 2002, from http://www.webct.com/company/viewpage?name=company_webct_customer

Wilson, J. P. (1999). *Human resource development: Learning and training for individuals and organizations.* London: Kogan Page.

Wilson, S., Liber, O., Beauvoir, P., Milligan, C., Johnson, M., & Sharples, P. (n.d.). *Personal learning environments: Challenging the dominant design of educational systems.* Retrieved October 12, 2006, from http://dspace.ou.nl/bitstream/1820/727/1/sw_ectel.pdf

Chapter III

The Context

Introduction

Today there is a range of technologies available to those who design learning events, from the old and simple to the new and complex. Key attempts have been made to develop theoretical frameworks of learning technologies and are reported in the literature of the fields of higher education, human resource development, and instructional design. These three fields are not discrete and some overlap occurs. For example, commentators in the field of instructional design state that their designs are intended for learning in many contexts including schools, higher education, organizations, and government (Gagné, Briggs, & Wager, 1995; Reigeluth, 1983). In many cases the theoretical frameworks are intended to guide the selection of learning technologies but often the conceptualizations have not kept pace with the changes in existing technologies and with the advent of new technologies. A review of the literature of these fields will help to evaluate the suitability of conceptualizations of learning technologies to their selection in the process of designing learning events.

Learning technologies are generally not applied to a whole subject, course, or program, rather they are applied to elements or groups of activities within a subject, course, or program, and it is argued that a conceptualization of these groups of learning activities to which learning technologies can be matched forms the basis of a sound technology selection method. The literature of the fields mentioned previously is reviewed to ascertain the suitability of existing conceptions of learning activities for this purpose.

A common, although not central, theme in the literature of these fields, is that a broad division of learning activities occurs when learning technologies are introduced. This is a division that is imposed by the limitations of individual technologies. While activities in face-to-face learning events may seamlessly change from one-way to two-way, when technologies are in place this is not always simple, as the technology suited to one-way activities may or may not be suited to two-way activities. One-way activities refer to those in which information flows predominantly in one direction, for example, a presentation by a student or an academic. Two-way activities are those in which information flows in at least two directions, for example, a discussion or conversation.

Categorization and Classification of Learning Technologies

In many instances attempts have been made to categorize and/or classify learning technologies. In the literature of several fields (for example: instructional design, higher education, human resource development) attempts have been made to classify learning technologies by the inherent characteristics of the technology or categorize them by the role they play in learning. As the number of technologies that are available to learning designers has grown, and continues to grow rapidly, many of the attempts to categorize them are outdated and others appear perfunctory in the context of the newer technologies.

Leshin, Pollock, and Reigeluth (1992) present a classification scheme for what they refer to as "media." The scheme is based on attributes of the media and learning technologies and are grouped into five classes referred to as "systems." Writing in 1992, just prior to the advent of the Web, Leshin et al. (1992, p. 256) include two high-tech systems, divided between audio visual technology and computer technology. The examples they quote for their audiovisual system include technologies that were state-of-the-art at that time, for example, video, slide-film programs, film, and live television. In their computer-based systems they include as examples, computer-based instruction, computer-based interactive video, and hypertext. The print-based system in their classification includes books, manuals, workbooks, job aids, and handouts and the visual-based system includes books, job aids, charts, graphs, maps, figures, transparencies, and slides. Curiously they add a media category entitled "human-based system," which includes teacher, instructor, tutor, role plays, group activities, and field trips.

Perhaps they include humans as human communications can conceivably be thought of as having the same characteristics of media in that the systems share the characteristic of carrying "a message (information) to a receiver (learner)" and that some "systems" can "process messages from the receiver" (Leshin et al., 1992, p 256). While there are clear issues with the model in terms of not applying to technologies that have been developed since 1992, it is also noteworthy that the implied conception of learning is one of information transmission. This is clearly at odds with the collaborative approaches that became fashionable in the late 1990s. Writing in the field of instructional design, Leshin et al. use their classification as a starting point from which technology-based learning events can be designed. They state that in the process of instructional design, that they refer to as "message design" the designer selects a particular medium or set of media (p. 256). Unfortunately they do not describe how the media are selected.

The approach taken to the classification of learning technologies by Leshin et al. (1992) does not result in tools that are suitable for the design of learning activities by teachers. The classification system provides little or no insight into the application of the technology and is not much more than a labeling system and, as they were writing prior to the development of the World Wide Web, the classification system does not include learning management systems (LMSs) or any of the newer, Internet technologies. They could easily be added to the last category: computer-based systems, but this adds little to our understanding of them or to their application to learning in an appropriate way.

Also writing in the literature of instructional design, Romiszowski (1988) classifies media by the sensory channels they support and provides examples such as telephone for the auditory channel, video for the "Audio/Visual" channel, chalkboards for the visual channel, and devices or models for the "Tactile or Kinaesthetic" channel. Romiszowski's approach is slightly more informative than that of Leshin et al. (1992), as he makes the conceptual connection between technologies and "sensory channels." However his system of classification is not suited to the design of learning activities for the same reason as Leshin et al.'s, that is, it provides only slightly more insight into the characteristics of the technologies that lead to the matching of them to learning activities in an appropriate manner.

Others in the field of instructional design take an even less rigorous approach to the categorization or classification of learning technologies. Reiser and Gagné (1983) argue that a "number of kinds of categories can be devised for the classification of media" and that "frequently employed categories include audio, print, still visual and motion visual, and real objects" (p. 13). They elaborate that the reasons for categorizing media are generally associated with their selection and that their application can be optimized through matching their characteristics to the task.

... a particular type of medium can best present a task having a similar classification. For example the learning of a task that requires differentiation of visual features can best be done with a visual medium. (p. 13)

Although Reiser and Gagné's (1983) categorization of media runs the risk of stating the obvious, it is appropriate for the selection of technologies for use as adjuncts to classroom teaching. However, it too, is limited to being applicable to the technologies available in the early 1980s and it does not have much to offer the selection of learning technologies when they are central elements of learning events. The model unfortunately does not easily expand to address technologies developed after their conceptualization was published.

Some other commentators have taken a more interpretive approach to the categorization of learning technologies. Contrary to the descriptive classification approaches, Laurillard (2002) categorizes learning technologies through the use of "pedagogical categories" and argues that there have been many attempts to categorize and classify the technologies in the literature. She states rather categorically that none of the attempts is "very illuminating for our purpose here" (p. 83).

Laurillard (2002) continues with the argument that educational media should be classified in terms of the categories and extent of learning processes they support and provides the four categories: "Discursive, Adaptive, Interactive and Reflective." Laurillard's categories provide limited insight to the nature and characteristics of learning technologies when used outside of her "teaching strategy" and hence are not suited to our purpose here. However, Laurillard does imply, unlike many others, that pedagogical decisions should be made before the technologies are selected. Laurillard does address the selection of technologies and a further discussion of her categorization for the purpose of technology selection is included in the next chapter.

In a similar fashion to Leshin et al. (1992), Romiszowski (1981), and Reiser and Gagné (1983), Bates (1995) classifies learning technologies in two ways. Firstly, according to the "medium they carry" and he states that there are five most important media in education, being: direct human contact (face-to-face), text (including still graphics), audio, television and computing (p. 31). Secondly, Bates distinguishes between technologies that are one-way and two-way. He argues that two-way technologies allow communications between people (p. 32).

Bates (1995), writing about open learning and distance education in the higher education sector, where in the past communications between learners and between learners and facilitators have been difficult due to the absence or lack of face-to-face opportunities, describes one-way and two-way technologies for four of the "five most important media." This correlation is shown in Table 3.1. The classification of learning technologies as being primarily one-way or two-way is reflected in Taylor's conceptual framework (see previous chapter) in which he classifies characteristics of technologies as "Highly Refined Materials" and/or "Advanced Interactive Delivery." Taylor (2001), citing Bates, makes it clear that there are two very different types of interactivity: social interactivity and interaction with resources.

This can confuse the notion of two-way technologies, and from Table 3.1, Bates' (1995) examples, with the exception of interactive databases all are of human interactions between learners or between learners and facilitators of learning. In the fourth and fifth generations of distance education as described by Taylor in the previous chapter, the technologies are characterized by both kinds of interactivity and unfortunately no differentiation between interactions between people and interactions with materials is provided. The congruency between Bates' approach to the classification of learning technologies as one-way or two-way and Taylor's approach, is supported by Rowntree (1994) who classifies learning technologies as:

- Print-Based,
- Audio-visual or technology-based
- Practical or project work, or
- Human Interaction
- others (p. 66)

Clearly the first three categories are one-way for the provision of, and interaction with, materials and the last category is clearly for the two-way interactions between people.

Table 3.1. One-way and two-way technology applications in distance education (Bates, 1995, p. 31)

Media	One-way technology applications	Two-way technology applications
Text	Course units; supplementary materials	Correspondence tutoring
Audio	Cassette programmes; radio programmes	Telephone tutoring; audio conferencing
Television	Broadcast programmes; cassette programmes	Interactive television (TV out; telephone in); video conferencing
Computing	CAL, CAI, CBT[*]; databases; multimedia	E-mail; interactive databases; computer conferencing

computer aided learning, computer aided instruction, computer based training

Conceptualizing Learning Technologies

The conceptualization of learning technologies as one-way or two-way provides a starting point for a theoretical framework of learning technologies that categorizes them according to the learning activities they support. This theoretical framework is developed further in Chapter VI.

From the generations of distance education discussed in the previous chapter, it is clear that in all but the first generation more than one technology is indicated and a combination of technologies is generally used within a subject or course. LMSs can be considered a single technological system and indeed they are packaged as such. However, for the purposes of the design of learning events that make appropriate use of them, LMSs can be considered to be collections of technological elements. Each technological element can have a separate role in the learning event such as the presentation of information, the facilitation of discussion, or others. The selection of appropriate learning technologies can then be seen as the matching of single technologies, or technological elements of LMSs, to sections of a subject or course or to categories of learning activities. The literature of higher education, human resource development, and instructional design was surveyed to ascertain the suitability of existing conceptualizations of learning activities to the process of technology selection.

Learning Activities

The design of learning is probably more clearly described as the design of learning activities, as it is the activities that are designable compared to *learning* which is the desired outcome of the activities. While the term *instruction* may be out of favor with some commentators, as it may imply a teacher-directed approach, *instructional design* has been used for some years to describe the design of the things learners and teachers or trainers do to facilitate learning. Gagné et al. (1995, p. 3) state that instruction is the sum total of the events that impact on students and result in learning. They go on to consider these events as mostly external to the learner and suggest that they might be encapsulated in a medium such as print or embodied in the words spoken by a teacher. They also note that some events of instruction might be internal or based on learner activity that they refer to as self-instruction.

One of the objectives of this chapter is to investigate the existing conceptualizations of learning activities in terms of their suitability for technology selection through matching them to learning technologies. Courses of study, subjects, or training programs are generally too large to be matched to a particular technology or technological element of an LMS. As mentioned earlier, distance education courses are generally characterized by a "package" of several technologies (Bates, 1995) or "combination of media" (Rowntree, 1994), which indicates clearly that more than one technology is generally used. In online learning or e-learning where an LMS is matched to a course, subject, or program the question remains of how to undertake the matching of each technological element of the LMS to subsections of the course, subject, or program. This chapter considers approaches to the categorization and classification of learning activities and in the following chapters reconceptualizes them in such a way as to facilitate their matching to learning technologies. However, before conceptualizations are considered some clarification and a definition of learning activities are required.

Gagné et al. (1992) use the term "events of instruction" to describe decisions made by teachers during a class.

The instructional events of a lesson may take a variety of forms. They may require the teacher's participation to a greater or lesser degree, and they may be determined by the student to a greater or lesser degree. In a basic sense, these events constitute a set of communications to the student. (p. 186)

The scale of each of the *events* or learning activities is temporally smaller than a lesson or class, as generally more than one would take place in a lesson or class. That is to find or develop a conceptualization of learning activities that is suitable for use in the selection of learning technologies, it is sufficient to define them as activities that are smaller than lessons or classes, where these are considered as time-tabled meetings between learners and facilitators or the equivalent in the context of flexible, online, or distance learning. The literature of instructional design places the design of learning activities as a step in the design of a larger course, subject, or curriculum.

With a small number of notable exceptions (Gagné et al., 1992; Laurillard, 2002) there is little reference in the literature to explicit methods of classification and categorization of learning activities. However, several commentators provide tacit classification as a by-product of discussions for other purposes.

Theories of Learning Activities

The approaches to the theorization of learning activities can be grouped into four categories. Some commentators categorize or classify learning activities for purposes other than the selection of learning technologies. Others do not overtly categorize or classify yet provide tacit conceptualizations while achieving other ends and yet others simply list methods or examples of learning activities in the absence of a more detailed conceptual framework. A fourth approach is to provide categories of learning activities that may ultimately assist in the selection of learning technologies in a way that is appropriate for the learners, the material, the context, and the budget.

Theories of Learning Activities for Purposes other than the Selection of Learning Technologies

Theories of learning activities for other purposes may appear to be a digression. However, a short discussion of them provides a background to the theoretical approaches taken hitherto as well as providing an insight to the temporal and other physical qualities of learning activities.

The approach taken by Gagné et al. (1992) and cited by numerous other commentators (Laurillard, 2002; Seels & Glasgow, 1990; Smith & Ragan, 1998) is to classify learning events in terms of their purpose and nature and then categorize them in terms of their chronological appearance in a lesson.

The events of instruction are designed to make it possible for learners to proceed from "where they are" to the achievement of the capability identified as the target objective. In some instances these events occur as a natural result of the learners interaction with the particular materials of the lesson...the exact form of these events (usually communications to the learner) is not something that can be specified in general for all lessons, but rather must be decided for each learning objective. The particular communications chosen to fit each set of circumstances, however, should be designed to have the desired effect in support the learning process. (Gagné et al., 1992, p. 189)

The scale of the *events of instruction* is implied in the previous quote as being temporally smaller than a *lesson* and Gagné et al. (1992) provide examples of learning activities for each of nine events of instruction and clearly indicate that all of the events fit within a lesson. To illustrate, the example provided for the first event of instruction, "Gaining Attention" is described as the opening section of a class in which activities such as providing initial instructions and drawing students' attention to them through the use of imperative terms such as "look!" and "watch!" (Gagné et al., 1992, p. 201). The activities described in this example of the gaining attention event obviously have a short duration that could be measured in minutes or seconds and hence represent the micro level of learning activities. Gagné et al. expand their concept of learning activities by a time-based list of sequential events of instruction. These are:

1. Gaining attention

2. Informing the learner of the objective

3.   Stimulating recall of prerequisite learning
4.   Presenting the stimulus material
5.   Providing learning guidance
6.   Eliciting the performance
7.   Providing feedback about performance correctness
8.   Assessing the performance
9.   Enhancing retention and transfer (p. 190)

The nine events of instruction form an often-used basis for the design of lessons and the activities that occur in them. A shortcoming of the events of instruction is the constraining of them to the duration of a lesson. While this is clearly appropriate for scheduled face-to-face classes, it is not necessarily suited to adult education where flexible approaches to time spent learning are essential for learning to fit with other time constraints such as family, work, and so forth. Although Seels and Glasgow (1990) also divide the process of instruction into a chronological sequence of learning events, which bears a close resemblance to the list provided by Gagné et al. (1992), they do not confine their steps, or events of instruction to a lesson of fixed length. They suggest that no matter how long the *instructional segment* is, there is a set of events that can be "prescribed for all learning situations" (Seels & Glasgow, 1990, p. 161). Seels and Glasgow continue by describing these events as:

1.   Introduction to gain students' attention
2.   Presentation of information, facts, concepts, principles or procedures
3.   Transitional practice designed to help students bridge the gap between entry level behavior and behavior required by the terminal objective(s)
4.   Criterion practice and
5.   Criterion test. (p. 160)

They also indicate that guidance is given and feedback received in steps three and four.

Romiszowski (1981) uses the terms "instructional method," "strategy," and "tactic" to describe what the instructor will do during instruction" (p. 276). He defines methods and strategies as broad approaches as in "the tutorial method" and "active learner participation" strategy that are broad, guiding philosophies of the instruction to be designed. He describes instructional tactics as the specific ways a particular method is implemented in detail and he suggests that they are often, in practice left up to the "classroom instructor." Romiszowski also describes "instructional exercises" as "the actual activities and events that occur when a particular tactic or set of tactics that make up the lesson are put into practice" but suggests that these too are "left to the classroom teacher" (p. 277).

The categorization of learning activities by the role they play is clearly very helpful in the design of learning activities, especially in the context of classroom teaching and learning as it provides designers with smaller chunks of activities to which instructional tactics can be applied. The conceptualization of learning activities by Seels and Glasgow (1990) and by Gagné et al. (1992) do not classify or categorize learning activities into groups that can then be applied to individual learning technologies, and especially in the case of Gagné et al. the activities are clearly intended to be used in classroom teaching where learning technologies are employed as adjuncts rather than as central to the learning process. These conceptualizations are thus not appropriate for use in a technology selection method where learning technologies are matched to learning activities.

Tacit Classification and Categorization of Learning Activities

Other contributors to the literature, while not setting out to overtly classify learning activities, have tacitly provided degrees of classification of them. In an earlier section of this chapter several classifications of learning technologies (Bates, 1995; Rowntree, 1994; Taylor, 2001) were discussed, each of which implies a classification of learning activities. Bates' descriptions of learning technologies as one-way or two-way implies that there are one-way and two-way learning activities and it follows that learning activities that utilize technologies in these ways can be classified as:

- Interactions with the material using the one-way technologies, and
- Interactions between people using the two-way technologies.

Taylor (2001) provides corroboration of this tacit conceptualization in the description of the generations of distance education in the previous chapter, where technologies are categorized as providing *highly refined materials* and/or having *advanced interactive delivery*. Further, Rowntree (1994) implies a similar tacit categorization of learning activities by categorizing media as those for human interaction and those for interaction with materials. It is not surprising that learning activities can be categorized as interactions with materials and interactions between people as this is reflected in many learning experiences.

While this tacit categorization of learning activities is a useful starting point for the conceptualization of learning activities, it requires further development and greater detail for it to be useful in the selection of learning technologies.

Classification and Categorization by Lists and Examples

In a number of instances in the literature (Beard & McPherson, 1999; Seels & Glasgow, 1990; Smith, 1992), rather than providing a conceptualization of learning activities, commentators have chosen to provide a list of instructional methods or examples of learning activities. Seels and Glasgow suggest that methods are instructional strategies or models of teaching, that "determine the nature of the lessons" and indicate a level of granularity by suggesting that a method is a way to provide structure to the learning "at the lesson level rather than the curriculum level" (p. 180). They go on to provide examples of methods that include: lectures, laboratory, discussions, readings, field trips, note-taking, demonstrations, programmed instruction, case studies, role plays, exercises, independent study, and simulations. Beard and McPherson (1999) provide a comprehensive list of 34 training methods that include classroom-based learning activities as well as some learning technologies. They provide a short description of each method and notes on the trainer's perspective and the end-user's perspective. While lists of methods are useful to the learning event designer they are not useful for designing for learning technologies, as they do not provide a direct link to any one learning technology, they do not facilitate an understanding of learning technologies, and in many cases the methods could be facilitated by any of a number of technologies.

Conclusion

Since World War II, learning technologies have changed in the role they play, their complexity, and their proliferation. In the first decade of 21st century, with the burgeoning adoption of the new Internet-based technologies and an accelerated rate of technological change, the role of learning technology is more entrenched in the institutions and organizations than ever before.

There are two different frameworks by which learning technologies are classified or categorized, and for clarity the following differentiation has been made. Learning technologies are classified according to the characteristics of the technologies and categorized according to the role they play in learning. For example Leshin et al. (1992) classify learning technologies as human, print, visual, audio/visual, or computer-based and Laurillard (2002) categorizes learning technologies as supporting "interpersonal and internal dialogue forms," namely discursive, adaptive, interactive, and reflective.

While classification of learning technologies according to their characteristics can be helpful to those who use the technologies at the time, such systems are not always sufficiently extensible to cater to new technologies, and classification systems are prone to limited currency in an environment of rapid technological change. Categorization systems of learning technologies, on the other hand, change only when new or different learning activities emerge.

As higher education and human resource development adopt flexible and online approaches to learning, the role of technologies changes from one of being an adjunct to the process of learning. Their new role is to be the mediators of communications between learners and between learners and teachers and to provide learners with access to the resources they need.

There are several reasons to classify and/or categorize learning technologies. On the broadest level such investigations, through the provision of conceptual or theoretical frameworks, assist our understanding through the indication of similarities and contrasts that can lead to generalization or specialization. On a more narrow and applied level, through the process of technology selection, a deeper understanding of learning technologies can assist in their application to the learning process in a fashion that is appropriate to the learners, the material, the context, and the budget.

The conceptualizations of learning technologies in the literature are not suitable for the selection of learning technologies. Some were found to be limited to descriptions of technologies by their form and as such add little to our understanding of their application to learning. However, the conceptualizations presented by Taylor (2001), Bates (1995), and Rowntree (1994) provide the basis of a theoretical framework through the division of learning technologies into categories of one-way and two-way. The technologies in the one-way category primarily facilitate learners' interactions with materials, while those in the two-way category facilitate interactions between people. The conceptualizations of learning activities in the literature are not suitable for the selection of technologies. In many cases they were designed for other purposes and generally were intended for application in face-to-face, classroom-based learning events. However, tacit conceptualizations of learning activities as by-products of the conceptualization of learning technologies provide the basis of a theoretical framework of learning activities that can be used in a technology selection method. As learning technologies can be grouped as one-way or two-way, it follows that learning activities, in the same context, can be grouped as one-way, interactions with materials, or two-way interactions between people. This symmetry of the bases of theoretical frameworks forms the foundation upon which the technology selection method, developed in subsequent chapters, is built. Before the theoretical frameworks and technology selection method are developed, the literature concerned with the selection of learning technologies in the fields of higher education, human resource development, and instructional design is reviewed to evaluate current and past practice.

References

Bates, A. W. (1995). *Technology, open learning and distance education*. New York: Routledge.

Beard, C., & McPherson, M. (1999). Design and use of group-based training methods. In C. Wilson (Ed.), *Human resource development: Learning and training for individuals and organizations*. London: Kogan Page.

Gagné, R., Briggs, L., & Wager, W. (1992). *Principles of instructional design*. Fort Worth, TX: Harcourt Brace Jovanovich.

Laurillard, D. (2002). *Rethinking university teaching: A conversational framework for the effective use of learning technologies* (2nd ed.). London: Routledge.

Leshin, C., Pollock, J., & Reigeluth, C. (1992). *Instructional design strategies and tactics*. Englewood Cliffs, NJ: Educational Technology Publications.

Reigeluth, C. (Ed.). (1983). *Instructional-design theories and models: An overview of their current status*. NJ: Lawrence Erlbaum.

Reiser, R., & Gagné, R. (1983). *Selecting media for instruction*. Englewood Cliffs, NJ: Educational Technology Publications.

Romiszowski, A. (1981). *Designing instructional systems*. London: Kogan Page /Nichols: New York.

Romiszowski, A. (1988). *The selection and use of instructional media*. London: Kogan Page; Nichols: New York.

Rowntree, D. (1994). *Preparing materials for open, distance and flexible learning*. London: Kogan Page.

Seels, B., & Glasgow, Z. (1990). *Exercises in instructional design*. Columbus, OH: Merrill.

Smith, A. (1992). *Training and development in Australia*. Sydney, Australia: Butterworths.

Smith P., & Ragan, T. (1983). *Instructional Design*. Merril: New York.

Taylor, J. (2001). *Fifth generation distance education* (Higher Education Series, Report No. 40). Canberra, Australia: Department of Education, Training and Youth Affairs.

Chapter IV

A Review of Methods for Selecting Learning Technologies

Introduction

In the recent past, the role of learning technologies in the human resource development and higher education sectors has changed, and today technology plays a central role in learning in many courses, subjects, and programs. In several places in the literature, learning technologies have been classified and categorized, resulting in the development of theoretical or conceptual bases upon which an understanding of the nature and role of learning technologies can be built. In many cases these bases are intended to inform the process of decision making regarding the planned use of learning technologies with some degree of confidence in the appropriateness of the result. Two clear levels of decision making regarding the use of learning technologies have been identified in the literature as the strategic and tactical (Bates, 1995).

The capital and infrastructural costs of some learning technologies dictate that decisions to use them are typically made at the executive level of the institution or organization. Less expensive, yet important to the learning process, are the decisions made by designers of learning events as to what material or learning activities are to be mediated or facilitated by each technology. These are referred to as strategic and tactical decisions, where strategic decisions are of the nature to invest, or not, in a technological system and tactical decisions are concerned with the nature of the use of the technology in the achievement of a particular learning objective. Both strategic and tactical decisions regarding learning technologies are made for development of human resources in organizations and for teaching and learning at universities and colleges.

An example of a strategic decision at the institutional or organizational level is the decision to invest in the equipment and infrastructure needed to offer Web-based online or e-learning, whether to purchase a commercial learning management system (LMS) or to build one that precisely suits the specific needs of the institution or organization. At the level of the designer of learning events, tactical decisions are made in terms of what technological elements of the LMS will be used and what parts of the learning events in the course, will they be used for. For example, will part of the course use text and images on Web pages in the LMS, or will a forum or forums be used for student interaction? What other techniques and technologies will be used?

As mentioned in the previous chapter, there are parallels between the history of the use of technology in human resource development, higher education, and instructional design. There are several instances in the literature (Berge, 2001; Gagné, Briggs, & Wager, 1992; Smith, 1992; Wilson, 1999) where changes in terms and approaches in the education sector have been adapted for use in training and development in the contexts of human resource development and instructional design. When compared to traditional classroom teaching and learning, open learning, distance learning, and flexible learning—as educational paradigms—have all impacted upon the way in which learning events are provided and the way that learning technologies are used. These new paradigms have impacted on organizations and when applied to training and development can provide reductions in costs of training and advantages in timing through the introduction of flexibility of when and where training occurs. As in higher education, the application of these paradigms in human resource development often involves an increase in the use of learning technology and the separation of learner from the facilitator. In particular the Internet and the World Wide Web have had an impact large enough to generate a new approach to training and development and the concomitant terms. For example Web-based training (WBT) (Khan, 2001) and technology-based training (TBT) (Kruse & Keil, 2000) provide approaches to training that rely on the World Wide Web alone in the case of WBT and the Web plus CD-ROM in the case of TBT. While the literature on these single or limited technology approaches to training is quick to point out the advantages to be gained, it does not dwell on the limitations inherent in an approach that is limited to one or two technologies even though one of them is as powerful and ubiquitous as the Internet. However, the purpose of this book is not the evaluation of technological approaches, rather it is the consideration of theoretical frameworks for learning technologies and learning activities as well as methods of technology selection. To achieve this purpose the middle section of the book presents three theoretical models for the matching of technologies to learning activities. The final section of the book details the process of selection and the application of technologies to online learning.

The adoption of the new learning paradigms has been facilitated in part by the advent and spread of the Internet and the World Wide Web. The flexibility of being able to learn when it best suits the task, the individual, or the organization has an obvious potential to increase productivity and has given rise to the concept of just-in-time training. Compared to face-to-face extraction training, just-in-time training is usually on-the-job and can provide gains due to the training being received precisely when it is required to perform a new task. Also, there is reduced disruption to working hours. Another benefit occurs if the training materials are encapsulated in, and delivered by, a learning technology, as they can be available for reinforcement when and where it is needed. Encapsulation also facilitates sharing and reuse of the resources. When encapsulated resources are stored in a content management system, metadata can be attached to them that can provide the teacher or designer with information about the resource and thus assist in the selection process. This is discussed in more detail at the end of Chapter IX. However, due to the absence of the instructor or trainer, to immediately interact with learners, the technology must be able to facilitate the complete learning experience or at least provide direction to the location of answers to learners' queries. The learning technology used must be appropriate to the learner and the organization and selected to do so efficiently and effectively so that the benefits of flexibility are maintained. Existing approaches to the selection of learning technologies are reviewed in the following sections. As the methods suggested in the literature of instructional design are limited and are generally applied to human resource development and higher education, the reviews of them have been combined and the following sections review methods of technology selection for human resource development and higher education. Another area that investigates methods of technology selection is organizational communications. As the efficiency of communications between managers and other members of an organization has clear links to profits, a sturdy body of literature that conceptualizes and theorizes the selection of technologies for communications has developed. This literature is reviewed later in this chapter.

Technology Selection in Human Resource Development

The literature concerned with the selection of technology for training and development in human resource development, appears under-theorized and characterized by guides to technology selection or lists of factors to be considered when selecting them. The guides to selection range in complexity and usually suggest one or more technologies from a finite list. For example "The Media Analysis Model" (Lee & Owens, 2001) is based on 24 questions to be answered on a scale of one to five. The questions are listed in Table 4.1.

In the Lee and Owens model (2001) the questions are grouped into two categories entitled, Instructional/Student factors and Cost Factors. The questions are mainly broad in nature and concern the characteristics of the material and the audience or are about the budget or the potential return on investment.

After collating the results, the Lee and Owens' (2001) media analysis model is proposed as a way to prescribe suitable learning technologies from a list. Lee and

Table 4.1. Instructional and cost factors: Questions in the media analysis model (Lee & Owens, 2001, pp. 8-13)

Instructional/Student Factors	Cost Factors
Content requires interactivity (computer)	Content has a short shelf-life or changes rapidly
Incidental learning may occur	Global audience—Multiple cultures or languages
Collaborative learning is desired	Materials must be available in a variety of formats
Content requires interactivity (human)	Audience level—Fewer than 200 per year need training/support
Audience requires motivation	Must accommodate large numbers of participants—2000 or more per four years of shelf life
Audience requires convenience – training at or near work site	Must train large numbers of employees quickly
Audience has limited access to required technology	Requires compression of training time
Audience has limited access to required expertise	Keep development costs per hour of instruction low
Students are resistant to new media	Keep travel expenses low
Employees must review the information frequently	Keep implementation delivery, and maintenance costs low
There is an immediate need for application of expertise to the job	Testing, evaluating or tracking student performance is necessary
Wide variation in entry-level background knowledge	Tracking course completion is necessary

Owens list of media from which the recommendations of the model are made is:

- Audio tapes,
- Audio teleconference,
- Computer-based,
- Satellite broadcast,
- Instructor-led,
- Performance support,
- Self-paced workbook,
- Video teleconference,
- Video tapes,
- Web-based (p. 14)

The confusion with the terms *media* and *technology* was discussed in Chapter I and it appears that the confusion is also evident here, in the field of human resource development as Lee and Owens (2001) use the term media to describe both technologies and media. For clarity in this book the terms media and medium are not preferred. The term technology is used to include the device or hardware, what is recorded or played with it, the software and the system that supports it. For example the technology *video* refers to the videodiscs (e.g., DVDs) and tapes as well as cameras, players, and screens.

Another example of a technology selection method used in human resource development is the "Training Design and Development Media Selection Model" (Scheer, 2001), which was developed to meet the *train the trainer* needs of the Internal Revenue Service (IRS) (U.S. taxation agency). The model is a complex flowchart containing 13 questions that lead to a range of technologies and methods that are suggested as suitable for the situation. In the *media selection* section of the model the questions asked concern the nature of the learning outcome or the demographics of the learners. For example, the questions ask:

- Are the trainees geographically dispersed?
- Is the same training is required by a number of trainees at the same time? and
- Is the content knowledge or skills?

Unfortunately the Lee and Owens (2001) model and the Scheer (2001) model are limited due to their prescriptive nature and that the technologies they prescribe are only those available when the models were published. Clearly for a model of technology selection to survive it must be capable of application to future technologies. As the models do not inform the user of the nature and characteristics of each technology they cannot be easily extended and used to select technologies developed after their publication.

Another approach to technology selection for human resource development, that is, a less instructive or prescriptive approach, is to provide a list factors to consider or questions to answer when selecting and to provide no directions for the selection process. For example, the Web site for Instructional Systems Inc. (2002) lists the following eleven points to be considered.

- What are my objectives?
- What learning styles am I attempting to address?
- What is the size of my audience?
- Will the training be self-instructional?
- What is cost-effective?
- How much time do I have to develop this?
- Is a high level of final performance required?
- How quickly will the media I am considering change in format and availability?
- How often will the training be updated?
- Should I buy off the shelf or create from scratch?
- Does it promote interest and interactivity?

As in the Lee and Owens (2001) model and the Scheer (2001) model, the questions in the Instructional Systems Inc. model can be seen as questions about costs and questions about instructional or student factors. The Instructional Systems model is certainly not prescriptive but it fails to guide users through the selection process. McPherson and Beard (1999) take a different approach to the selection of technology. They do not differentiate between the selection of technology and the selection of methods. They provide no model, method, or process of technology selection, rather they provide a limited number of examples and a large table of methods and technologies. However, they do not explain how any technology on the list can be used for particular *methods*. Their table lists methods and technologies and contains a short description of each as well as notes on the perspectives of the *trainer* and the *end user*. For clarity the elements of the their table have been listed in Table 4.2 and have been annotated by the author. The lack of distinction between technologies, activities, and other, for the elements of the list, implies interchangeability.

Table 4.2 The methods of training as suggested by McPherson and Beard (1999)

"Method"	Annotation
Action Learning Sets	Resource
Action Maze	Resource
Brainstorming	Activity
Business Game	Activity
Simulations	Activity
Buzz Groups	Activity
Case Study	Activity/Resource
CD-ROM	Technology
Computer Based Training (CBT)	Technological approach
Computer Conferencing/Newsgroups	Technology
Discovery Learning	Approach to learning
Discussion	Activity
Exercise	Class of Activities
Experiential Exercises	Activity
Films and Videos	Technology
Fish Bowl Exercises	Activity
Instruction	Approach to teaching
In-tray Methods	Activity
Language Laboratory	Technology
Lecture	Approach to Teaching
Multimedia	Technology
Video Conferencing	Technology
Open Forum	Activity
Outdoor Development Programmes	Activity
Project	Activity
Prompt List	Activity
Radio and TV Broadcasts	Technology
Role-play	Activity
Role-reversal	Activity
Self-managed Learning/Reading	Activity
Study Groups	Activity
Syndicates	Activity
T-group	Activity
Training	A subset of education
Virtual Reality Training	Application of technology
Web-Based Learning	Application of technology

For example, videoconference is on the list and it can certainly be used in training (also on the list) but no clarification exists to suggest methods that best suits the use of videoconference for training.

In a similar fashion Smith (1992) does not provide a method, model, or process for the selection of technology. Rather, in a chapter entitled: "Methods and Media," he describes in some depth the technologies of video, computer-based training, and interactive video. Others also appear to limit the technologies recommended for human resource development. As mentioned earlier, Kruse and Keil (2000) present the TBT approach in which the technological options are limited to multimedia CD-ROM and Web-based training. While this may appear to be a technological limitation, Kruse and Keil point out that the two technologies have many benefits, such as flexibility of time and place of learning. They also point out that for asynchronous training using these technologies, one of the disadvantages is the reduction or elimination of social interaction. They propose a simple decision grid to select the more appropriate of the two technologies based on the two criteria: (1) frequency of updates and (2) whether or not audio and video are required. Romiszowski and Chang (2001) analyze the uses of the World Wide Web in training and categorize them as individual and group study modes. The details of this categorization are shown in Table 4.3.

Romiszowski and Chang (2001) address the question of which is the appropriate variety of WBT for a subject or course by arguing that all four categories: (1) individual/synchronous, (2) individual/asynchronous, (3) group/synchronous, and (4) group/asynchronous have "their respective roles to play in modern education and training systems" (Romiszowski & Chang, 2001, p. 110). However they single out the asynchronous/group category for treatment and argue that it has the most to offer education both now and in the future, particularly in the corporate training context.

Both Kruse and Keil (2000) and Romiszowski and Chang (2001) concentrate on one or two technologies and suggest they can meet most training needs. Unfortu-

Table 4.3 CBT-WBT and CMC-WBT (Romiszowski & Chang, 2001, p. 109)

	Individual Study Mode (CBT-WBT*)	Group Study Mode (CMC-WBT*)
Online Use or Synchronous Communication	Browsing the Web, accessing Websites for information or CBT modules	Internet relay chat (IRC) or Web-based videoconference sessions
Offline Use or Asynchronous Communication	Downloading courseware from the Web for later study on local computers	Asynchronous CMC tools such as e-mail, discussion lists and groupware environments

CBT: computer-based training, WBT: Web-based training, CMC: computer mediated communications

nately this approach to the application of technology to learning is limited by the same characteristics as the Lee and Owens (2001) and the Scheer (2001) models. By prescribing one or two technologies little opportunity for the provision of an insight to other technologies and no allowance in the selection method for technologies developed later.

Importance of Training

Training and development is important to individuals, as there is little doubt that opportunities for increased income and job satisfaction can be gained. Training and development is also important to organizations. While it is difficult but not impossible to find a direct correlation between development and the performance of the organization, the importance of training is that it can increase the performance of employees and thereby increase efficiency and competitive advantage. However, training has real associated costs and ways to quantify costs must be available if the organization is to calculate the return on the training or development investment. As the selection of appropriate learning technologies can be reflected in the efficiency of training and as training can result in increases in productivity, it follows that a correlation can exist between the selection of appropriate learning technologies and productivity.

Human resource development is not the only area in which the selection of technology is practiced in organizations. For some years managers have been considering the selection of technologies for communications within organizations. The depth of consideration is reflected in a body of literature that is larger than that of technology selection for human resource development. While there is an obvious overlap between communications and human resource development this is not reflected in the literature of technology selection of each area. In fact the discourses are quite discrete. However, the literature of selection of technologies for organizational communications is briefly surveyed here for comparison and to investigate the application of its theoretical and conceptual frameworks to technology selection for learning.

Technology Selection for Organizational Communications

Selecting appropriate technologies for communicating within an organization is important to managers and there are many instances in the literature of management and organizational communications where quite clear definitions of the outcomes of appropriate technology selection are provided. For organizational communications, the outcome of the selection of technologies that are appropriate to the task and personnel is the reduction of uncertainty, ambiguity, or equivocality (Carlson & Davis, 1998; Guthrie, 2001). This quite conceivably leads to increases in profit through increased efficiency. For training the outcome is an increase in human performance (Nadler & Nadler, 1994; Nordhaug, 1993; Wilson, 1999), which again is conceivably linked to increases in performance through increased productivity.

Studies have shown that the majority of a manager's time is spent communicating (Rice & Shook, 1990). Carlson and Davis (1998) reinforce this thus: "Communications activities account for a significant portion of the working time of managers" (p. 1) and other commentators indicate the significance of communications to management. Some commentators have extended this further by considering organizations as "communication phenomena" (Farace et al., 1997; Weik, 1979 in Carlson & Davis, 1998, p. 1), and suggest that organizations can only be maintained and developed through continuous communications between members of their staff as well as others. Through this significant proportion of time spent communicating, managers are coming to terms with their environments, reaching decisions, and coordinating activities of the organization. The centrality and importance of communications to management is reflected in the degree of theorization and discourse on the selection of technologies with which the communications are made.

Trait Theories and Technology Selection

Many studies have developed theories of the selection of technologies for organizational communications. The theories have been divided into two categories and are referred to as "Trait Theories of Media Selection" and "Social Interaction Theories of Media Selection" (Carlson & Davis, 1998; Guthrie, 2001). Trait theories suggest that users match the medium to the communications task. For example, media richness theory, developed by organizational scientists (Daft & Lengel, 1984), describes *media* as having degrees of richness depending on the number of communication cues available (for example, vocal attributes and/or body language), the ability to provide immediate feedback, personalization, and others factors. Media richness theory then states that the higher the equivocality or uncertainty in the communication the richer the *medium* needs to be.

Another of the trait theories, social presence theory, states that technologies differ in the extent to which a user "psychologically perceives other people to be physically present when interacting with them" (Carlson & Davis, 1998, p. 4). This theory suggests that users understand that different technologies support different levels of social presence and that their choice of technology is based on the level of social presence required by the task or type of communication. Media richness and social presence theories are very similar and both rank technologies in the same order with face-to-face communications being the richest or supporting the greatest level of social presence at the top of the scale and written communications at the bottom of the scale.

Later research (Carlson & Davis, 1998; Guthrie, 2001) has indicated that the choice of media has been complicated by the introduction of the recent information and communications technologies (ICTs) and that the approach taken by the trait theorists fails to take into account the attributes offered by these new technologies. For example, media richness theory suggests that the telephone is richer than written communications as it can provide the *communication cues* of vocal attributes such as emphasis, pauses, pace, timbre, as well as words. However, the new capabilities of e-mail and computer-mediated communications, such as:

- Storage
- Retrieval options
- Control over participation and access
- Raising and lessening of status
- Choice of synchronous or asynchronous communication

are not taken into account as only communication cues are compared.

Social Interaction Theories and Technology Selection

The second category of theories of technologies selection, the social interaction theories, suggest that the technology selection process is vastly more complex than simply matching attributes of technologies to tasks. In addition, these theories provided a response to the problems ICTs posed for media richness theory and the other trait theories by considering that a combination of social factors was the prime influence on technology selection. While matching of technologies to tasks using the media richness or social presence scales was appropriate in some cases, there were other cases where other attributes of the technologies were as important, or more important, in the selection of one technology over another. Each of the theories in the social interaction category approach technology selection from the perspective that organizations involve complex patterns of communications or "webs of interaction" (Carlson & Davis, 1998, p. 5). Further, they argue that through interactions members of an organization form a system of meaning in collaboration.

The preeminent theories in this category include symbolic interactionism (Carlson & Davis, 1998), social information processing, and structuration theories. Structural symbolic interactionism, a framework based on symbolic interactionism, proposes that social context is the major influence on technology selection. For example, within this framework, the decision-making process of technology selection is based on such factors as distance between participants, time constraints, and access or connection to the technology. Also based on symbolic interactionism, social information processing theory has the basic premise that meaning is socially constructed. This theory describes specific mechanisms by which interpretations and descriptions of the work environment influence behavior and attitudes. It suggests that workers in the same environment develop criteria with which they point out the salient features and interpret the features of technologies.

Structuration theory, another of the social interaction theories, describes social interaction as an iterative process compared to the sequential processes described in social information processing and symbolic interactionism. Adaptive structuration describes the structure of a group as both a medium and an outcome of group interaction with technology. Members of the group select specific features of the medium to use in interactions and thus shape the way the medium affects the group. The technology is then both a medium and an outcome of human interaction. Similarly properties of institutions are both an influence on, and are influenced by, interactions with technology.

Clearly the factors impinging on the decision-making process of technology selection are many, complex, and contextual. In the absence of a single, robust theory of technology selection managers need to examine the fundamental aspects of the technology as well as the social context in which it is to be used if they are to select technologies that are appropriate to the task.

For the past 20 to 30 years, research regarding a theoretical basis for selecting technologies to be used for organizational communications has been as widespread as it has been inconclusive. The volume of research published in the area is testament to the importance with which the development of a single and robust theory of technology selection is viewed but as yet the quest for such a theory continues. If such a theory will lead to an increase in communications efficiency, which in turn will result in a decrease in uncertainty or equivocality within organizations, it is almost certain that productivity will increase. It is then easy to understand why managers are prepared to foster the high degree of research in this area. Likewise the literature of human resource development is clear in stating that development of the human resources of an organization should lead to increased productivity. However, it is clear that the area of technology selection for human resource development is considerably less theorized than its organizational communications counterpart. While the establishment of the reasons for this discrepancy would in all likelihood form a fascinating study it is beyond the scope of this book to do so.

Of the families of theories of technology selection for organizational communications, the trait theories have the greatest to offer as the basis of a theoretical framework that can be used in technology selection. Trait theories such as the media richness theory rank technologies in order of the communications cues or channels they support. In this way a hierarchy of technologies can be constructed in which *rich* technologies such as videoconference with visual and vocal communications channels would be rated as having a different level of attributes when compared to technologies like e-mail, which is generally limited to text.

Technology Selection in Education

The literature regarding technology selection in education reflects the changed role of learning technology in flexible approaches to education. Learning technologies as described in the literature can be quite easily divided between those for traditional classroom teaching and learning, and those for flexible learning. The literature describing technology selection for traditional, face-to-face, classroom teaching and learning does not agree on a single coherent statement of purpose or outcome for the selection of appropriate technology. Some commentators give no reason other than that educators and designers of courses spend a great deal of time and effort engaged with the task of technology selection while others cite reasons of enhancing the teaching presentation (Seels & Glasgow, 1990; Romiszowski, 1988). Later commentators on distance education, open learning, and flexible learning cite other, quite different reasons for the selection of appropriate technologies such as cost benefit, innovation (Bates, 1995), widened access, and increased flexibility (Bates, 2000), or to support the process of learning (Laurillard, 2002).

The key factor differentiating the role of learning technology in flexible learning from traditional face-to-face learning is the degree of the centrality of technology to the learning process. In flexible learning, technologies play a central role, while in traditional learning the role is generally as an adjunct. Reports of the approaches to technology selection for flexible learning and traditional learning in the literature are reviewed in the following sections.

Technology Selection in Traditional Classroom Learning

In traditional learning, technologies are typically used only as adjuncts to face-to-face, classroom teaching, while in flexible learning, technologies provide materials to learners and mediate the communications between learners and between learners and the facilitator. In traditional learning, learners and the facilitator are in the same place at the same time and the technology in this setting has adjunct and illustrative uses, for example:

- To display records of events or phenomena that are difficult to reproduce in the classroom, are expensive, or dangerous.
- To screen movies of theatrical performances of plays and literary works.
- Illustrations that exemplify or explain difficult concepts.

Most commentators on technology selection for traditional learning recognize that selection is part of the design process (Gagné et al., 1992; Reiser & Gagné, 1983; Romiszowski, 1988; Seels & Glasgow, 1990). However, only a limited number go further than recognition and put forward lists of factors to be considered or models for technology selection. For example Gagné et al. (1992) suggest that there are three categories of factors contributing to media selection. They call these "models of media selection" and state that they include categories of factors that can be used in the selection process. The categories are the physical attributes of the technology, the characteristics of the task and the learners.

While lists of factors to be considered, or models for technology selection have been developed and have been used for many years for selecting technologies that are appropriate for use in the classroom, they are limited to classroom use as the technologies are generally used for very small parts of the learning event. These models are limited in their applicability to the selection of technologies that can be used for larger sections of learning events, and it has been argued (Bates, 1995) that the limitations of these models are sufficient to render them not suitable for the selection of appropriate technologies for use in flexible learning.

In traditional learning, apart from the standard equipment (e.g., whiteboards, over-head projectors, etc.), the decision of what technology to use is typically made by the teacher and based upon resources that are available, relevant, and affordable. There is little or no reason for other technology selection decisions to be made at the level of the institution unless it is for the installation of a major facility such as a computer laboratory or a network of television receivers.

In flexible learning, technology selection is of greater importance due to its centrality to the process of teaching and learning. The decision to use a particular technology is made at a strategic level and the ways in which the technology is used is made at a tactical level.

Technology Selection in Distance Education, Open Learning, Flexible Learning, and Online Learning

In the previous chapter, predominantly through the work of Taylor (1995, 2001) a link was shown to exist between distance education, open learning, flexible learning, and online learning, and it has been argued that flexible learning and online learning form a later "Generation" of distance education (Taylor, 2001). For this reason as well as the following shared characteristics they are treated here as one group:

- They share the characteristic that for at least some of the teaching time students and teachers are separated in time and or space.
- They require some level of technology selection at an institutional level.
- Technology is used to provide materials and as the central or only communication between teachers and students.

Technology selection in distance education, open learning, flexible learning, and online learning has two levels; the strategic and the tactical, as described in the beginning of this chapter. Strategic decisions, usually made at the upper management levels of institutions might concern investment in technologies such as videoconference system or a Web-based LMS. Tactical decisions, usually made at the level of designer or facilitator of learning events, might concern what parts of the learning to use videoconference for or what parts of the LMS should be used for particular parts of the learning.

Rowntree (1994), writing about tactical decisions in "An Action Guide for Teachers and Trainers," situates a section called "Choose Your Media" in the planning stage of his diagram entitled "Route Map for Materials Preparation" (Rowntree, 1994, p. 5). The suggested route map divides the process into three stages and suggests that forwards and backwards interaction between each stage should take place. The stages are entitled planning, preparing for writing, and writing and rewriting. In the first stage he includes the task of selecting media. As a guide to the process of selecting media he puts forward 11 possible questions to be considered in the selection of learning technologies.

1. Do any of the learning objectives dictate certain media?
2. Which media will be physically available to the learners?
3. Which media will be most convenient for the learners to use?
4. Are any media likely to be particularly helpful in motivating learners?
5. Are you under pressure from the organization to use/avoid certain media?
6. Which media will you (the teacher/trainer) be most comfortable with?
7. Which media will learners already have the skills to use?
8. Which media will you (the teacher/trainer) have the necessary skills to use?
9. Which media will you be able to afford to use?
10. Which media will learners be able to afford to use?

11.   Which media might you call on to back up the main media and/or to ensure adequate variety? (p. 67)

Rowntree (1994) goes on to list a range of media and provides a matrix in which some media are prescribed for some learning tasks. For example, he links *telephone tutoring*, which he labels as one of the available media, to the tasks; "build each learner's ideas into the teaching" and "ask learners to answer questions about the subject" (Rowntree, 1994, p. 68). The matrix lists: print, audio, video, interactive video, practical work, computer tutoring, computer simulation, multi-media, computer conferencing, lecturing, face-to-face tutoring, telephone tutoring, and correspondence tutoring as some of the "more common media" (Rowntree, 1994, p. 68). Rowntree's questions and matrix can clearly be helpful to designers who wish to use technology in the learning events they design. While the questions are broad and could be applied to most technologies, the matrix is limited to the finite number of technologies it contains. Rowntree's matrix is prescriptive and does not provide designers with an insight to the characteristics or nature of the technology. For these reasons Rowentree's matrix is of limited value to designers today whose designs may include technological elements of Web-based LMSs, a technological system that was not available at the time that Rowntree was writing.

Bates (1995, p. 49) proposes a "Course Development Process," which has been designed for a particular need that was relatively new when he was writing in the mid-1990s. At that time the needs for training a vast increase of people had become obvious to managers of educational institutions, government departments, and businesses. A more cost-effective approach to education and training was sought and technology was seen as the way to achieve this. The course development process, described by Bates has four stages. The second stage: entitled "Selection of Media" contains a model for the selection of media. Bates advocates the use of a model and argues that the desirable characteristics of a model for technology selection are as follows:

•   It will work in a wide variety of contexts;

•   It allows decisions to be taken at both a strategic, or institution-wide, level and at a tactical, or instructional, level;

•   It gives equal attention to instructional and operational issues;

•   It will identify critical differences between different technologies, this enabling an appropriate mix of technologies to be chosen for any given context.

•   It will accommodate new developments in technology. (p. 35)

Bates (1995) states that his model or practical decision-making framework, entitled the "ACTIONS model" (Access Costs Teaching functions, Interactivity, Organizational issues, Novelty, Speed) can be used by "policy-makers, education and training planners, senior education administrators, teachers and trainers" (Bates, 1995, frontispiece). However, the lack of a method or model of the selection process limits the suitability of this model for the designer making tactical decisions. Bates was writing in the context of the United Kingdom Open University, a distance education/open learning university of over 100,000 students and while his process is useful to large distance education providers where the team approach to all stages of curriculum design, including selection of media, can be afforded, its value is limited in cases where the designer is the facilitator or the design team is very small.

Also contributing to the distance education literature, Moore and Kearsley (1996) propose a "Systems Model for Distance Education" in which they attempt to broaden the approach taken by Bates (1995), by including the learning environment in the model. However, like Bates' model, Moore and Kearsley's model is designed for large distance education organizations that can afford a team approach and while their model is suited to this approach it provides limited guidance for individual designers who are not skilled in instructional design or in cases where the designer is also the facilitator or the design team is very small. Moore and Kearsley are quite clear in specifying a team approach to the design of learning events using their model. They go so far to say that even where the content expert has instructional design skills and is well versed in the technology it is still better if the instructional design is carried out by a team consisting of media specialists, graphic designers, and instructional designers. Moore and Kearsley maintain that in this way high quality course materials and programs will be generated (p. 9).

Moore and Kearsley (1996) provide a limited treatment in the area of selection of technology. They argue that it is most important to remember the strengths and weaknesses of each medium. They then continue to outline the strengths and weaknesses for print, audio/video, radio/television, teleconferencing, and computers. Moore and Kearsley state that other considerations in the selection process include the degree to which students require motivating, the budget and the context. They then provide four main steps in technology selection.

1.   Identify the media attributes required by the instructional objectives or learning activities.

2.   Identify the student characteristics which suggest or preclude certain media.

3.   Identify characteristics of the learning environment which favor or preclude certain media.

4.   Identify economic or organizational factors which may affect the feasibility of certain media. (p. 97)

The approaches taken to the selection of technology by Bates (1995) and by Moore and Kearsley (1996) are clearly very informative and helpful in the context of large distance education or open learning institutions. Like Bates, Moore and Kearsley were writing in the context of large institutions. Moore was writing at the Pennsylvania State University, where he was academic director of the Center for the Study of Distance Education and Kearsley was lecturing at the University of Wisconsin, Madison. Like the United Kingdom Open University, Pennsylvania State University and the University of Wisconsin all have significantly large enrolments of distance education students and hence can provide instructional design resources for the design of learning events including the selection of technology.

Although the approaches taken by Bates (1995) and Moore and Kearsley (1996) probably work well in the context of a design team of specialists, they do not provide individual designers, with no instructional design training, with either a concise method to guide them through the technology selection process or a method that leaves the designer with an understanding of the technology from which they may extend or change the application of the technology to the learning events they design.

In the evolution of distance education, represented by Taylor (2001) as the fourth and fifth generations of distance education (see previous chapter), the most recent stages involve the use of the Internet and the World Wide Web and are commonly referred to as online learning or e-learning. For the sake of simplicity the term *online learning* is used here to describe learning events in which materials are distributed, in part or whole, and dialogue hosted in part or whole, by an Internet technology. Often this technology is an LMS. With online learning there is a clear differentiation between strategic and tactical technology selection decisions. Online learning in many cases uses several technologies within the technological system of the Internet. These may include Web pages for the display of learning materials, e-mail for one-to-one or one-to-many communications, and discussion lists to emulate classroom discussions. Also, there are other specialized tools that can be used to facilitate collaboration between learners using online workspaces. Strategic technology selection decisions in online learning concern choices in the purchase, installation, and maintenance of the necessary hardware and software such as LMS servers and commercially available LMS software. Strategic decisions are typically made at the executive level of the institution due to the high cost and systemic nature of such hardware and software. Tactical decisions in online learning are in many cases, especially in the medium and small institutions and organizations, made at the level of the individual designer of learning events. The designer may consider what part of the content of a subject the LMS will carry and whether it will be reinforced by other methods or technologies.

Two approaches to online learning are emerging in the literature (Bates, 2000; Harris, 1999; Palloff & Pratt, 1999). They are not mutually exclusive within the context of a course or subject and are:

- Learning as the provision of materials.

- Learning as communications between learners and between learners and the facilitator of learning.

The technological functions provided by LMSs can be divided, more or less, in the same fashion. For example, material can be provided through Web pages of text and graphics as well as through streamed video and audio. Communications between learners and between learners and the facilitator can be mediated by e-mail, discussion lists, notice boards, and synchronous tools such as chat rooms and desktop videoconference. Often online learning is not used as the sole learning technology, as print, lectures, tutorials, residential schools, and other technologies and methods can form part of the learning experience.

In many institutions and organizations the facilitator of learning undertakes the design of online learning events. This includes the selection of technology at the tactical level where learning activities are matched to some or all of the technological elements of the LMS. While the literature contains little regarding the selection of these elements, in several cases institutions have provided guides, which generally do not differentiate between the technical elements of LMSs and other technologies. For example the guides provided by the Digital Media Centre at the University of Minnesota (USA), the Outreach Unit at Pennsylvania State University (USA), and the Centre for Educational Development and Interactive Resources at the University of Wollongong (Australia) all combine technologies of LMSs with others. The guides typically list technologies and provide examples, to differing depths, of the application of some of the technologies to learning. The University of Wollongong's, Web-based, Media Matrix, which was developed separately from the author's work, clearly indicates the Web as a method of presentation, interaction, and delivery for a number of the technologies. The Media Matrix is presented as a tool for the selection of learning technologies and is described on the Web site as a simple model for course designers. It invites them to: "explore options and to creatively integrate four dimensions: media for presentation and interaction, presentation of the subject message, interaction to support teaching/learning process and a delivery method for presentation and interaction" (Centre for Educational Development and Interactive Resources [CEDIR], 2003). The Media Matrix is two-dimensional and has three columns on one axis and four on the other. The horizontal axis is divided into Presentation (one-way), Interaction (two-way) and Delivery. The vertical axis lists four media: Print, Audio, Video, and Multimedia. The body of the matrix is composed of cells that contain examples such as cassette tapes and audioconferences at the junction of the Audio row and Interaction column.

Guides for the selection of learning technologies, such as the Media Matrix often do not differentiate between technologies that are part of the LMS and those that are not. Clearly, technologies in the Media Matrix, such as audiocassettes and textbooks cannot be part of an LMS while e-mail and Web-based study guides could easily be so. The combination of LMS technologies and others implies that they are intended to be selected at the same time in the design process. Many of the technological elements that make up an LMS are analogous to other methods or technologies that are not Web-based, and this is reflected in the naming of them; for example: e-mail, chat room, Web page, discussion list, video stream, and audio stream. It follows that as other technologies can be used in conjunction with LMSs, and as the technological elements of LMSs are analogous to other non Web-based technologies, that the technology selection methods for individual learning technologies can be generalized for use in the selection of technological elements of LMSs. The guides provided by institutions and organizations for the selection of technologies are generally helpful in the process of selection but limited as they tend to be prescriptive, are restricted to currently available technologies, and provide little insight into the nature of the technologies being selected hence limiting experimentation.

In Chapter II the work of Laurillard (2002) in the classification of learning technologies and a *teaching strategy* was discussed. Laurillard takes a different approach to the selection of learning technologies, which is worthy of investigation as her purpose is similar to that of this book, which is to develop a framework within which learning events may be designed that make appropriate use of learning technologies by matching them to learning activities. Laurillard develops her own teaching strategy, as described later on and discounts the approaches taken in two major areas of enquiry. She argues that instructional design theory has limited application as it is not empirically based and is logically principled. She argues that therefore it cannot be used to design teaching that is based on how students learn (Laurillard, 2002, p. 77). Further, she discounts constructivist approaches as their focus is predominantly on the relationship between students and teachers and their interactions. She also argues that a detailed link is missing between teaching, student activity, and interaction with the subject" (Laurillard, 2002, p. 77). Laurillard provides a classification system for learning technologies by classifying them by *media form*. Laurillard is quite blunt in her discounting of other attempts to categorize and classify forms of media, stating that none of them "is very illuminating or useful for our purpose here" (Laurillard, 2002, p. 83).

Taking a phenomenographic approach, Laurillard (2002) develops what she refers to as: "the best expression of an empirically based teaching strategy so far" and states that it is an "iterative dialogue between the teacher and student focused on a topic goal" (p. 77). She then provides four aspects of the progression of the dialogue and details the responsibilities of the teacher and student in each. The aspects of teaching strategy are described as discursive, adaptive, interactive, and reflective.

Laurillard (2002) states that there are five principal media forms and connects them to the learning experiences they support and the associated methods and technologies. These are reproduced in Table 4.4.

Laurillard (2002) provides examples of learning technologies for each category of media form and provides an insight into their effective use in learning through a

Table 4.4. Laurillard's five principal media forms and learning experiences, methods and technologies. (Laurillard, 2002, p. 90)

Learning Experience	Methods/Technologies	Media Forms
Attending, apprehending	Print, TV, video, DVD	Narrative
Investigating, exploring	Library, CD, DVD, Web resources	Interactive
Discussing, debating	Seminar, online conference	Communicative
Experimenting, practising	Laboratory, field trip, simulation	Adaptive
Articulating, expressing	Essay, product, animation, model	productive

matrix that indicates which of the 12 activities are supported by each example of learning technology.

While Laurillard's (2002) approach appears to be conceptually strong, in practice its uptake has been limited, probably as to do so would require complete and systemic changes to institutional and individual teaching philosophies. Laurillard writes in the context of the United Kingdom Open University (UKOU), of which she holds the office of deputy vice-chancellor. The UKOU is an extremely large university with enrolments in excess of 100,000 and hence has large resources for the design of learning events and the selection of technology. Laurillard's framework, is clearly designed to be used as a complete package or systemic approach in which the design of learning events matches learning *strategies* to learning technologies and given the resources available at the UKOU, the adoption of it is quite feasible. However, it is difficult to address the question of adopting her framework in the context of smaller institutions or organizations where resources are limited. Laurillard's framework is strategic and does not appear to translate to the work of individual designers in many smaller institutions and organizations, that is, the selection of technology at the tactical level. If the technology selection section of her framework is isolated from the overarching framework it becomes cumbersome to the extent of impracticality. In practice the uptake of Laurillard's framework has been limited, probably as at the strategic level institutions and organizations are reluctant to undertake a systemic change to their teaching approach and at a tactical level individual designers apply their own approach or philosophy.

Criteria of Technology Selection

The criteria by which learning technologies in human resource development and in higher education are selected share some similarities across the various methods, models, and lists. At the simplest level the costs of technologies are considered in all the selection methods surveyed in this chapter. Some researchers provide cost criteria in detail (Lee & Owens, 2001), while others simply mention it in broad terms (Bates, 1995; Moore & Kearsley, 1996; Rowntree, 1994). All the selection methods surveyed also consider criteria that are determined by the nature of the subject and those that have implications for the learners or the facilitator of learning. Several of the models surveyed separate these two groups of criteria while others consider them at the same time. For example Lee and Owens (2001) put "Content requires Interactivity (computer)" (p. 8) in the same category of criteria as "Students are resistant to new media" (p. 9), while Moore and Kearsley (1996) separate consideration of how well a learning technology will meet instructional objectives from identification of "student characteristics that will suggest or preclude" (p. 97) certain learning technologies.

The criteria by which learning technologies are selected in the methods surveyed in this chapter can be grouped as:

- Cost
- Nature of the subject
- Implications for learners and facilitators of learning

Conclusion

In the last 10 years the role of learning technologies has changed significantly. In the contexts of human resource development and higher education, online learning is providing increased opportunities and flexibility, with the Internet providing a cheap and almost ubiquitous technology for the delivery and mediation of learning events.

The selection of learning technologies takes place on two levels in both the field of human resource development and higher education. At the strategic level the decisions concern high-cost systems of technology that are generally organization or institution wide. At the tactical level decisions are usually made by designers of learning events and generally concern which learning activities will be delivered or mediated by which learning technologies. The theoretical frameworks developed later can be applied to both the strategic and tactical decision-making levels.

The literature concerning the selection of technology for learning in higher education and human resource development is characterized by case studies and appears to be under-theorized as it presents little in the way of generalization of individual experiences to the field as a whole. This contrasts markedly with the selection of technologies for organizational communications in which not only theories, but families of theories have been developed. While organizational communications might appear outside the scope of this book, a discussion of the central theories developed in this area has been included as a comparison to the relative lack of theorization in the other areas and as they will be used in the development of the theoretical framework for learning technologies in Chapter VII. The methods and guides for the selection of learning technologies located in the literature are not suited to the selection of learning technologies by individual designers of learning events for a number of reasons. Some methods have been developed for use in classroom teaching where technologies are adjuncts to the teacher's presentation and hence they are not suited to the selection of technologies that are central to the process of learning. Some methods or guides have been developed in the context of large organizations or institutions where resource levels are such that instructional designers will bring their specialized, technology selection skills to the design team. Other methods or guides are prescriptive and propose a limited number of technologies from which the designer selects. While this approach might be effective it does not actively encourage the designer to use the technologies in new and different ways. Also, many guides or methods of this type do not readily or easily expand to include new technologies and hence quickly become obsolete.

Researchers and designers of learning events require theoretical frameworks of learning activities and theoretical frameworks of learning technologies if they are to gain an understanding of the application of learning technologies. Designers working by themselves, who are often facilitators of the learning events they design, require a technology selection method that matches learning technologies to learning activities in an appropriate manner that provides the designer with an understanding of the nature of the technology, does not prescribe technologies, and can easily expand to include new technologies. In the next chapter existing approaches to theoretical frameworks of learning activities and learning technologies are explored and the case is presented for new theoretical frameworks that are suited to the needs of designers of e-learning.

References

Bates, A. W. (1995). *Technology, open learning and distance education.* New York: Routledge.

Bates, A. W. (2000). *Managing technological change: Strategies for college and university leaders.* San Francisco: Jossey-Bass.

Berge, Z. (2001). *Sustaining distance training: Integrating learning technologies into the fabric of the enterprise.* San Francisco: Jossey-Bass.

Carlson, P., & Davis, B. (1998). An investigation of media selection among directors and managers: From "self" to "other" orientation. *MIS Quarterly, 22*(3), 335-363.

Centre for Educational Development and Interactive Resources (CEDIR). *Media matrix.* Retrieved March 18, 2003, from http://cedir.uow.edu.au/programs/flexdel/cedir/matrix.html

Daft, R. L., & Lengel, R. H. (1984). Information richness: A new approach to managerial behavior and organizational design. In L. L. Cummings & B. M. Staw (Eds.), *Research in organizational behavior* (pp. 191-233). Homewood, IL: JAI Press.

Gagné, R., Briggs, L., & Wager, W. (1992). *Principles of instructional design.* Fort Worth, TX: Harcourt Brace Jovanovich.

Guthrie, C. (2001). Selecting and switching media features and the performance of distributed multi-trade workgroups. In *Proceedings of the 9th European Conference on Information Systems,* Bled, Slovenia. Retrieved July 5, 2002, from http://ecis2001.fov.uni-mb.si/doctoral/Students/ECIS-DC_Guthrie.pdf

Harris, D. (1999). Creating a complete learning environment. In D. French et al. (Eds.), *Internet based learning: An introduction and framework for higher education and business.* Sterling, VA: Stylus.

Instructional Systems Inc. (2002). *How can we help you?* Retrieved June 5, 2003, from http://www.isinj.com/helpYou/

Khan, B. (2001). A framework for Web-based learning. In B. Khan (Ed.), *Web-based training.* Englewood Cliffs, NJ: Educational Technology Publications.

Kruse, K., & Keil, J. (2000). *Technology-based training: The art and science of design, development and delivery.* San Francisco: Jossey-Bass/Pfeiffer.

Laurillard, D. (2002). *Rethinking university teaching: A conversational framework for the effective use of learning technologies* (2nd ed.). London: Routledge.

Lee, W., & Owens. (2001). *A systematic approach to media selection.* ASTD learning Communities. Retrieved June 5, 2003, from http://www.astd.org/virtual_community/Comm_elrng_rdmap/whitepapers.html

McPherson, M., & Beard, C. (1999). The selection, design and use of individualized training methods. In J. Wilson (Ed.), *Human resource development: Learning and training for individuals and organizations.* London: Kogan Page.

Moore, M., & Kearsley, G. (1996). *Distance education a systems view.* Belmont: Wadsworth.

Nadler, L., & Nadler, Z. (1994). *Designing training programs.* Houston, TX: Gulf.

Nordhaug, O. (1993). *Human capital in organizations.* Oslo, Norway: Scandinavian University Press.

Palloff, R., & Pratt, K. (1999). *Building learning communities in cyberspace: Effective strategies for the online classroom.* San Francisco: Jossey-Bass.

Reiser, R., & Gagné, R. (1983). *Selecting media for instruction.* Englewood Cliffs, NJ: Educational Technology Publications.

Rice, R., & Shook, D. (1990). Relationships of job categories and organizational levels to use of communication channels, including electronic mail: A meta-analysis and extension. *Journal of Management Studies, 27*(2), 195-229.

Romiszowski, A. (1988). *The selection and use of instructional media.* London: Kogan Page/New York: Nichols.

Romiszowski, A., & Chang, E. (2001). A practical model for conversational Web-based training: A response from the past to the needs of the future. In B. Khan (Ed.), *Web-based training.* Englewood Cliffs, NJ: Educational Technology Publications.

Rowntree, D. (1994). *Preparing materials for open, distance and flexible learning.* London: Kogan Page.

Scheer, T. (2001). Distance learning at the IRS. In Z. Berge (Ed.), *Sustaining distance training.* San Francisco: Jossey-Bass.

Seels, B., & Glasgow, Z. (1990). *Exercises in instructional design.* Columbus, OH: Merrill.

Smith, A. (1992). *Training and development in Australia.* Sydney, Australia: Butterworths.

Taylor, J. (1995). Distance education technologies: The fourth generation. *Australian Journal of Educational Technology, 11*(2), 1-7.

Taylor, J. (2001). *Fifth generation distance education* (Higher Education Series, Report No. 40). Canberra, Australia: Department of Education, Training and Youth Affairs.

Wilson, J. P. (1999). *Human resource development: Learning and training for individuals and organizations.* London: Kogan Page.

Chapter V

Existing Theoretical Approaches to Learning Technologies, Learning Activities, and Methods of Technology Selection

Introduction

In the 1990s, flexibility of where and when learning took place grew in significance to learners and providers of learning. For learners it meant they could learn at times and in places that suited them. Flexibility gave many students access to education that had previously been denied due to commitments such as work and family. Managers of higher education saw flexibility as a way to increase participation rates without a concomitant increase in resources and staff. In human resource development, flexibility meant that learners could learn when it suited the organization or the task and hence maximize performance gains while minimizing time away from work. In both contexts, flexibility of the time and place of learning was seen a way to increase the efficiency and effectiveness of learning. Flexibility in learning is generally characterized by the use of information and communication technologies (ICTs).

These are generally used for some or all of the:

- Provision of learning materials.
- Mediation of interactions between learners.
- Mediation of interactions between learners and facilitators.

If ICTs are used to provide flexibility of where and when follows learners learn, it follows that the design of online learning or e-learning entails the selection of ICTs used in learning. For the purposes of this book these are referred to as learning technologies.

The selection of learning technologies in the contexts of higher education and human resource development occurs at two levels: the strategic and the tactical. At the strategic level an institution or organization may decide to invest in a high-cost technological system such as an learning management system (LMS) or a system of videoconference endpoint and bridging technology. At the tactical level, personnel responsible for the design of learning events will match technologies, or elements of them, to learning activities. To do so in a manner that is appropriate to the learners, the material, the context, and the budget, designers of learning events often need guidance. It is argued that this guidance can be provided by tools that provide theoretical understanding of the technologies; the activities faculty and students undertake in the process of learning; and a practical method for the selection of appropriate technologies. Specifically, they need a theoretical framework of learning technologies, a theoretical framework of learning materials, and a technology selection method that matches technologies to activities using the frameworks. In the following chapters these frameworks and method are described and exemplified. The literature on learning technologies, learning activities, and technology selection in the contexts of higher education and human resource development has been investigated to ascertain the suitability of existing theoretical frameworks in these areas to the purpose of technology selection. Unfortunately, while rich in case studies, this literature remains under-theorized.

As discussed in Chapters III and IV, attempts have been made to categorize and classify learning technologies with the intention of providing guidelines, methods, and models for the selection of learning technologies. However, the attempts reported in the literature are not suitable for the design of online learning for the following reasons. The older of the attempts have little relevance to contemporary learning event design as the technologies they were designed for have been superseded or newer technologies are now used in parallel with them. Some attempts have little to offer the designer of learning events as they appear to state the obvious by classifying technologies by their characteristics. For example, Leshin, Pollock, and Reigeluth (1992) classify learning technologies as "human, print, visual, audio/visual or computer-based" (p. 256). Other attempts categorize technologies by the learning functions they serve. For example Laurillard (2002) develops a "teaching strategy" and divides it into several sections. She then categorizes learning technologies into equivalent categories and hence describes the suitability of individual technologies to the sections of her teaching strategy. While Laurillard's approach appears to be conceptually strong in practice, its uptake has been limited. To do so would require systemic changes to institutional and individual teaching approaches. Hence, in many institutions, the adoption of her "conversational framework" has little to offer the designer at the tactical level of technology selection.

One-Way and Two-Way Technologies

In traditional face-to-face teaching and learning, technology usually was used as adjuncts. In e-learning, technology takes a central role. The design of learning where technology has a central role concerns the matching of technologies to learning activities. The literature of learning activities was reviewed to determine the suitability of classification systems of learning activities to this purpose. Unfortunately little has been written about learning activities and much of what has been written is not suited to technology selection, as it is intended for other purposes, in particular the design of classroom-based teaching. The few attempts that consider learning activities in the design of technology-rich learning events are generally confined to lists and examples. However, a closer examination of the literature on learning technology provides a number of examples of tacit classifications of learning activities. For example Rowntree (1994), Bates (1995), and Taylor (2001) all indicate in their descriptions of learning technologies, either implied or explicitly, a differentiation between one-way and two-way technologies. It is not difficult then to infer that learning activities can be broadly categorized as one-way, or interactions with materials, and two-way, or interactions between people and this is often reflected in learning experiences. While this tacit categorization of learning activities does not provide sufficient conceptual detail for it to be useful in detailed selection of learning technologies at the tactical level, it is a starting point for a theoretical framework of learning activities.

The literature contains several tools for the selection of learning technologies in human resource development and higher education. Unfortunately many of these tools are superficial or under-theorized and hence have limited applicability to learning event design. For example, many of the tools are lists of factors to be considered or matrices that prescribe technologies. In sharp contrast, the slightly related field of organizational communications contains a well-theorized literature on technology selection. Although the purposes and reasons for the selection of technology are somewhat different, one of the theoretical approaches has been adapted for use in the development of the original theoretical framework of learning technologies presented in this book.

As mentioned earlier, one purpose of this book is to provide and exemplify a conceptually rich method for the selection of learning technologies that is appropriate to the learners, the material, the context, and the budget. To do this at a tactical level, learning technologies must be matched to learning activities. To appropriately match learning and technologies, tools are needed such as sound theoretical frameworks of learning activities and learning technologies, and these are the foundations upon which a solid technology selection method can be built. The literature provides some key elements that provide the starting points for the theoretical frameworks of learning activities and learning technologies.

Key Elements in the Literature

Of the points in the literature concerning learning technologies, one key point provides the notion that forms the basis of the theoretical frameworks described in the following chapters. That is, as mentioned earlier, that learning technologies have been categorized as one-way or two-way. One-way technologies have been described as those with which learners interact with materials and two-way technologies as those with which learners interact with other humans. As there appears to be agreement between several commentators, and as the division of technologies into one-way and two-way is congruent with the author's experience, it is used as the formative basis of a theoretical framework of learning technologies.

Where learning technologies are central to the process of learning, for example, in online learning, they can be used to provide a categorization of the learning activities they facilitate. As technologies can be categorized as those that provide and facilitate interactions with materials and those that facilitate interactions with other humans, so learning activities can be categorized as interactions with materials and interactions between people. In the following chapters, this categorization is expanded to provide the basis of the theoretical framework of learning activities.

Another key element that emerges from the literature concerns the criteria used in existing methods of technology selection. While the literature contains many different lists of technologies and methods of technology selection, the individual criteria from the lists and methods can be easily grouped into:

- Cost factors.
- Factors determined by the nature of the subject.
- Implications for learners and facilitators of learning.

A further key element from the literature forms part of the basis of the original theoretical framework of learning technologies. Drawn from the literature of organizational communications, this key element is the based on the family of trait theories of technology selection. The trait theories categorize technologies by their traits, or communications channels available and rank different technologies by this criterion. Although, for the selection of technologies for organizational communications, trait theories have been superseded by later theories that are more germane, the ranking of technologies by traits provides a comparative understanding of the technologies and as such is worthy of inclusion as a defining criterion of the theoretical framework.

Shortcomings in Theoretical Frameworks of Learning Technologies

Several systems of classification and categorization of learning technologies were located in the literature and investigated for their suitability to the technology selection process. Several commentators have provided frameworks for the classification of technologies, none of which are completely suitable for the design of online learning. Several of the classification systems simply group technologies by their characteristics (Leshin et al., 1992), which adds little to users' understanding of them. Others provide superficial classifications, for example one-way and two-way, which while being sound starting points for understanding, are not sufficiently complete for use in the design of online learning due to a lack of development into tools that can be readily applied during the design process (Bates, 1995; Rowntree, 1994; Taylor, 2001). Laurillard (2002) proposes a classification system in which learning technologies are grouped into five *media forms*. Unfortunately this system of classification provides little help in the selection of technologies unless it is used in conjunction with her teaching strategy and as this would require changes in teaching philosophy at a strategic or institutional level the use of her system has been limited and the media forms are not relevant to designers of learning events making tactical, learning technology decisions.

Shortcomings in Theoretical Frameworks of Learning Activities

As mentioned earlier, part the process of the design of learning events that use technologies in central roles is the matching of learning activities to learning technologies. An appropriate theoretical framework of learning activities would provide designers with a conceptual tool and assist in the matching process.

The literature of learning activities is small, and generally not suited to the purpose of this book as the theorization is often for different purposes. For example, Gagné, Biggs, and Wager (1992) divide learning activities into chronological categories for classroom teaching and this book is concerned with the design of learning that will generally not take place solely in a classroom. Other classifications of learning activities in the literature have limited application to the design of technology-based learning. Some commentators provide lists of activities and suggest that the design process is simply one of selection from it (Wilson, 1999). This approach has obvious shortcomings that severely limit its application to the design process. As it is prescriptive, learning designers are not provided with an understanding of the technologies involved and hence extension of them beyond the prescribed activity is not encouraged. Also, the list is constrained to the technologies available at the time of its compilation, which in a world of rapid technological change is a limiting characteristic.

Shortcomings in Technology Selection Methods

The literature that covers the selection of learning technologies in higher education and human resource development is characterized by case studies and is markedly less theorized than the literature of the selection of technologies for organizational communications within the field of management. One of the theoretical approaches developed for technology selection in the field of organizational communications is used as part of the basis for the theoretical framework of learning technologies described in the following chapters. The higher education and human resource development literature contains several technology selection methods that are well theorized but are not useful for the selection of appropriate technologies in the design of online learning. They have been developed for use in contexts where technology is an adjunct to the teacher-in-a-classroom, face-to-face learning approach, or they do not include recently developed technologies such as the Internet and World Wide Web. The literature of distance education provides a number of technology selection methods for the strategic and tactical levels. The technology selection methods aimed at the strategic level are clearly differentiated from those intended at the tactical level, as they generally concern high-cost, institution-wide systems of technology and are often presented within managerial contexts such as cost-scale, cost-benefit analyses, and other institution-wide issues. The recent literature on technology in learning is concerned in large part with Web-based technologies and in particular LMSs. As with the earlier literature, it is characterized by case studies and a lack of generalization that can lead to a theoretical approach to technology selection. In several places guides have been produced to assist designers at the tactical level in the selection of technologies, or technological elements of an LMS. These guides to technology selection at the tactical level are prescriptive, do not extend to include new technologies when they become available, and as mentioned earlier are under-theorized.

To select learning technologies at the tactical level in a way that provides a considerable degree of confidence in the appropriateness of the selection for the learners, the material, the context, and the budget, a robust theoretical framework is required which has the following characteristics:

- It must be sufficiently flexible to operate within institutional or organizational approaches to, and philosophies of, education.
- It must be easily generalized across disciplines.
- It must provide designers with an insight into the characteristics and nature of the technologies they are selecting and hence lead to individual decisions that are not general, simple and prescriptive.
- It must lead to decisions that are appropriate to the learners, material, context and budget of each case.

Conclusion:
New Theoretical Frameworks and Method

The next section of this book addresses the aforementioned deficiencies in existing conceptualizations of learning technologies and learning activities by the presentation of two new theoretical frameworks and a practical method. A theoretical framework of learning activities, entitled learning activities model (LAM), categorizes learning activities based on the notion that the activities of the process of learning can be described as the provision of materials and interactions. The second theoretical framework categorizes and classifies learning technologies. Entitled, the learning technologies model (LTM) this framework has two dimensions. In the first dimension technologies are classified as one-way, for the provision of materials or two-way for interactions between humans. In the second dimension technologies are classified by the communications cues that they support. The theoretical frameworks are then brought together to form an original method for the selection of learning technologies. This technology selection method (TSM) is based on matching technologies as analyzed by the LTM to categories of the LAM. A four-step process is suggested in which technology options are narrowed until an appropriate match is made. In this way online or e-learning events that make appropriate use of technology can be designed and hence lead to learning events that achieve the learning objectives in an efficient and effective manner.

References

Bates, A. W. (1995). *Technology, open learning and distance education.* New York: Routledge.

Gagné, R., Briggs, L., & Wager, W. (1995). *Principles of instructional design.* Fort Worth, TX: Harcourt Brace Jovanovich.

Laurillard, D. (2002). *Rethinking university teaching: A conversational framework for the effective use of learning technologies* (2nd ed.). London: Routledge.

Leshin, C., Pollock, J., & Reigeluth, C. (1992). *Instructional design strategies and tactics.* Englewood Cliffs, NJ: Educational Technology Publications.

Rowntree, D. (1994). *Preparing materials for open, distance and flexible learning.* London: Kogan Page.

Taylor, J. (2001). *Fifth generation distance education* (Higher Education Series, Report No. 40). Canberra, Australia: Department of Education, Training and Youth Affairs.

Wilson, J. P. (1999). *Human resource development: Learning and training for individuals and organizations.* London: Kogan Page.

Chapter VI

The Learning Activities Model

Introduction

The effects of open, distance, and flexible learning, and the changed role of technology in learning have been felt in almost all educational sectors and institutions. Technology in many subjects now plays a central role and learning management systems (LMSs) are part of the standard software of higher education institutions. However the influence of learning technology has not been limited to education. The literature on human resource management (HRM) recognizes that there are benefits to be gained through the application of some of the techniques and technologies of flexible learning to training and development (Smith, 1992; Wilson, 1999). For example, LMSs are also providing efficiencies to organizations in the development of their human resources. As mentioned earlier in this book, the term *flexible learning* is used here to refer collectively to the approaches of open, distance, online, and e-learning and to the literature that is concerned with them. More recently terms such as *blended learning* and *e-learning* have appeared to refer to learning experiences that incorporate an electronic element. Typically flexible learning or e-learning would involve the use of the learning technologies discussed here.

In earlier chapters the literature of flexible learning has been shown to support the notion that the process of learning can be described as consisting of the provision of materials and interactions. Also, the literature was interpreted as providing tacit conceptualizations of the process of learning as the provision of materials and interactions. In this chapter, this description is defined, described in greater depth, and interaction is also subdivided into several categories. The categories of interaction and the provision of materials are then brought together to constitute the theoretical framework, the learning activities model (LAM).

This model is the first of two theoretical frameworks described in this book and provides the field with a new analytical tool and as well as informing the learning technology field. The model is intended to assist designers of learning events and is based on the thesis that categories of activities that are subdivisions of the learning process can be matched to techniques, technologies, and methods as part of the design process. While the literature, in many places (Bates, 1995, 2000; Taylor, 1995, 2001), implies that the process of learning can be described as interactions and delivered things, previous investigators have chosen not to use these categories of learning activities as overt tools for the analysis of the learning process. The research reported here conceptualizes learning activities and presents a theoretical framework within which the process of all learning events can be described and analyzed. This framework is the LAM. When the selection of learning technologies is addressed in Chapter VIII, the categories of activities form identifiable elements to which appropriate technologies can be matched. This chapter concludes with several examples, which analyze fictitious learning events and illustrate how the model can describe the learning process.

Provision of Material

Traditionally, the predominant approach to undergraduate university teaching consisted of mainly a presentational approach. Most lectures were primarily concerned with the provision of material, as learning seemed to be equated with the transfer of knowledge as opposed to the development or construction of it by students. A similar approach occurred in human resource development and many programs have been conducted in venues using the model of a trainer presenting material to a group of trainees. In these cases material was provided by the words the lecturer or trainer spoke and the words written on the board, overhead projector, screen, or handout. The material provided in traditional presentations like this resulted in the notes and memories that learners took away from the training room or lecture theatre.

In e-learning and flexible learning, the provision of material is usually by different means. It may be provided in the form of printed materials or by other technologies. In this book the term *material* is used for several reasons, firstly to differentiate between human and non-human resources. In a face-to-face presentation material is the thing or *stuff* that is provided by the presenter to the audience as opposed to the human resource that is the presenter. The difference becomes clear in technology-based learning events, where learners interact with a recording of the presenter, or materials rather than the presenter themselves or the resource. The primary difference between the two is the nature of the interactions. In face-to-face events learners can interact with the presenter while in the case of the recording, learners are limited to interacting with the material. Of course, in flexible learning and e-learning there are other channels that are often used for interaction with the presenter, however, these generally constitute a separate technological channel from that used for the provision of materials. Chapter VII provides further clarification of this differentiation in the discussion of the learning technologies model (LTM).

The term *material* has been selected to describe what is provided. This term is preferred to *knowledge, information,* or *data* as it reinforces the notion that the materials themselves are passive, inert and do not constitute learning until learners do something with them. The term, *knowledge* is not used, as knowledge is generally considered to be one of the possible outcomes of learning. For example, the work of Bloom, Krathwol, and others refers to the outcomes of learning as consisting of skills, knowledge and attitudes (Gronlund, 1978) while Gagné, Briggs, and Wager (1992) list the outcomes as:

- intellectual skills (or procedural knowledge);
- cognitive strategies;
- verbal information (or declarative knowledge);
- attitudes and
- motor skills (p. 13)

Another reason for referring to that which is provided as material is to highlight the difference between data, information, and material. The term, *information* implies an interaction, or the process of informing someone or something. The meaning of data is restricted as they are often thought of as simply numbers. In this book the term *material* is used to clearly indicate the words, pictures, sounds, and other things that form part of the learning event.

The first category of the LAM consists of activities concerned with the provision of material and is referred to as *provision of materials*. Materials may be provided in the classroom, training room, or lecture theatre where they are part of the learning process. Alternatively, in e-learning, materials may be provided away from designated learning venues. Materials can be provided in a number of ways, including:

- The voice of the presenter or facilitator in a training program, lecture, tutorial, seminar, laboratory, study group, residential school.
- Visual aids to the aforementioned items.
- Printed materials—for example, prescribed texts, references, and manuals.
- Other printed materials such as training notes study guides, lecture notes, handouts.
- Other media—for example, radio and television programs, audio and video, Web pages, multimedia, podcasts, vodcasts (video podcasts), streams, and Webcasts.

Interactions

The provision of material alone is generally not considered sufficient to produce the desired outcomes of a learning event. For learning from materials to occur, learners have to interact with it and, clearly, in many learning events other types of interactions occur. These other interactions can be identified through the analysis of distance learning and flexible learning as practiced in higher education and human resource development (HRD) in general and specifically in the following example.

Correspondence courses represent one of the earliest forms of distance learning. In correspondence courses, learners interacted with printed materials that were sent to them through the postal service. Sometimes there was opportunity for limited interaction with the facilitator in the form of comments and corrections on assignments and assessments. Usually there were few, if any, opportunities for interaction between learners. When technology was added to correspondence courses, and the term *distance learning* (or *distance education*) applied to it, there was greater opportunity for interaction between learners. However, in many cases this was limited due to the high cost of conferencing technology or other communication technology.

Distance learning presents a clear comparison to face-to-face learning where there usually are many opportunities for learners to interact with facilitators and with other learners. From the general comparison between distance learning and face-to-face learning, three discrete categories of interaction can be identified. They are:

- *Interaction with materials*
- *Interaction with the facilitator*
- *Interaction between learners*

As the terms *interactive, interaction,* and *interactivity* are used widely and applied in many fields and places, they need to be clarified. The Oxford English Dictionary (1992) defines interaction as "reciprocal action; action or influence of persons or things on each other" and interactive as:

1. Reciprocally active; acting upon or influencing each other.
2. Pertaining to or being a computer or other electronic device that allows a two-way flow of information between it and a user responding immediately to the latters input.

In this book the term *interaction* is used in preference to interactive or interactivity. Apart from the grammatical constraints, this is done to avoid the confusion that can occur with the term *interactive*. Interaction in several dictionaries is defined as action on each party or reciprocal action. There are usually two definitions of interactive, one that describes things that interact and another that describes computers that react immediately to the input or commands of the operator. So that there is no confusion between what is meant here by interactive and the computer definition of interactive the use of interaction is retained, and defined as reciprocal action. This is broader than, but includes, the interactivity of computer programs. For example, a conversation in which each party tries to change the attitude of the other can be described as interaction. To further clarify the concept of interaction in learning it is compared to the provision of material that was mentioned earlier. The provision of material can be seen as a one-way process as when learners interact with it material flows from the providing technology or person to the learner and usually not the other way, that is, from the learner to the technology or person. However, interaction is essentially a two-way process allowing information to flow back and forth between learners, facilitators, and other people or things. For example, when a learner (or for that matter any viewer) watches a broadcast of a television program, material is provided to them. If they make a video recording of the program and replay it, pause, rewind, and replay parts of it, the process gains an aspect of the two-way, and to a limited degree they interact with it.

The three categories of interaction are clearly identifiable in learning although not all categories are present in all learning events. The first category of interaction, and the second category in the LAM, is interaction with materials.

Interaction with Materials

As well as the different categories of interaction that can be identified in learning events there are different levels of interaction that can be present within each category. Obviously there are many levels and styles of interaction and although the interaction of the learner or viewer in the example of the videotape (seen previously) is rather basic, it could serve to help achieve the desired learning outcomes through the removal of the ephemeral characteristic of the broadcast once the program is encapsulated in a video recording. interaction with materials is the second category in the LAM and some examples of activities in this category include:

- Looking up a definition in a reference book.
- Pausing, rewinding, and replaying sections of a video or audio recording,
- Searching the Internet or World Wide Web.
- Interacting with computer-aided learning packages, for example, multimedia.

In face-to-face learning, the boundary between the provision of material and interaction with it can be difficult to distinguish. In a presentation, material is provided by the voice of the presenter and by any visual aids used. By definition interaction with the material only happens when a learner does something with it. In flexible learning the boundary between provided material and interaction with it is usually clearer than in traditional face-to-face learning. Often the material is recorded and provided by a technology and in such cases the boundary is defined by the boundary of the technology.

Interaction with the Facilitator

Interaction with the teacher or trainer plays an important role in many learning events and for simplicity's sake this person is referred to in this book as the *facilitator*. The role of the facilitator in traditional face-to-face learning will be different to their role in flexible learning. In flexible learning the role can include some or all of the following:

- Design of materials
- Consultation with learners
- Assessment of learners' work
- Answering learners' questions
- Provision of materials

In some contexts, for example, in-house training in a small company, these activities might be undertaken by one person. In traditional face-to-face learning at a university it could be a team consisting of a lecturer, a coordinator, and one or more tutors. In flexible learning, learning events can be the result of single or team efforts. The teams can consist of academics who provide the content material, tutorial staff who answer learners' questions and assess their work, as well as instructional designers, administration, and other infrastructural staff.

In a face-to-face learning environment, learners interact with facilitators by interjecting in a presentation or asking questions during a consultation with the facilitator in their office or elsewhere. An example of interaction with the facilitator in higher education can be a discussion taking place between a teacher and student in a tutorial or seminar. An example of interaction with the facilitator in training could be the discussion between a participant and the trainer in an in-service workshop. Tutorials, consultations, and workshops traditionally have been face-to-face meetings; however, interaction with the facilitator can happen in flexible learning through the use of technologies like e-mail, audio conferencing, videoconferencing, and online discussion forums. While face-to-face interaction is obviously synchronous, the technologies used for interaction may be either synchronous or asynchronous. Some examples of the techniques and technologies that can be used in interactions with the facilitator are:

- Questions and answers in lectures
- Questions and answers in workshops
- Tutorial discussion
- Phone calls
- E-mail
- Instant messaging
- Letters
- Facilitator/learner consultation (face-to-face)
- Audioconferences, video chat, or videoconference discussions
- Feedback on assessments
- Chance meeting and social events

Generally interaction is a valued quality of learning. The author was a member of the Education Committee of the National Tertiary Education Union (NTEU), the peak academic industrial union in Australia, which developed a policy statement that echoes this sentiment.

NTEU recognises the increase of flexible teaching and learning in tertiary education and while the benefits of flexible teaching and learning are also recognised it must be remembered that education is an interactive process, at the heart of which lies the relationship between student and teacher. (National Tertiary Education Union, 1997, p. 12)

In many universities, it is part of teachers' duty statements to be available for a number of hours per week for student consultation or *office hours*. Also many teachers cultivate an attitude of questioning in their students, hence engendering a learning style that is highly interactive. In HRD interaction is also valued and considered vital to learning. Kruse and Keil (2002) go further and argue that a collaborative approach should be the theoretical guide to training and that a vital component of human learning in interaction between humans.

Interacting with the teacher, trainer, or facilitator is the third category of the LAM and is referred to as interaction with facilitator. The third type of interaction and the fourth category of the LAM is interaction between students, trainees, or participants and is referred to as interaction between learners.

Interaction Between Learners

Interaction between learners can be formal or informal. The most formal would be in events such as student presentations in tutorials or participant interaction in workshops. Other examples of formal interaction between learners occur where they work as a group or team on a project for assessment. Less formal interaction between learners can occur at any time or place where they talk about their learning.

These last two categories, that is, interaction with the facilitator and interaction between learners, are both dialogic. Dialogue can have different attributes depending on the technology it is mediated by. For example, e-mail is generally limited to text while a videoconference can include body language and vocal attributes as well as the *text* as spoken words. Dialogue here is defined as a conversation and is not limited to a duologue. The nature of dialogue is expanded further in Chapter VII within the context of the second theoretical framework: the LTM.

The Fifth Category of Learning Activities

The first four categories of the LAM describe the learning process as consisting of provided materials, interactions with materials, interactions with the facilitator, and interactions between learners. This is not a complete description of all learning activities, rather it is a description of the activities that can be planned and undertaken in order to facilitate learning. There are a number of things that learners do in order to learn or as part of the learning process that the designer of the learning event can facilitate but generally cannot control. These activities do not fit into the first four categories of the LAM and include activities such as:

- Learners' informal reflection on what they have heard or read,
- Formal, directed, or structured reflective practice,
- Critical thinking,
- Refining ideas, opinions, and attitudes,
- Comparing new to existing knowledge and experiences, and
- *The penny dropping* or sudden realizations that are apparently not stimulated.

As these activities are outside of the categories mentioned so far, and so that the model can represent all learning activities, a category for these activities is added to the LAM. This is the fifth category and is referred to as *intra-action*, a term coined by the author to describe action within. Intra-action as a category of activities is worthy of investigation. However, such an investigation, while helpful to understanding learning, is outside the scope of this book.

The five categories of learning activities combine to form a theoretical framework or model of the activities in the process of learning. While the first four categories of learning activities can be determined in the design process, intra-action is very difficult, if not impossible, to ensure. The opportunities for intra-action can be maximized through thorough and appropriate design of the learning activities and environment. However, as learners bring their own psychological baggage to their learning and as achieving the desired learning outcomes is ultimately dependent on them, intra-action cannot be prescribed or guaranteed.

The Learning Activities Model

The five categories described are brought together to form the LAM. This model is a theoretical framework of learning activities and is the first theoretical framework presented in this book. It has theoretical and practical applications and is represented graphically in Figure 6.1.

In Figure 6.1 the space enclosed by the circle represents the total of all activities that happen during the process of learning and can be applied to complete programs of structured learning in a range of granularity. At the most coarse level the model can be used to analyze or describe the approach taken to learning by an institution or organization and the activities listed for each category of the model would reflect

Figure 6.1. Graphical representation of the learning activities model

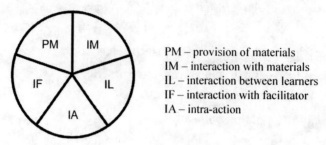

PM – provision of materials
IM – interaction with materials
IL – interaction between learners
IF – interaction with facilitator
IA – intra-action

the approach. At a finer level the model can be applied to courses or programs or to subjects or modules of a program or subject. At the finest level of granularity the model can be applied to short discrete learning events such as using a set of instructions to perform a task. The five categories of the model; (1) provision of materials, (2) interaction with materials, (3) interaction with the facilitator, (4) interaction between learners, and (5) intra-action are indicated by the segments or *piece-of-pie* shapes.

It is not suggested that all categories of the model need to be present for learning to occur or that there is a relationship that always correlates the presence of more elements with increases in the effectiveness and efficiency of learning. Some successful learning events may use all five categories, and others may use only two or three. There are many factors to be considered in the design of the number of categories of the model to include in learning events. For example while interaction between learners is generally considered desirable in learning events it may be reduced or not occur where the number of learners is small, the duration of the learning event is short and flexibility of time is desired. In such cases it would be conceivable for no interaction between learners to occur during the process of learning.

The model is proposed as a theoretical framework for the analysis of planned or existing learning events. It also provides a framework within which the activities of learning events can be mapped and as a tool for the design of future learning events. The following examples are provided to illustrate the model in general terms and to demonstrate the applicability of the model to commonplace learning environments.

The Model Exemplified

This group of examples concerns a simple, everyday learning event: preparing and cooking food from a recipe for the first time. The desired learning outcome can be easily, although subjectively, measured as the successful production of the food. The first example is the simplest, containing only two categories of learning activities. In subsequent examples further categories of the model are added expanding and developing the activities of learning. In the simplest case of the example, the learner is the person preparing the food and they interact with the learning materials. In this case the learning materials are the recipe and other relevant information, for example, a conversion chart for weights and measures. We all know that food can be prepared this way and that the results can be anywhere in the spectrum of taste. So it would be reasonable to suggest that effective learning can happen this way.

Example 1

The materials are already on hand and not provided as part of the learning event. The facilitator (assuming the facilitator is the person who prepared the recipe and instructions) is not present and the learner works by himself or herself. The activities are:

- Interaction with the materials (the materials being the recipe book, not the ingredients).
- Intra-action (where the intra-action is the comparing and critical evaluation of the process with recipes prepared earlier and other experiences).

This is represented graphically in Figure 6.2.

Example 2

In the second example the learner prepares the food in much the same way but this time the materials include a videotape of a television program, and through the

Figure 6.2. Example 1: Interaction with materials and intra-action

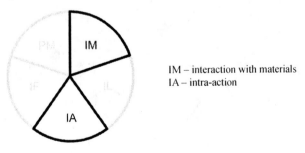

IM – interaction with materials
IA – intra-action

recorded program activities in the category of Provision of Material are introduced. As well as interacting with the recipe some limited interaction with the videotape (i.e., replaying, pausing, etc.) is possible as well. The graphical representation (Figure 6.3) is the same as in the earlier example with the addition of the Provision of Material category.

Example 3

In the third example the learner prepares the food in much the same way interacting with the materials including the television program. However, the learner is not alone. They work and interact with another learner, discussing aspects of the food preparation, sharing information, experiences, knowledge, and reactions. Hence the category of interaction between learners is added and the graphical representation is presented in Figure 6.4.

Figure 6.3. Example 2: Provision of materials, interaction with materials, and intra-action

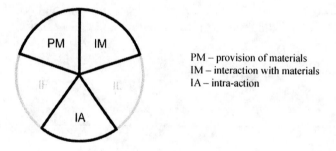

PM – provision of materials
IM – interaction with materials
IA – intra-action

Figure 6.4. Example 3: Provision of material, interaction with material, interaction between learners, and intra-action.

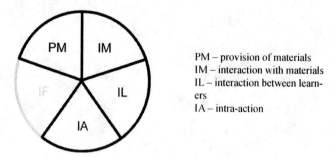

PM – provision of materials
IM – interaction with materials
IL – interaction between learners
IA – intra-action

Example 4

In the fourth example, the learner is a member of a face-to-face cooking class. They still interact with the materials and the other learners, and material is provided by the words spoken by the facilitator. The category of interaction with the facilitator is introduced as opportunities exist for learners to question and interact with the facilitator. In this example, all five categories of learning activities are present.

The examples of the cooking class show how the model can be used to analyze existing learning events in a general everyday learning environment. The category, intra-action has been included in each example and as mentioned earlier this category is one that the learner controls rather than the facilitator or designer and is included here as an indication that it is possible for activities in this category to take place in these examples.

As the context for the research described in this book is not a cooking class but rather learning in HRD and in higher education, the following fictitious examples are provided to clearly describe the application of the LAM in the appropriate contexts. The examples and the accompanying analysis of each category of activities within them, provide a guide to the application of the model to other learning events. The examples are in two groups: higher education and HRD.

Higher Education Examples

The first group of examples provides three comparative analyses of learning events that are common in higher education—large lectures are compared to small lectures; tutorials are compared to seminars; and traditional teaching is compared to flexible learning.

Figure 6.5. Example 4: All categories

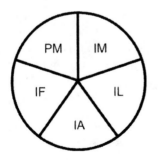

PM – provision of materials
IM – interaction with materials
IL – interaction between learners
IF – interaction with facilitator
IA – intra-action

For literally hundreds of years, lectures have been used as one of the major learning activities at universities. They have certainly ranged in quality from being dull, boring, and poorly delivered to well presented, engaging, and exciting, and likewise their effectiveness and efficiency as learning events has ranged just as widely. Lectures have been presented to audiences of varying sizes—ranging from first year core subjects in large universities with hundreds of students to small groups studying esoteric postgraduate subjects. The presentation styles and learning activities afforded vary significantly along with the range of lecture size and it is clearly not practical to analyze examples of every different lecture size here. Two typical examples are provided in which the LAM is applied to a large lecture and a small lecture.

Large and Small Lectures

Usually in large lectures the range of learning activities that is practicable is limited, and in many large lectures the most obvious learning activities consist of the lecturer speaking to the group and using audio/visual aids. The words, vocal attributes and body language of the lecturer plus the words, sounds, and pictures in the audio/visual material comprise the things that are transmitted or provided by the lecturer. In terms of the LAM these activities are in the category of the Provision of Material. As was mentioned earlier, it is not suggested that this alone is sufficient to engender the desired learning outcomes. Learners need to interact with the provided material and to undertake activities in the interaction categories for learning to occur.

While many lecturers would not hesitate to answer questions during a lecture, interaction with the lecturer in large lectures is usually limited to those learners who have the ability, motivation, and/or confidence to ask. Of course learners do benefit from hearing their colleagues' questions answered but interaction with the lecturer is often limited by the large physical size of the group. So in terms of the LAM, activities in the category of interaction with the facilitator (in this case the lecturer) are limited.

In a lecture to a large group of learners (for example, 100 or more) the management of group activities becomes difficult or impossible. Hence in terms of the LAM, activities in the category of interaction between learners are limited and often do not exist in practice. A lecture that engages a large group of learners, that is well presented, and makes appropriate use of well-designed audio/visual materials can provide opportunities that allow for interaction with the material presented, but it is generally limited to the notes learners take or in new or changed attitudes or ways of thinking about an idea, concept, or issue. In terms of the LAM, in a large lecture, activities in the category of interaction with material are thus limited.

In analyzing a typical large lecture in which the lecturer presents and the audience is passive, it can be seen that opportunities for activities in the categories:

- Interaction with the facilitator (in this case the lecturer)
- Interaction with the materials
- Interaction between learners

are limited due to the physical size of the audience and the concomitant lack of practicability. Conversely, large lectures can provide opportunities for efficient and effective activities in the Provision of Material category.

In small lectures, where the lecturer has more control over the mechanics and physical arrangement of the learners, a greater range of activities is practicable. As in large lectures, the typical learning activities of the lecturer speaking to the group and using audio/visual materials can provide an efficient and effective way to provide material. However, if the numbers of learners are small enough, group or individual activities can easily be structured as part of the lecture, which provide opportunities for interaction with the facilitator (in this case the lecturer) and interaction between learners. In terms of LAM, this would increase the activities in these two categories.

The analyses of large and small lectures can now be compared for each of the categories of the LAM as shown in Table 6.1. Intra-action is possible in large and small lectures but, as mentioned earlier, it is dependent on learners and cannot be prescribed by the facilitator or designer of the learning event. Intra-action is included in Table 6.1 to indicate that it is possible but should not be considered to be inevitable.

Table 6.1. Learning activities model: Analysis of large and small lectures

LAM Category	Large Lecture	Small Lecture
Provision of material	Yes, if well presented and A/V used appropriately	Yes, if well presented and A/V used appropriately
Interaction with material	Limited	Yes
Interaction with facilitator	Limited	Yes
Interaction between learners	Limited	Yes
Intra-action	Possible	Possible
Model		

It is tempting to compare small lectures with large lectures, as analyzed by the LAM, and arrive at the conclusion that in all cases small lectures would be better at achieving the desired learning outcomes. While this may be so, such a conclusion is specious as there can be many other factors that need to be considered. These can include the suitability of the material to the various activities as well as the efficiency of a large lecture. In cases where the desired learning outcome is the transmission of information and the student numbers are great, a well-presented large lecture can provide the outcomes in an efficient and effective manner.

Tutorials and Seminars

Other traditional learning events that are commonplace in higher education are tutorials and seminars. For this book, a tutorial is described as a meeting of learners and facilitator (in this case the facilitator is a tutor or a lecturer) where problems are discussed and/or solved. Group and individual work can be undertaken. Seminars are described as presentations by a learner (or small group of learners) to a larger group of their peers followed by a discussion. Both the presentation and discussion would normally be in the presence of a facilitator (in this case a tutor or lecturer).

In tutorials, as described previously, there are opportunities for activities in the categories interaction with material, interaction with the facilitator, and interaction between learners. There are also opportunities for intra-action. In this type of tutorial, the provision of material is usually restricted. Examples of activities in the interaction with material category in tutorials include: things learners look up in texts; references or notes; and the occasional reinforcement of a point by the facilitator.

The provision of material in a presentation by learner(s) is a central part of a seminar. Presentations are generally followed by discussions between the presenter, the other learners, and the facilitator. Some material can be provided by the presentation and learners interact with the material presented in order to contribute to the ensuing discussion. The discussion provides opportunities for interaction between learners and interaction with the facilitator, who in this case would typically be a lecturer or tutor.

The analyses of seminars and tutorials can now be compared by each of the categories of the LAM and are represented in Table 6.2. Intra-action is possible in seminars and tutorials but, as mentioned earlier, as it is predominantly dependent on learners, the facilitator or designer of the learning event cannot prescribe it. The category intra-action is included in Table 6.2 to indicate that it is possible but it is certainly not inevitable.

As with the comparison between large and small lectures, it would be inappropriate to assume that seminars are more efficient or more effective learning events when compared to tutorials simply because more elements of the model are present.

Table 6.2. Learning activities model analysis of tutorials and seminars

Category	Tutorial	Seminar
Provision of material	Limited	Student presentation
Interaction with material	Limited	Limited
Interaction with facilitator	Yes	Yes
Interaction between learners	Yes	Yes
Intra-action	Possible	Possible
Model		

Rather, this analysis highlights the different nature of the learning events. It also draws attention to the differences in the characteristics and nature of these learning events, which can inform the design process and result in more effective and efficient learning events.

The use of the LAM in the analysis of learning events in higher education serves a number of purposes. Later the LAM will be used as part of the technology selection method. In addition, the LAM can be used to analyze learning events. For example, the previous analyses of learning events in higher education (small and large lectures, tutorials, and seminars) serve to remind the facilitator (or designer of learning events) that there are strengths and weaknesses in each and that when these are matched to:

- the needs of the learners,
- the requirements of the content,
- the context, and
- the budget,

the design of the learning events can be optimized for the desired learning outcomes.

Traditional and Flexible Learning

In the next pair of examples a traditionally taught subject is compared to one that is taught flexibly. A face-to-face language class is compared to a CD-ROM–based, flexible language-learning package. The traditionally taught language subject was Spanish and offered at first year university level. It was a basic course designed for beginners to achieve a level of spoken and written literacy. The subject was two semesters long and involved six hours of face-to-face classes each week for 13 weeks. The classes were in three blocks of two hours for day students and two blocks of three hours for part-time students (after hours). Class activities consisted of short lectures, whole class activities such as reading, individual activities, presentations, and group work. The facilitator used an overhead projector and handouts as well as the prescribed text and activities books. Each learner was expected to provide their own Spanish/English, English/Spanish dictionary and to use the resources of the university library. Assessment was by presentation, examination, and assignments. An analysis of the traditionally taught Spanish class, using the LAM yields the following list of activities.

Provision of material:

- Material was provided by the facilitator's voice, the text and activities books, the overhead projector slides, handouts, dictionaries, and reference books.

Interaction with materials:

- Learners interacted with the material in a number of ways. They looked up rules of grammar in the text, they carried out the exercises in the activities book, and they looked up words in the dictionary and other information in reference books. Interaction with the materials occurred in the classroom but was not limited to it. It could occur in the library, at the learner's home, or wherever learners chose to study.

Interaction with facilitator (lecturer):

- Learners interacted with the facilitator in several ways. During class the facilitator circulated while learners were working individually or in groups. She answered their questions and checked grammar and pronunciation. Other interaction between the facilitator and learners occurred in consultations and in the comments made by the lecturer on returned assessments.

Interaction between learners:

- Learners interacted with each other in the classroom while carrying out group activities. Outside of the classroom they interacted while preparing joint presentations and in other more informal ways.

Intra-action:

- Intra-action, as discussed earlier, is largely dependent on learner-controlled factors. While it can be stimulated or inhibited by learning activities, it can also be independent of them.

The flexible learning package consisted of a study guide and a CD-ROM. The commercially produced CD-ROM was purchased by learners and used either at home or in the university computer laboratory. It was in two parts: Beginners Level and Intermediate Level. Each level contained 10 chapters or work sessions. Each session required learners to recognize Spanish words in text or sound and learners responded by clicking on the text of a word or a picture. While there appeared to be less grammatical information provided in the package, the advertising material suggested that the philosophy of language learning employed was the same as that of learning a first language, or immersion as a central part of the process, hence the rules of grammar would be learned through usage. Each work session or chapter had to be completed in one sitting or restarted from its beginning if the student exited the program before finishing. Students could ask questions of the teacher by e-mail or during consultation. Using the LAM to analyze the flexible learning package yields the following list of activities.

Provision of material:

- Material was provided by the CD-ROM in the form of pictures and text on the computer screen, sounds, and the text of the study guide. The package was designed to be used in conjunction with other provided materials such as dictionaries and indexes of verbs.

Interaction with the material:

- Interaction with material in the package happened in several ways, all of which required learners to be at a computer. While the predominant interaction was pointing and clicking on a word or picture, learners could also type words and phrases for the CD-ROM to verify or correct.

Interaction with facilitator:

- As the package was flexible in terms of when and where learners learned, interaction with the facilitator was more limited that for the classroom subject. Learners could e-mail or phone the facilitator or visit them during the designated consultation hours. Some interaction with the facilitator also occurred through the feedback provided in notes on work learners submitted for assessment.

Interaction between learners:

- No interaction between learners was designed into the package. However, if learners were working on campus (for example in computer labs) such interaction could be constructed. Of course there was no way of defining the exact level and amount of informal (or social) interaction between learners.

Intra-action:

- As has been discussed earlier, the final category of activities, intra-action is dependent on many factors. While most of these are determined by learners others may be dependent on the degree of encouragement or stimulation produced by the activities in the other categories.

Table 6.3 compares the two modes of learning and lists the details of the activities in each category. This representation indicates the differences between the modes for each category of the LAM, as well as the absence of activities in one category for one of the modes. The differences between modes within each category cannot be directly related to the effectiveness of learning without considering factors that are outside of the LAM and beyond the scope of this book. For example, it may have been decided that interaction between learners was *traded off* in favor of participation for students who were widely distributed geographically.

Table 6.3. Learning activities model analysis of a traditionally taught class and a flexible learning package

Category	Traditionally Taught Class	Flexible Learning Package
Provision of material	Facilitator's voice, slides, textbooks, handouts, reference books	CD-ROM, reference books, study guide
Interaction with material	Taking notes, looking up rules in reference books, activities in text	Computer-based point and click
Interaction with facilitator	Q+A in classroom, consultation	E-mail, phone Consultation
Interaction between learners	Group work in classroom Informal	None planned
Intra-action	Possible	Possible
Model		

Human Resource Development Examples

Training has been undertaken for as long as it was considered important to pass on skills from one generation to the next and the learning model of master and apprentice is not a new one. Traditionally training in organizations was practiced in several ways. Extraction training, in which learners were *extracted* from the workplace, was traditionally popular for the training of the workforce but has obvious costs. On-the-job training reduces these costs but does so at the expense of the rich learning experience that can be provided by including the presence of a facilitator and other learners.

Four fictitious examples of training are provided and analyzed using the LAM. They are:

- An extraction training program,
- Collaborative Web-based training,

- Print-based independent learning, and
- Independent Web-based training.

The examples are intended to illustrate the use of the LAM in the analysis of various modes of training.

Extraction Training and Web-Based Training

Many organizations have successfully used training programs for many years in which participants are extracted from their workplace and gathered together, often in a designated training environment. The training may be for a multitude of purposes and training sessions can vary in length from minutes to days or be scheduled periodically over a number of weeks or years. While presentations are viewed by many as the basis for this type of training program, there is agreement that presentations are not considered appropriate in many cases (Moss, 1993; Nadler & Nadler, 1994) and that a more participatory approach is generally preferable. Participatory learning activities can involve things like, brainstorming, case studies, debates, demonstrations, forums, games, peer teaching, simulations, workshops, and many more. Of course presentations are not ruled out completely as they can be efficient ways to transmit information or provide material.

Analysis of extraction training programs using the LAM indicates that material can be provided through the voice, handouts, and audiovisual aids the presenter uses or through materials distributed or encountered in the program and learners can interact with the materials in a number of ways. Opportunities for interaction with the facilitator can be provided in extraction training and can be in the form of questions and answers or comments. Opportunities for interaction between learners can be structured, as in group work, or can be informal such as a lunchtime discussion. As was the case in the higher education examples, the final category of activities, intra-action is dependent on many factors. While learners determine most of these, others may be dependent on the degree of encouragement or stimulation produced by the activities in the other categories or by other factors.

The development and proliferation of the Internet and the World Wide Web in years since the mid-1990s, has made Web-based training possible. Many organizations use the Web for training with examples ranging from the simple, such as information retrieval, to the complex in which learners may engage in online discussions and work in virtual groups. The earliest use of the Web was for the provision of material, which was in the form of text, pictures, diagrams, charts, and audio and video clips. More recently the Web has also been used to host collaboration through tools such as text-based discussions, wikis, and blogs. These have been included in Web-based training to allow for interaction with the facilitator and interaction between learners. The presence of a cohort of learners can be the factor that determines which of these approaches to Web-based training is used. Where a cohort is absent learning is primarily an individual process and is independent of other learners and the facilitator and the learning activities are carried out independently. Devices such as lists of frequently asked questions (FAQs) can provide an emulation of interaction with learners and interaction with the facilitator. To clearly differentiate between these two approaches they are referred to here as collaborative Web-based training and independent Web-based training.

One of the benefits of Web-based training over face-to-face extraction training is the flexibility of time and place of training. Learners can undertake training during downtime or when it suits the task as collaboration in Web-based training can be asynchronous. They can also undertake training without having to travel to a training venue.

Table 6.4 compares the analysis of extraction training and collaborative Web-based training. It lists the details of the activities in each category and indicates the differences between the modes for each category of the LAM. The differences between modes within each category cannot be directly related to the effectiveness of learning

Table 6.4. Learning activities model analysis of extraction training and collaborative Web-based training

Category	Extraction Training	Collaborative Web-Based Training
Provision of material	Facilitator's voice, audiovisual aids, textbooks, handouts, reference books	Text, photographs, pictures, diagrams, charts, audio and video clips
Interaction with material	Taking notes, looking up information in reference books	Reading, viewing, point and click
Interaction with facilitator	Q+A, and comments during training session	Text-based discussion forum—e-mail
Interaction between learners	Group work in training session. Informal	Text-based discussion forum
Intra-action	Possible	Possible
Model		

without considering factors that are outside of the LAM and beyond the scope of this book. For example, a cost-benefit analysis in which costs include transporting learners to the learning venue and time off the job could be a deciding factor.

Independent Learning

Independent learning is common in many organizations. In contrast to extraction training, independent learning is often on-the-job and is, by definition, undertaken by individuals in the absence of other learners or a facilitator. Independent learning can be used for a range of purposes including the acquisition of skills, know-how, or procedures. It follows that, in a broader context, independent learning happens whenever a learner consults a manual or set of instructions and successfully completes a new or difficult task. Material for independent learning can be provided by a technology such as the Web or in print. For example, a software designer might learn a new programming sequence from a book or an accounts clerk may consult online help to undertake a new accounting procedure. When the learning is on-the-job, interaction with material is often through reading, viewing, or pointing and clicking, and the learner usually applies what they have learned to the job immediately. One of the benefits of independent learning is that it can be undertaken at a time that suits the learner, the organization, and the task. Learners may interact with the materials through direct application or by following instructions. As the training is carried out independently there is usually no interaction with the facilitator or between learners. Of course there are exceptions, such as cases where the learner does not achieve the learning outcome and may consult with a peer or ask a supervisor. As in other modes of training intra-action is possible, but determined by the learner and hence difficult to prescribe.

Table 6.5 compares the analyses of print-based independent learning and independent Web-based training. It lists the details of the activities in each category and indicates the differences between the modes for each category of the LAM. The differences between modes within each category cannot be directly related to the effectiveness of learning without considering factors that are outside of the LAM and beyond the scope of this book. For example while Web-based training can easily deliver recently updated information to many locations, it is necessary to have access to a networked computer to access it, which could be problematic in remote or difficult locations. This contrasts to the use of print-based field manuals which may used some distance from a computer, network connection, or power source.

Table 6.5. Learning activities model analysis of print-based and Web-based independent learning

Category	Independent Web-Based Training	Print-Based Independent Learning
Provision of material	Web material—text and graphics	Manual/instructions in print, reference books
Interaction with material	Reading, viewing, point and click	Reading
Interaction with facilitator	Not planned	Not planned
Interaction between learners	Not planned	Not planned
Intra-action	Possible	Possible
Model	PM IM IA	PM IM IA

Conclusion

The LAM has been developed for two types of purpose. Firstly it provides a theoretical framework for the analysis of learning activities and secondly it can be used to assist facilitators and designers of learning events in the design process by subdividing learning events or programs into categories of activities. It can be used in a formative way to analyze a proposed learning event or program or in a summative way to assist in the revision of an existing learning event or program. The LAM can also be used to compare different methods and modes of achieving learning goals.

There are some things that the LAM cannot, and is not intended, to do. It will not prescribe the best mixture of activities to use for a particular learning event or content area. It is not sensitive to the cultural and demographic make-up of learners. The facilitator is usually the expert in the content, and the facilitator or designer should have created a profile of the learners and hence they are best placed to match the activities of the model with the content and the learners.

The LAM is the first of two theoretical frameworks that have been developed and can be combined to form a technology selection method for the design of learning events. In the next chapter learning technologies and techniques are analyzed, and a LTM is presented. In Chapter VIII the two models (LAM and LTM) are brought together to form the technology selection method in which technologies, analyzed by the LTM, are matched to categories of activities in the LAM.

References

Bates, A. W. (1995). *Technology, open learning and distance education.* London: Routledge.

Bates, A. W. (2000). *Managing technological change: Strategies for college and university leaders.* San Francisco: Jossey-Bass.

Gagné, R., Briggs, L., & Wager, W. (1992). *Principles of instructional design.* Fort Worth, TX: Harcourt Brace Jovanovich.

Gronlund, N. (1978). *Determining accountability for classroom instruction.* New York: Macmillam.

Kruse, K., & Keil, J. (2000). *Technology-based training: The art and science of design, development and delivery.* San Francisco: Jossey-Bass/Pfeiffer.

Nadler, L., & Nadler, Z. (1994). *Designing training programs.* Houston, TX: Gulf.

National Tertiary Education Union (NTEU). (1997). *Policy document.* Australia: Author.

Smith, A. (1992). *Training and development in Australia.* Sydney, Australia: Butterworths.

Taylor, J. (1995). Distance education technologies: The fourth generation. *Australian Journal of Educational Technology, 11*(2), 1-7.

Taylor, J. (2001). *Fifth generation distance education* (Higher Education Series, Report No. 40). Canberra, Australia: Department of Education, Training and Youth Affairs.

Wilson, J. P. (1999). *Human resource development: Learning and training for individuals and organizations.* London: Kogan Page.

Chapter VII

The Learning Technologies Model

Introduction

The learning activities model (LAM) developed in the previous chapter provides a theoretical framework for the analysis of the process of learning through the categorization of activities. During the design of learning events, different techniques, methods, and technologies can be applied to activities within each category or to complete categories of the LAM. This matching process is, in essence, the basis of the technology selection method (TSM), presented in Chapter VIII. However, before technologies that are appropriate to learners and learning events can be selected it is essential to have a clear understanding of the nature and capabilities of the technologies. To assist in the understanding and analysis of learning technologies, a theoretical framework of them, called the learning technologies model (LTM), is presented.

Learning technologies differ in the function and roles they can play in the process of learning. In past times when learning technologies were simple and limited they were used primarily as adjuncts to face-to-face teaching and learning. Teachers had little difficulty in coming to terms with them and generally used them in pedagogically appropriate ways. However, particularly in e-learning, learning technologies have increased in number, complexity, and diversity to such an extent that a theoretical framework is needed to help teachers and designers understand the nature of different technologies and hence apply them appropriately.

At many universities and colleges, and in the training of human resources, a range of learning technologies is used in an approach to learning that blends face-to-face and online methods. Often those who design blended courses are teachers and not specialized designers. These teachers/designers need tools to guide their decisions of which technology to match to learning activities. The LTM was developed to assist teachers/designers in making appropriate use of learning technologies by classifying them within a simple system. The model produced is sufficiently robust for general application and simple enough to be accessible to busy staff such as academics who most likely have areas of research outside of educational technology and the design of technology-rich learning events.

Theoretical Basis of the LTM

The theoretical basis for the LTM is provided, in part, by researchers in the field of distance education through their description of learning technologies as one-way or two-way (Bates, 1995; Rowntree, 1994; Taylor, 2001). Writing in the area of open and distance learning, Bates distinguishes between one-way and two-way technologies by stating that two-way technologies are those that support communications between humans. He suggests that while they are significant for communications between learners, instructors, and tutors they have probably greater significance for communications between learners (Bates, 1995, p. 32).

The research reported on here takes this rather basic conceptual approach, redefines it, and juxtaposes it with theories developed for technology selection in the field of organizational communications to produce a new theoretical framework for the analysis and categorization of learning technologies. This forms the basis of the LTM. The LTM is the second original theoretical framework discussed in this book and can be used to assist learning designers in the analysis of learning technologies as well as in their selection. When the selection of learning technologies is addressed in Chapter VIII, learning technologies, as analyzed by the LTM, will be matched to categories of the LAM.

The LTM has been developed in two stages. Firstly, the two theoretical dimensions are juxtaposed to form a matrix. Secondly, the matrix is placed into a context that includes two further criteria by which characteristics of learning technologies can be classified—these are: the categories of the LAM to which the technology is inherently suited, and the degree to which the technology supports synchronous or asynchronous interactions. Examples of the analysis of several technologies by the LTM are provided later in this chapter to illustrate the model.

As mentioned earlier, part of the theoretical basis of the LTM is drawn from the literature of distance education. Another area of inquiry that forms the second part of the theoretical basis of the model comes from the field of organizational communications and is broadly termed *media richness theories*.

Media Richness Theories

As with different methods of communication, different teaching techniques, methods, and technologies support or require different attributes or communication channels. For example, a discussion where learners are gathered at the same time and in the same place can consist of a dialogue in which several levels of attributes can be present. Learners hear the text of the speech. They also hear the emphasis, pace, volume, pitch, inflection, and other vocal attributes of the speech. Also, they see the body language and other non-verbal communications of the speakers. In addition, learners may have the opportunity to question the speaker and hopefully achieve the desired goals of the learning event. In a second example where material is provided by a textbook, learners read the text and view the diagrams in it. While, the vocal and non-verbal attributes of the first example are not available, the learner has the option to find their own way through the book. They can elect to read from beginning to end or to repeat or dwell on salient sections and skim through others. They can refer to the index and other devices in the book.

In Chapter IV, theories for the selection of technologies for organizational communications were discussed. Two early trait theories developed scales of richness or ability to facilitate social presence. The media richness theory (Daft & Lengel, 1984) and the social presence theory (Carlson & Davis, 1998) both describe technologies as having degrees of richness based on:

- The number of communication channels or attributes available.
- The ability to provide feedback.
- Personalization, and other factors.

For example, both theories determine that face-to-face communication is richer than telephone, which in turn is richer than a written letter or memo. Later research (Carlson & Davis, 1998; Guthrie, 2000) has indicated that the choice of technology is more complex and has been made so by other factors such as the introduction of information and communication technologies—late last century—as these technologies often have other attributes that impact on their choice. For example, while e-mail messages equate with written letters and memos in terms of communications channels or attributes (both are usually text only) other features of e-mail can affect its choice in organizational communications. The ease with which e-mail messages can be stored and retrieved, sent to multiple recipients, access controlled, and priority assigned are features that can play a role in the process of deciding on a choice of technology.

While it is recognized that the trait theories fall short of providing an inclusive description of the factors that impact on the selection of technologies, they do provide a convenient hierarchy within which an analysis of technologies can be undertaken. The hierarchy is adopted as one dimension of the matrix that forms the basis of the theoretical framework, the LTM, as it allows the differentiation of technologies based on communication channels, or attributes. When technologies are then matched to categories of the LAM, it can be ensured that each technology is suited to the corresponding category and that it can support the communication attributes necessary or desired for learning.

Learning Technologies

Compared to face-to-face learning, when learning technologies are used to provide, facilitate, or mediate learning activities, they can impose restrictions on the communication channels available. For example, if a discussion is facilitated by an audioconference, participants at one site cannot see those at other sites and hence the non-verbal attributes of the dialogue of speakers at the other sites are not available. Further, if the discussion was mediated by e-mail or Internet chat, the only available attribute of the dialogue would be text.

There are too many variables for it to be argued that fewer available communication cues or attributes in a learning technology will always equate to a reduction in the quality of the learning experience. Such an argument would be a reductionist one for the same reasons that trait theories do not provide a complete comparison of all aspects of the technologies. In some cases a reduction in the set of attributes or communication cues can enhance the learning experience through the provision of a narrower focus. In other cases there may be *trade-offs* that are worthwhile. For example, if learners elect to study at times and places that suit themselves they may be limited to interacting with other learners and the facilitator by asynchronous and communicatively limited means such as e-mail. For them the trade-off is a reduction in the attributes or communication cues in favor of a flexible learning program.

Based on research in the area of open and distance learning (Bates, 1995; Rowntree, 1994; Taylor, 2001), in the LTM, learning technologies are first categorized as those that support:

- The one-way representation of material.
- Two-way interactions between humans or dialogues.

The one-way learning technologies are labeled as *representational* and the two-way as *collaborative*. The division is not always complete or clean for all technologies and there are examples of learning technologies that perform in both categories, although usually their performance in one category is more effective and/or more efficient than in the other. This division is helpful in the selection of technologies that provide appropriate communication for the achievement of the planned learning objectives. In representational technologies the flow of information is generally one-way from the technology to the learner. In collaborative technologies the flow of information is two-way between users of the technology. For example, the information in printed materials (a representational technology) clearly flows from the text to the reader. However, it is only by interacting with the text that the reader makes sense or meaning of the text. Collaborative technologies facilitate a dialogue or two-way flow of information between humans. When a telephone call is made between two parties the information is usually two-way and flows between them.

Representational Learning Technologies

The term *representational* is used here to describe the nature of the communication in the one-way representation or provision of material. Different technologies used for the provision of material have different channels or attributes of representation. For example, while printed materials can only represent material as text and still images (and in many cases as text alone), video can represent material with full motion pictures and audio. The available attributes of representational learning technologies can be broadly categorized as:

- Text only
- Audio only
- Text and still images
- Audio and still images
- Audio and moving images

Within the representational category of learning technologies the level of the available attributes of representation is presented as a means of analysis and as a way to further understand the technologies and to assist in the selection of them for use in learning events.

Collaborative Learning Technologies

For the second category of learning technologies, the term *collaborative* is used to describe the nature of the two-way communication. In a fashion similar to the first category, different technologies within this category support different collaborative attributes or channels of collaboration. For example, while telephones support dialogue in which the words, or text, of each speaker contributes to the interaction, they also support vocal characteristics such as timbre, inflection, emphasis, pitch, pace, tone, and volume. Within the collaborative category of learning technologies the level of the available attributes of communication is presented as a tool to further understand the technologies and to assist in the selection of them for learning. The attributes can be broadly grouped as:

- text only
- voice only, and
- voice and non-verbal attributes

In the previous list, voice could be thought of as consisting of text plus the vocal attributes mentioned earlier. The non-verbal attributes refer to eye contact, body language, and so forth. Hence voice plus non-verbal attributes can be thought of as text plus vocal attributes plus non-verbal attributes. Table 7.1 shows the cumulative or developmental nature of the attributes of collaborative technologies.

As existing technologies develop and new technologies are created it is reasonable to expect that a theoretical model that describes them must expand and change to

Table 7.1. Attributes of collaborative technologies

	Channel	Communication Channels
1	Print	Text
2	Voice	Text plus vocal attributes
3	Face-to-face	Text plus vocal attributes plus non-verbal attributes

remain germane. Recent additions to learning technologies include tools that allow students to collaboratively create products in online environments. For example, Wiki's (http://wikimediafoundation.org/wiki/Home), collaborative, user-produced Internet documents (CUPIDS) (or dynamically created Web pages) (Caladine, 2005), and blogs can be used to create products such as group reports or create glossaries online. Shared eWhiteboards and application sharing are further examples of collaborative learning technologies that support two-way communications and facilitate the creation of products. Therefore the subcategories of the collaborative technologies category are termed *dialogic* and *productive*. Dialogic learning technologies are defined as those that are confined to the support of dialogue alone: for example, telephone. Productive learning technologies combine two-way communications and facilitate the creation of products.

Basis of the LTM

The attributes of most learning technologies can be grouped into three levels of communications cues (as indicated in Table 7.1) and used as one axis or dimension of the matrix that forms the basis of the LTM. The second axis of the matrix is based on the work discussed earlier that describes learning technologies as one-way or two-way, referred to in this book as representational or collaborative. When the

Table 7.2. The basis of the LTM

Attributes - Channels	Representational	Collaborative
Level 1	• **Text only** • Text and still images • E.g., printed material	• **Text only** • E.g., e-mail or CMCs
Level 2	• **Voice and other audio** • Sound effects • Found sound • Music and other sounds • E.g., radio broadcast, audio tape	• **Voice only** • E.g., telephone—compressed hence vocal attributes may be less apparent.
Level 3	• **Voice and moving pictures** • Plus other audio • Plus non-verbal when presenter on screen and close. • E.g., movie or video tape	• **Voice and image (face to face)** • Plus non-verbal attributes (if resolution is sufficient) • Plus other audio • Plus other images still or moving • E.g., videoconference

categories of attributes are generalized for both collaborative and representational technologies, the resulting matrix forms the basic element of the LTM as shown in Table 7.2.

While the two dimensions: level of attributes or channels supported and representational or collaborative nature, present a valuable start to a framework for the analysis of learning technologies, there are other characteristics that impact on the activities of learning and hence need to be considered in the framework in order to increase the applicability and general usefulness of it. These characteristics are whether the technology supports synchronous or asynchronous interactions and the learning activities to which the technology is inherently suited.

Other Characteristics of Learning Technologies

Learning technologies can be described as either synchronous or asynchronous. This refers to the interactions between learners; between facilitators and learners; and between learners and materials. Synchronous interactions are those that happen more or less at the same time. Asynchronous ones do not. For example, videoconferences are described as synchronous, meaning that learners, or learners and the facilitator participate in the conference at the same time. E-mail and Internet chat (both are described later in this chapter) provide good examples of the difference between synchronous and asynchronous technologies. E-mail is usually responded to at the discretion of the user and hence is described as asynchronous. However, when in a chat session each participant knows that the others are waiting for their responses. The resulting *conversations* are synchronous, develop at their own pace, are quite different from e-mail interactions, and hence serve different learning purposes.

In the early days of the Internet, and as its use for learning increased, the debate over the benefits of asynchronous versus synchronous communication gained momentum as the Internet provided efficient and available applications for both synchronous and asynchronous communications. Some proponents suggested that asynchronous communication was, by its very nature, of a higher quality (in both the learning and communications senses) as learners had time to consider their responses. Others maintained that the spontaneity learners were used to with face-to-face communication was all-important. It is argued that both types of communication have roles to play in learning. Asynchronous communications certainly provide opportunities for learners to meet learning objectives that require them to consider their responses, while synchronous communications can help learners develop skills such as "thinking on their feet." Both forms of communication have valid and different uses in learning and surely the best use of a learning technology occurs when it is selected to meet a synchronous or asynchronous learning need.

Synchronous communication on the Internet can be as fast as face-to-face but this is rarely the case. For example, to *chat* on the Internet the *speaker* types their message, which is then loaded to the chat room or host. All of this takes time and reduces the speed of the interaction. Experienced *chatters* obviously dislike this delay and have developed a shorthand and system of language shortcuts and icons (often called *smilies* or emoticons) to speed up the typing of the conversation. Of course the video communications technologies are inherently synchronous and slight delays due to network or other technology issues can adversely impact on the effectiveness of the communications.

Another characteristic of learning technologies incorporated into the LTM is the technology's inherent suitability to particular learning activities. As mentioned earlier, some technologies are one-way or representational and suited predominantly to the categories of the LAM of *provision of materials* and *interaction with materials*. Other technologies are collaborative and more suited to the interaction categories of the LAM and the matching of technologies to categories of the LAM, forms the basis of the TSM, discussed in Chapter VIII.

The LTM

The LTM brings together the nature and attributes of learning technologies, as illustrated in Table 7.2 with the criteria mentioned previously, of synchronous/asynchronous nature and suitable categories of the LAM.

Figure 7.1 is an example of the graphical representation of the LTM. When technologies are analyzed by these criteria, and the results represented in tabular form, the resulting robust tool provides a theoretical framework of learning technologies that has theoretical and practical applications.

Many other conceptualizations of learning technologies are less robust than the LTM as they are either simple and only classify technologies by their characteristics or relate only to a finite group of technologies available and in favor at the time of publication.

The LTM links learning technologies to applications and as well provides an insight into the nature and characteristics of the technology, which makes possible the extension of the use of the technology. The framework can also be used to analyze future technologies.

As the LTM is presented as a model that can be used to describe future technologies and as it is beyond the scope of this book to analyze all information and communication technologies, a number of learning technologies that can reasonably be expected to be available to designers for use in learning events is analyzed using the LTM. The technologies are:

Figure 7.1. An example of the LTM

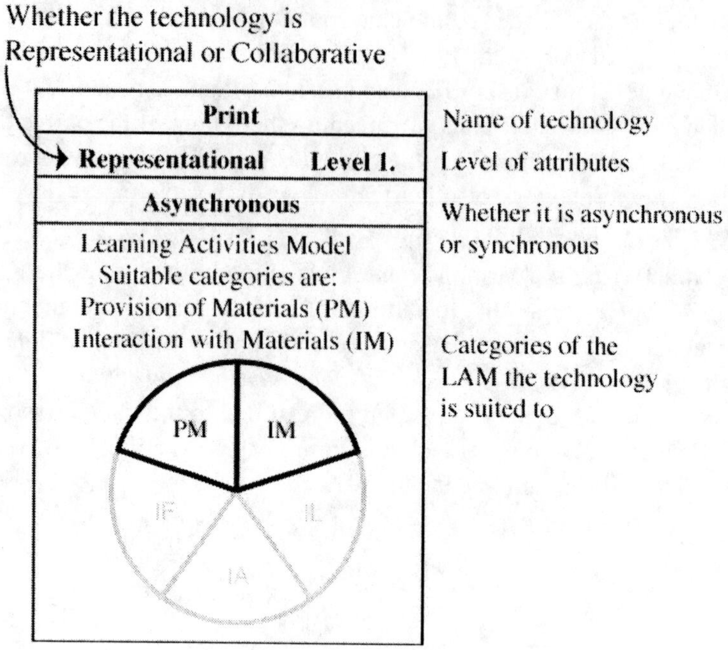

- Print,
- Radio, podcasts, and recorded audio,
- Television and video,
- Videoconference and video telephony
- Multimedia,
- Internet, consisting of:
  - World Wide Web,
  - Internet chat,
  - Online discussion,
  - E-mail and list servers, and
  - World Wide Web including learning management systems.

An analysis of each of the aforementioned technologies is provided to illustrate the LTM.

Print

Print is defined here as printed symbols (letters, numbers, diagram, pictures, etc.) on paper. Typically in learning events print appears as manuals, handouts, textbooks, study guides, course notes, and so forth. Print is probably one of the oldest learning technologies and generally considered central to learning. Bates (1995) suggests that print has been the foremost educational technology at least "ever since the invention of the Gutenberg press" (p. 116). Further he suggests, almost with surprise, that it is still dominant today especially in distance education as well as face-to-face learning.

The use of print in education has been described as primarily being one of presenting information or the representation of things. Bates (1995) argues that is use is mainly in the precise presentation of facts, abstract concepts or ideas, rules, and principles. He also suggests it is suited to the presentation of detailed, long, or complex arguments and that as mentioned earlier is the predominant learning technology or medium (p. 119). Kemp and Smellie (1989) argue that many materials when presented on paper can be used for instructional purposes or to at least inform learners. They subdivide printed materials into three categories: aids, materials and informational materials (p. 45).

As well as the presentation, or provision of material, Bates (1995) argues that students need to interact with print if they are to derive meaning from it.

Thus a text is not a neutral object; its meaning depends on the interpretation of the reader, whether it is a work of great literature or a car repair mechanic's manual. Therefore if the reader is to obtain meaning from a text, there has to be an interaction. (p. 120)

It is generally known that the predominant use of print in learning is for the presentation of material in a form that can be conveniently accessed by learners. To learn from it, learners need to interact with the text on a cognitive level, mentioned by Bates (1995), as well as on a physical level through access devices such as indexes, headings and sub-headings, summaries, self assessment questions, glossaries, and so forth. By contrast and implicitly, print as described here does not play a great role (if any) in the categories of: *interactions between learners* and *interaction with the facilitator* in the LAM. Print is obviously suited to the categories: *provision of materials* and *interaction with materials*. While print can be used to host a dialogue through letters, today this is rarely the case in a learning context outside of correspondence courses.

The literature concurs that print is generally used for the presentation of material and it follows that print is a representational technology in the LTM. As print consists of text and still images, it is of level one attributes. Print is generally considered to be an asynchronous technology as the preparation of it is generally performed

Table 7.3. Learning technologies model: Print

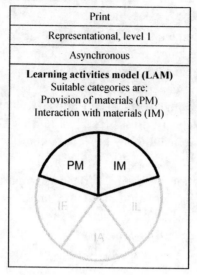

Print
Representational, level 1
Asynchronous
Learning activities model (LAM) Suitable categories are: Provision of materials (PM) Interaction with materials (IM)

prior to its use. The analysis of the learning technology, print—using the LTM—is shown in Table 7.3.

Radio, Podcasts, and Recorded Audio

Radio and recorded audio have been used in learning for some time. Podcasts, a more recent arrival, are functionally similar as they are audio recordings that are automatically delivered to users' computers (and perhaps connected iPods) via the Internet. Bates (1995) describes radio as having a number of uses in learning contexts. He suggests it has a role in school broadcasts as well as in general educational programs that can benefit from its broadcast nature. These can include programs of adult or social education (p. 139).

Writing in 1995, Bates also describes audiocassettes as the most cost-effective learning technology. In some cases audiocassettes have been used as a vehicle for learners' feedback to facilitators. For example, in some language learning where learners record oral exercises on tape and deliver them to the facilitator for evaluation and/or examination. However, in the main, audio programs in education are of the pre-recorded type. Today audiocassettes have all but been replaced by audio CDs as a recorded audio technology. Of course the future of CDs appears to be challenged by online delivery of audio, which can include the purchase of music of the podcasting of radio programs. Once popular, today live radio broadcasts have limited use in online learning. However, in the past few years podcasts have become increasingly popular.

Moore and Kearsley (1996) suggest that recorded audio can be used for a number of learning purposes that include:

- Talking learners through printed resources, real objects and/or practical procedures
- Analyzing human interactions, and
- Providing aural experiences. (p. 84)

With the exception of student recorded podcasts, recorded audio is generally used to present material and as such audio recordings are asynchronous, one-way technologies and are described as representational in the LTM. In addition, they have level two attributes as they can contain text (spoken) and vocal attributes (see Table 7.2). Interaction with audio is usually limited to replaying sections of the program and the categories of the LAM this technology is suited to are provision of material and interaction with material. The analysis of the leaning technologies, radio, podcasts, and recorded audio—by the LTM—is shown in Table 7.4.

Table 7.4. The LTM: Recorded audio

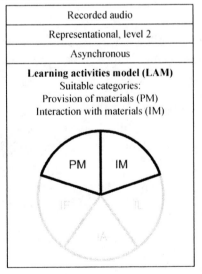

Television and Video

The reporting of the use of television in the literature concerned with learning technologies is confused by the problems of definition. In North America many reports on educational television refer to the technology as interactive videoconferences. These use broadcast television and students communicate with the *on-air* teacher via a telephone. For the sake of clarity, here television is restricted to prepared programs broadcast with no intention of interaction with the on-screen identities. That is, programs that are generally encapsulated in a medium such as videotape, videodisc, or DVD and the material has been prepared before its broadcast or viewing.

The video replay technology, DVD, and the second generation variants of it, Blu-ray and HD-DVD, have the potential to provide rich learning materials as they can combine a menu structure with full screen, high quality video and have the unique capabilities to replay different pieces of video in a seamless manner. Unfortunately this recently arrived second generation of DVD has two competing and incompatible formats, Blu-ray and HD-DVD. Both formats can store more information on a disc of the same diameter. These have the ability to provide high definition images and sound to learning. As menu and chapter structure of the DVD technologies allow navigational option to users, its potential in teaching and learning is increased as students can navigate the resources in ways that best suit them. This provides somewhat of a challenge to the creators of such resources as writing for them is obviously quite different from writing a linear video or film script. DVD scripts need to be branched allowing students to select scenes, images, and text in ways that suit their learning needs. In this way students can customize the resources to their own needs.

Television and video have been used in learning contexts for many years as useful adjuncts to learning and have been used to provide educational course material, especially in distance, open, and flexible learning programs. It is generally known that television and video are suited to the display of action, objects, color, and motion. If action or movement is not required then a still photograph may be cheaper and probably have more clarity or resolution. Television is suited to the display of moving things and three-dimensional objects, for example: the training of sales staff in new product knowledge. Berge (2001) suggests television can be used to train large audiences in things such as product knowledge and do so in a short period of time. Berge suggests the use of television for this kind of training should have high production values and works well for the transfer of knowledge.

Clearly when television or video is used in this way, it is an asynchronous, one-way technology and can be described by the LTM as a representational technology of level three attributes. As interaction with television is rather limited and interaction with video is limited to pause, rewind, and replay, it is suited mainly to the category of

Table 7.5. The LTM: Television and video

| Television and video |
| Representational, level 3 |
| Asynchronous |
| **Learning activities model (LAM)**
Suitable categories:
Provision of materials (PM)
Interaction with materials (IM) |

LAM of provision of materials. Learners can interact with the material on videotape, disc, or DVD through stopping and reviewing sections of the material.

This mechanical type of interaction can lead to clarification and the desired learning outcomes and hence video is suited to the interaction with materials category at this level. The analysis of the learning technologies, television and video—by the LTM—is shown in Table 7.5.

Video has been used in education for many years with basically two types of programs. Firstly, there have been many video programs designed specifically for educational purposes, such as training tapes. In addition, many video programs, created for other purposes, have been used for educational purposes. In recent years do-it-yourself videos have been used in teaching and learning and its future looks particularly bright in online learning. In recent years the costs of video cameras have dropped and the ease of editing increased. This has been made possible by programs such as Movie Maker in the Windows platform and iMovie on the Apple, which are both supplied at no extra cost with the operating system. When this is combined with the ability to upload video to the Internet for distribution, the use of video is considerably easier than it was a few years ago.

Videoconference

In the literature, and as mentioned in the previous section, the term *videoconference* is used to describe two different technologies. For some it refers to a one-way broadcast television program with participation from students through telephone calls to the presenter while he or she is on air. For clarity, in this book, the term videoconference is used to describe a technology which generally uses publicly or privately owned telecommunications lines or the Internet to transmit and receive two-way audio and two-way video. In these two-way videoconferences, participants gather at videoconference equipped rooms or studios and connect to parties at other such rooms or studios. The technology is appliance-based and typically consists of:

- Video cameras to capture the images of participants, documents, and so forth,
- Microphones to capture the audio,
- Television style monitors to view and hear the other parties, and
- Compressor/decompressor or coder/decoder (CODECS) to reduce the size of the signal (video and audio) to a level suitable for transmission.

While much has been written on the technical details of videoconferences, only a limited amount has been written on the use of this technology for learning. However, the literature concurs on the issue of the importance of interaction to the process of learning using videoconference. Latchem (in Mitchell, 1993) suggests that video-conferences work best with small- to medium-sized groups of students at each site who are encouraged to interact with each other as well as trainers, tutors, or teachers. He further suggests that videoconferences are excellent in the support of learning activities such as simulations, role plays, case studies, brainstorming, problem solving, and in general cognition building. Daunt (1997) reinforces the importance of interaction in videoconferences and describes facilitators of videoconferences in learning as "teleteachers."

Most teleteachers agree that interaction is an important element in their teaching—after all it is the only thing that distinguishes teleteaching from a video tape! Interactivity takes many forms; it is not just limited to audio and video, or just teacher-student interactions. It represents the connectivity students feel with the teacher, the local tutors and their peers. (p. 109)

Laurillard (1993) describes videoconferences as a discursive media and suggests that they are not suited to the transmission of presentations or lectures. She continues to argue that video would be more appropriate for this. Kobayashi, Tanaka, Yamaji, and Otsuka (1997) reflect on their experience with videoconferences in higher education and argue that the least effective forms of discourse for this technology were those characterized by presentations—monologues where the sole purpose was the one-way transfer of information. The author's experience with videoconference in learning is congruent with the view that they are suited to interaction rather than presentation. Many times he has been faced with teachers who ask why the students go to sleep in their videoconferences. The answer is usually that one-way lectures are not suitable for videoconferences. Videoconferences rely on interaction to be effective and there are a range of technologies that are more suited to the encapsulation and delivery of one-way materials.

The literature concurs that videoconference is best used as an interactive technology in learning. Hence in the LTM, it is a collaborative technology and as it supports voice and image, has level three attributes. As such it is clear that videoconference is suitable for the categories of the LAM that concern interactions between humans: interaction between learners and interaction with facilitator. As all parties need to be connected to the videoconference at the same time it is a synchronous technology. The description of the learning technology, videoconference—by the LTM—is shown in Table 7.6.

Multimedia

The term *multimedia* is often used to describe a style of computer-mediated presentation or program that incorporates two or more specific elements. Often the elements

Table 7.6. The LTM: Videoconference

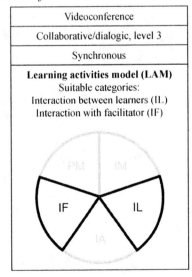

number more than two and can include: audio, still pictures, moving pictures, and text. One of the many definitions contained in the literature, states that multimedia is defined by the elements it contains. Tannenbaum (1998) argues that the defining characteristics of multimedia are interactivity, computer presented, and at least two of "the following elements: text, sound, still graphic images, motion graphics and animation," (p. 4).

Tannenbaum's (1998) definition is rather broad and can describe electronic books, streamed video, and World Wide Web pages. For clarity, multimedia is defined here as a computer program that contains at least three of the elements mentioned previously and is usually distributed on a Web page, CD-ROM, or is used from a computer hard drive. Multimedia as defined here cannot host interaction with the facilitator, designer, or interaction between learners. While the interactions learners have with multimedia can emulate interactions with other humans, they are limited by two factors. Firstly, interaction is not with a live facilitator or designer, rather it is with the essence of them encapsulated in the program. Questions and answers contained in a multimedia program are usually assumed by the designer or are those frequently asked when the material is presented in a different format. In this way the emulation of interaction with the facilitator is limited. Secondly, as the material and essence of the facilitator or designer is encapsulated within the technology, the material is fixed in time thus imposing a potential limit to the new knowledge that can be constructed in this way. Unfortunately the nature of multimedia does not lend itself to easy or inexpensive updating, hence shelf-life has to be a major consideration in the planning and use of multimedia in learning. However, within the limitations mentioned multimedia has many uses in learning that range in complexity from skills acquisition, for example in language learning, through to complex simulations. Kruse and Kiel (2000) describe multimedia as CD-ROM and suggest that if offers advantages over traditional modes of training as they provide a "more engaging Learning experience" (p. 45) and can contain video and animations. They suggest the educational benefits of multimedia are in their use of text, audio, animation, and video to convey information.

Clearly, while multimedia can be apparently synchronous as learners interact with the material in real time, it is argued that it should be considered an asynchronous technology as the material is gathered, authored, and encapsulated prior to its use. In the LTM multimedia is a representational technology but as well can be considered a collaborative one if a dialogue can be had with a computer. This question has philosophical dimensions that are beyond the scope of this book. Some multimedia programs are highly representational and others can be highly interactive. In Chapter III the dual definition of interactivity was discussed and the use of the term *interaction* was adopted to mean interactions that are reciprocal and to include the *interactivity* of a computer responding to a user's input. However, as the interaction is limited to a computer program, multimedia is described here as a representational learning technology. As multimedia can contain audio, video as well as text and animations it

Table 7.7. The LTM: Multimedia

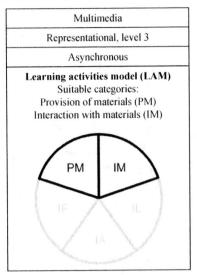

Multimedia
Representational, level 3
Asynchronous
Learning activities model (LAM) Suitable categories: Provision of materials (PM) Interaction with materials (IM)

has the capacity for level three attributes. As multimedia does not provide interaction between learners or interaction with the facilitator the categories of the LAM it is suited to, are provision of materials and interaction with materials. The analysis of the learning technology, multimedia—by the LTM—is shown in Table 7.7.

Internet

The use of the Internet for learning in the higher education and human resource development contexts has grown with remarkable speed. Most universities have some degree of online learning and many organizations use, or plan to use, the Internet for training. The rapid uptake of the use of the Internet for learning is probably due to its almost ubiquitous and pervasive nature and the concomitant efficiencies of communication it offers. The use of the Internet can clearly be divided into two distinct categories of functions that reflect the primary differentiation of technologies in the LTM: representational and collaborative.

Initially, representational uses of the Internet were limited to the retrieval of files from servers. More recently, with the advent of the World Wide Web, representational uses have been dominated by the viewing and reading of Web pages as well as the retrieval of files linked to them. The files may be of any format such as portable document format (PDF) or files created with word processing applications, graphics files, streamed audio, or video.

One of the first collaborative uses of the Internet was e-mail. E-mail is still one of the most used applications of the Internet. As well as e-mail two other collaborative applications of the Internet can be used in learning events. They are Internet chat and online discussions. E-mail, Internet chat, and online discussions can be situated within a Web page or can be stand-alone applications and detailed descriptions and analyses of these collaborative Internet technologies are given later in this chapter. The most recent uses of the Internet, and these are predicted to be of significance for online learning, can be broadly classified as social software and media sharing software. Social software covers a range of applications that allow users to tell others about themselves through a presence on the Web and hence rendezvous, connect, and collaborate. Sharing applications allow users to upload files to be shared with others. Commonly uploaded files include bookmarks, blogs, audio, and video.

World Wide Web Pages for Information Retrieval

The World Wide Web (or Web) came into being in 1993 and within a few years became the way most people use the Internet. This revolution in Internet use was primarily due to the user-friendly nature of the Web afforded by its graphic user interface (GUI). The following definition of the Web is taken from a Web-based encyclopedia of computer terms.

A system of Internet servers that support specially formatted documents. The documents are formatted in a language called HTML (HyperText Markup Language) that supports links to other documents, as well as graphics, audio, and video files. This means you can jump from one document to another simply by clicking on hot spots. Not all Internet servers are part of the World Wide Web. There are several applications called Web browsers that make it easy to access the World Wide Web; Two of the most popular being Netscape Navigator and Microsoft's Internet Explorer. (http://www.pcwebopedia.com/ 1998)

There are tens of millions of Web pages on servers (or host computers) in many countries in the world and they are used for many purposes including, business, e-commerce, learning, social interaction, and so forth.

In a learning context, using the Web for information retrieval clearly fits within the provision of material and interaction with materials categories of the LAM. Learners interact with material on the Web by searching, navigating, selecting, assessing, evaluating, and managing information. However, evaluating information takes on a greater significance for information that is on the Web. For a small price almost anyone can put anything on the Web and so learners need to develop keen evaluation skills and hence use the material they have retrieved appropriately. Designers or facilitators of learning events need to ensure that learners develop a set of skills that includes these evaluation skills as well as search and retrieval skills.

The majority of the information on the Web is in text and still images. Hence, when the Web is used as a resource for the retrieval of this type of information, it is being used as a representational technology with level one attributes. Through the use of streaming or progressive download technologies, video and audio files can be placed on Web servers and retrieved by users. However, such files are usually large in size and take time to download. While in the past, download time has probably been the main reason against the widespread use of video and audio on the Web, the growth of broadband connections to the Internet and recent advances in compression technology are reducing the download time with tolerable losses in quality of image and sound. When video and audio are included in Web pages the capability of the technology rises to level three. As Web pages are generally constructed prior to their hosting and use they are considered an asynchronous technology. The description of the learning technology, the World Wide Web, for information retrieval, by the LTM is shown in Table 7.8.

Internet Chat or Instant Messaging

Internet chat is a synchronous, text-based emulation of a conversation that uses the Internet to connect participants. A similar form is instant messaging that is primarily designed for, but not limited to, text chatting between two users. It can be

Table 7.8. The LTM: World Wide Web pages for information retrieval

World Wide Web pages
Representational, level 1 (level 2 and 3 with streamed audio and video)
Asynchronous
Learning activities model (LAM) Suitable categories: Provision of materials (PM) Interaction with materials (IM)

point-to-point where the communication is simply between two parties who have the same chat software package and have logged onto it at the same time or it can be multipoint where more that two chatters log onto a server, or chat room and *talk* to whomever else is logged on. Internet chat applications are usually free or at least inexpensive. Chat programs can be stand-alone or located within a Web page, for example a Web-based learning environment. To use a chat program, comments are typed into the input box and then sent to the server by pressing the enter key or clicking on a button. The comment then appears in the chat window. Chat technology has evolved in recent years and is often referred to as instant messaging (IM). IM was first limited to text interchanges and most of the applications contained a *presence* function that notified other users of their availability or otherwise. IM has evolved to include audio and video communications and are referred to by a number of names including video chat and video telephony.

As chat is synchronous the text-based conversation style tends short, to the point, and highly interactive and chatters have developed a shorthand and use emoticons (smilies) to assist the conversation. It follows then that the use of Internet chat in education is best where this type of conversation is desired. This technology has been used successfully to host tutorial style discussions after the participants have read a prescribed paper or position paper. In many cases chat has been used in conjunction with e-mail or a Web-based learning environment. For example:

[Chat provides] The ability to conduct a conversation among a group of learners by typing back and forth. For example, a group of human resource managers studying flexible benefit packages may be asked to discuss the advantages and disadvantages of cafeteria benefit plans. (Driscoll, 2001, p. 179)

Due to its synchronous nature and conversational style, chat is a collaborative technology and is not appropriate for predominately one-way provision of material or as a representational technology. For the same reasons it is generally not suitable for discussions where learners are required to give deep consideration to their responses. It is suitable for discussions where learners need to develop the skills of thinking on their feet and the required conversation style is quick, light, and highly interactive. In the LTM chat is clearly a collaborative technology and as it is text-based technology it has level one attributes. Chat is suitable for activities in the categories of the LAM: interactions between learners and interaction with facilitator. The analysis of the learning technology, Internet chat—by the LTM—is shown in Table 7.9.

Internet chat has been used for some years for social purposes and a chat sub-culture has developed. It has had wide acceptance and large, international groups of enthusiasts have emerged. On occasion some users have become addicted to this

Table 7.9. The LTM: Internet chat

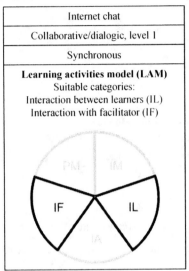

Internet chat
Collaborative/dialogic, level 1
Synchronous
Learning activities model (LAM) Suitable categories: Interaction between learners (IL) Interaction with facilitator (IF)

form of communication and others have found it a pathway to personal relationships (Parker, 1997).

One of the disadvantages of Internet chat, which is a disadvantage of other communication applications that are text-based or have attributes of level one, is the ability to watch rather than participate. The term *lurker* has been coined to describe those who join an Internet chat session (and other online discussions) but do not participate. One of the advantages of Internet chat is that the *conversation* is logged on each participant's computer and can be saved for future reference or evaluation of levels of participation.

Online Discussion

While similar in many ways, the salient differentiating characteristic between chat and online discussions is that chat is synchronous and online discussions are usually asynchronous. Online discussion software is basically a virtual space where users can leave messages for other users to read. Subsequent users of the discussion can either post new messages or respond to existing messages. Hence subsequent users add to the content of the page.

The asynchronous nature of online discussions comes about as each learner can choose when to access the discussion and it is generally not expected that users access them at the same time. They are primarily a two-way or collaborative technology as users can add new messages or respond to existing ones. However, they have a limited capacity to be used as a host for information and in this sense are representational although practice has shown that their predominant use is collaborative. For example, Khan (2001) extols the virtues of online discussion for students who are not geographically proximate. He suggests it can be used to share ideas and attitudes between students and teachers with shared interests.

In learning contexts, online discussions have been used successfully for several purposes. While they are used to host discussions (Khan, 2001) they can also be used as a place for the posting of news, announcements, and administrative information, such as assignment questions and due dates, exam dates, and other important deadlines. Originally online discussions were stand-alone applications but the technology has converged with the World Wide Web and most online discussions are now found integrated into Web pages or Web-based learning environments.

As mentioned earlier, apart from use as announcement tools, the predominant use of online discussions in learning is as an asynchronous, two-way conversational tool. Hence in the LTM they are a collaborative/dialogic technology and as they are text-based they are of level one attributes. It follows then that as facilitators and learners can interact using online discussions that they support activities in the categories of the LAM: interaction between learners and interaction with facilitator. The analysis of the learning technology, online discussion—by the LTM—is shown in Table 7.10.

Table 7.10. The LTM: Online discussion

Online discussion
Collaborative/dialogic, level 1
Asynchronous
Learning activities model (LAM) Suitable categories: Interaction between learners (IL) Interaction with facilitator (IF)

E-Mail and List Servers

E-mail is one of the more common communications applications of the Internet. It is a system for the sending and receiving of messages between networked computers. Usually e-mail is stored on a host or server and as messages are retrieved and responded to by users at their convenience it is asynchronous. When a message is responded to e-mail becomes a two-way or dialogic technology.

A unique e-mail style of conversation has emerged and generally messages tend to be longer than those in Internet chat but have more of an informal style than that of printed memos. Although many e-mail messages contain images, particularly those marketing products and services, personal e-mail messages are generally limited to text with limited formatting to ensure high-speed communications. However, files of any kind can be attached to e-mail messages. While most e-mail programs limit the size of attached files the limit is usually high enough to permit medium to large text files.

E-mail has been successfully used in e-learning for messages between learners and between learners and facilitators. Assignment or exam questions can be sent to learners by e-mail and completed assignments can be submitted from distant and local learners as e-mail attachments. However, e-mail can also be used as a discussion tool in e-learning.

While e-mail is a convenient method for one-to-one communications, it can also be used as device for discussion between members of a group. This can be done in a number of ways. As mentioned earlier, online discussions can be used for asynchronous discussion and Internet chat for synchronous discussion. However, both of these technologies require the participant to log onto the chat or discussion space. E-mail lists allow messages to be distributed to members of a group and hence arrive with the individual's other e-mail messages. One of the most popular kinds of list technology is the list server.

Once a list server has been set up it can host many different lists. Open lists can be subscribed to by anyone who owns an e-mail account. Subscription to closed lists has to be approved by the list owner. Subscription is usually a matter of sending a brief, specific e-mail message to the list server program. Once users have subscribed, messages sent to the list are forwarded to all subscribers and generally subscribers who reply to a message on the list have their replies automatically forwarded to all subscribers.

List servers have been used in learning for many types of discussion in many discipline areas. They can be used to pass information from the facilitator to the learners such as forthcoming television programs or newspaper articles that are pertinent to the course. They can also be used as an alternative or extension to class discussion. Moore and Kearsley (1996) list several benefits of the use of e-mail for class discussion particularly in an e-learning environment that uses other communications technologies. They suggest that discussions that started in a virtual classroom can be extended by e-mail and not be constrained by the allocated time of the class and with more modest costs. Further, they suggest that as many students have access to the Internet at home or at work, they can contribute to the discussion when it suites them and hence increase the potential for a richness in the discussion. E-mail can also assist students whose first language is not that of the class. As e-mail is asynchronous they can take time to compose their replies, consulting dictionaries and other language texts as they do so.

Clearly e-mail and list servers are appropriate technologies for asynchronous two-way communications and hence are categorized by the LTM as collaborative technologies. As they are text-based they have level 1 attributes. It follows then that when facilitators and learners use e-mail and list servers that they support activities in the categories of the LAM: interaction between learners and interaction with facilitator. The analysis of the learning technologies, e-mail and list servers—by the LTM—is shown in Table 7.11.

Web-Based Learning Environments or Learning Management Systems

A few years after the arrival of the World Wide Web, some representational and collaborative functions of the Internet were combined within the context of the World

Table 7.11. The LTM: E-mail and list server

E-mail and list server
Collaborative/dialogic, level 1
Asynchronous
Learning activities model (LAM) Suitable categories: Interaction between learners (IL) Interaction with facilitator (IF)

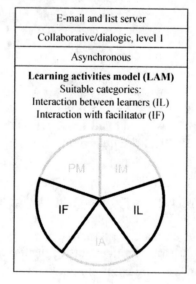

Wide Web and the first online learning environments were created. Today Web-based learning environments combine learning activities with those that permit learners and teachers to track their progress through a course or learning event and are called learning management systems (LMS), course management systems (CMSs), or virtual learning environments (VLEs). The most popular, commercially available, LMS is Blackboard and it represents the majority of the market and provides learners with a collection of technological elements to use while engaged in online learning. The technological elements can be readily divided into those for the process of learning and those for the management of learning. Those for the process of learning can be further subdivided into representational and collaborative technological elements. Table 7.12 shows the representational and collaborative technological elements of the LMS, Blackboard.

LMSs have enjoyed rapid and wide acceptance in higher education and to a lesser degree in human resource development. Describing itself as "the world's leading provider of e-Learning solutions for higher education" (Blackboard, 2007) Blackboard claims that over 2,200 institutions in worldwide are licensed to use its learning environment. This widespread use of LMSs has been partly responsible for new terms entering the parlance of higher education and Web-based learning is often referred to as online learning. Human resource development has also adopted new terms such as *e-learning* and *Web-based training* to describe the learning with LMSs.

As LMSs consist of technological elements that can be easily differentiated, and as the technological elements can be used individually and are very similar to those used independently of an LMS, rather than analyze the complete LMS, it is more useful to analyze individual elements. The analysis of the LMS Blackboard, by the LTM, is then the analysis of the technological elements it is comprised of and is shown in Table 7.13. This analysis draws on the previous analyses of learning technologies that are the same as the technological elements of the LMS.

From the description of Blackboard by the LTM it is apparent that the analysis of Blackboard is the sum of the analyses of its parts. However, the description is only of some parts of Blackboard. It is beyond the scope of this book to consider the

Table 7.12. Blackboard LMS learning elements as representational and collaborative technologies

Representational	Collaborative
Text	Online discussion
Graphics	Chat
Audio recordings	E-mail
Video recordings	

Table 7.13. The LTM: Blackboard

Representational	Collaborative
Text and graphics Asynchronous Level 1 Provision of material, interaction with material	**Online discussion** Asynchronous Level 1 Interaction with facilitator, interaction between learners
Recorded audio Asynchronous Level 2 Provision of material, interaction with material	**Chat** Synchronous Level 1 Interaction with facilitator, interaction between learners
Recorded video Asynchronous Level 3 Provision of material, interaction with material	**E-mail** Asynchronous Level 1 Interaction with facilitator, interaction between learners

elements of Blackboard that are designed for the management of learning, such as the collection or marks and the tracking of student progress through a course.

Analysis of Technologies and Techniques

To assist in the comparison of technologies Table 7.14 lists a range of learning technologies and techniques that can typically be found in higher education and human resource development contexts. Several traditional techniques are listed in the table as they are often used in conjunction with online learning, and as they serve to provide a comparison to learning technologies.

Table 7.14. Analysis of techniques and technologies

Technique or Technology	Learning Technologies Model (LTM)		
	Synchronous/ Asynchronous	LTM Basic Analysis	LAM Suitable Categories
Audioconference/ phone	Synchronous	Collaborative Level 2	Interaction with facilitator, interaction between learners
Audio tape	Asynchronous	Representational Level 2	Provision of materials, interaction with materials
E-mail	Asynchronous	Collaborative Level 1	Interaction with facilitator, interaction between learners
Face-to-face consultation	Synchronous	Collaborative Level 3	Interaction with facilitator
Face-to-face lecture	Synchronous	Representational and collaborative Level 3	Provision of materials, interaction with materials, interaction with facilitator, interaction between learners
Face-to-face tutorial	Synchronous	Collaborative Level 3	Provision of materials, interaction with materials, interaction with facilitator, interaction between learners
Facsimile	Asynchronous	Representational Level 1	Provision of materials, interaction with materials

continued on following page

Table 7.14. continued

Internet chat	Synchronous	Collaborative Level 1		Interaction with facilitator, interaction between learners
List server	Asynchronous	Collaborative Level 1		Interaction with facilitator, interaction between learners
Multimedia	Asynchronous	Representational Can be all levels		Provision of materials, interaction with materials
Print	Asynchronous	Representational Level 1		Provision of materials, interaction with materials
Residential, school or block teaching	Synchronous	Can be both representational and collaborative All levels are possible		Provision of materials, interaction with materials, interaction with facilitator, interaction between learners
Video tape	Asynchronous	Representational Level 3		Provision of materials, interaction with materials
World Wide Web for information retrieval	Asynchronous	Representational Level 1		Provision of materials, interaction with materials

The list of learning technologies described in Table 7.14 is not fixed in time. Indeed as other learning technologies become available for use in higher education and human resource development, they can easily be classified by the LTM and then added to the table. For example, at the time of writing, the very successful simulation environment, Second Life (SL) has just announced a transition from text to voice communications. Analyzing SL is easily achieved with the LTM. Interactions

Table 7.15. The LTM: Second life

Second Life (text interactions)	Second Life (voice interactions)
Collaborative representational, level 1	Collaborative representational, level 2
Synchronous	Synchronous
Learning activities model (LAM) **(all categories)**	**Learning activities model (LAM)** **(all categories)**

in SL are generally synchronous as users avatars interact. Currently avatars are not capable of facial expression and body language is significantly limited. Therefore, if the interactions are in text them the attributes are level 1. If the interactions are by voice the attributes are level 2. In SL materials can be left for other users who can interact with them in the environment. So SL can facilitate all categories of activities in the LAM. An analysis of SL by the LTM is displayed in Table 7.15.

Also, different organizations and institutions have greater ranges of, preferences for, or investments in, specific learning technologies. It these cases it is appropriate to construct a table similar to 7.14 for the institution or organization within which the technologies are to be used.

Conclusion

The LTM has been developed for two types of purpose: firstly, to inform the field as a framework for analysis and secondly as a practical device for use in the design of learning events in which technology plays a central role. The LTM represents the juxtaposition of two theoretical approaches as it draws upon media richness theory from the organizational communications field and on the LAM. The LTM is simple enough for relative novices to use in the process of learning technology analysis and selection. Compared to other conceptualizations of technologies, the model links uses and characteristics of technologies that provide an insight to technology, which fosters an approach to the application of technology to learning, that promotes new and extended uses of learning technologies. In addition, the LTM is not fixed in time and hence is not limited to the technologies available at the time of publication and new technologies can be analyzed by the model. The LTM is robust and plays a significant role in the selection of learning technologies and the TSM which is presented in Chapter VIII.

References

Bates, A. (1995). *Technology, open learning and distance education.* New York: Routledge.

Blackboard. (2007). *Global in practice.* Retrieved March 19, 2007, from http://www.blackboard.com/inpractice/global/

Berge, Z. (2001). *Sustaining distance training: Integrating learning technologies into the fabric of the enterprise.* San Francisco: Jossey-Bass.

Caladine, R. (2001). Learning environments of the future: Narrowband to broadband via DVD. In *Proceedings of the 18th Annual Conference of the Australian Society for Computers in Learning in Higher Education (ASCILITE),* Melbourne, Australia.

Caladine, R. (2005). The use of database-driven Web pages to increase the functionality of current online learning technology. In P. McGee (Ed.), *Course management systems for learning: Beyond accidental pedagogy.* Hershey, PA: Information Technology Science.

Carlson, P., & Davis, B. (1998). An investigation of media selection among directors and managers: From "self" to "other" orientation. *MIS Quarterly, 22*(3), 335-363.

Daft, R. L., & Lengel, R. H. (1984). Information richness: A new approach to managerial behavior and organizational design. In L. L. Cummings & B. M. Staw (Eds.), *Research in organizational behavior* (pp. 191-233). Homewood, IL: JAI Press.

Daunt, C. (1997). Is teleteaching different? In J. Osborne (Eds.), *Open, flexible and distance learning: Education and training for the 21st century.* Proceedings of the 13th Biennial Forum of ODLAA; Launceston, Australia.

Driscoll, M. (2001). Developing synchronous Web-based training for adults in the workplace. In B. Khan (Ed.), *Web-based training.* Englewood Cliffs, NJ: Educational Technology Publications.

Kemp, J., & Smellie, D. (1989). *Planning, producing and using instructional media* (6th ed.). New York: Harper & Row.

Khan, B. (2001). A framework for Web-based learning. In B. Khan (Ed.), *Web-based training.* Englewood Cliffs, NJ: Educational Technology Publications.

Kobayashi, T., Tanaka, K., Yamaji, H., & Otsuka, Y. (1997). Crosscultural joint classes between Japan and Australia using ISDN. In J. Osborne (Eds.), *Open, flexible and distance learning: Education and training for the 21st century.* Proceedings of the 13th Biennial Forum of ODLAA; Launceston, Australia.

Kruse, K., & Keil, J. (2000). *Technology-based training: The art and science of design, development and delivery.* San Francisco: Jossey-Bass/Pfeiffer.

Mitchell, J. (1993). *Video-conferencing in higher education in Australia: An evaluation of the use and potential of video-conferencing facilities in the higher education sector in Australia.* Occasional Papers Series, Department of Education Employment and Training, Higher Education Division. Canberra: Australian Government Printing Service.

Moore, M., & Kearsley, G. (1996). *Distance education a systems view.* Belmont, CA: Wadsworth.

Parker. C. (1997). *The joy of cybersex.* Kew, UK: Mandarin.

Rowntree, D. (1994). *Preparing materials for open, distance and flexible learning.* London: Kogan Page.

Tannenbaum, R. (1998). *Theoretical foundations of multimedia.* New York: Computer Science Press.

Taylor, J. (2001). *Fifth generation distance education* (Higher Education Series, Report No. 40). Canberra, Australia: Department of Education, Training and Youth Affairs.

Chapter VIII

The Technology Selection Method

Introduction

In the previous chapters the learning activities model (LAM) and the learning technologies model (LTM) have been developed and examples of their use have been
provided. These tools are individually useful as they provide theoretical frameworks
for the analysis of learning activities and learning technologies. However, they can
be put to a different use and meet a far greater need. They can also be used together
in the practical process of the design of learning events and specifically for the
selection of learning technologies that are appropriate to the learners, the material,
the context, and the budget. This chapter forms the conceptual center of this book
as it brings the first two models together to form the technology selection method
(TSM). The TSM, an original tool or method, is presented. Examples of the method
are provided and it is placed within the context of a generic flowchart for the design
of learning events. The TSM can also be used in the conversion of existing learning
events from traditional, face-to-face techniques to online learning events.

Traditionally, facilitators of learning events undertake the design of learning events as part of their role. However, in the past when learning technologies were expected to be a central component of the learning process, usually in distance education or open learning, specialized instructional designers typically undertook the design. Currently in higher education and in human resource development, where online learning is burgeoning, many designers of learning events are not equipped to undertake the selection of appropriate learning technologies yet there is a growing expectation by management that they undertake this task as part of the design of online learning events.

The TSM, presented here, is a robust tool for the selection of appropriate learning technologies. It assumes no specialist knowledge in the field of instructional design and provides users with an understanding of the technologies as well as the selection process.

The Selection of Learning Technologies

In traditionally taught subjects the techniques are often predetermined, such as seminars, workshops, tutorials, presentations, laboratories, and so forth. The technologies are also often limited to traditional classroom technologies, for example, overhead projectors, computer slideshows (such as PowerPoint), and whiteboards or blackboards. In online learning the opportunity exists to select from a range of technologies that in combination will play a central role in learning events. In Chapter VI, the LAM was presented and has as its basic premise that the process of learning can be described as provided materials and interactions. In Chapter VII, the LTM was presented in which learning technologies were classified as representational or collaborative. The TSM has as its basis, the matching of technologies, as defined by the LTM, to categories of activities in the LAM. Broadly, representational technologies are matched to the *provision of materials* and *interaction with materials* categories of the LAM and collaborative technologies are matched to the *interaction with facilitator* and *interactions between learners* categories.

Criteria for the Selection of Learning Technologies

As well as matching technologies to activities there are other criteria, sometimes external or peripheral to the process of learning, that must be considered if the selected technologies are to be appropriate for the learners as well as the material, the context, and the budget. In Chapter IV it was reported that researchers in the areas of human resource development and higher education, generally grouped these criteria into instructional factors, learner factors, and cost factors. As these three groups of criteria were found to be common to the TSMs reviewed and are congruent with the author's experience they are used, with the extension of learner factors to include facilitator factors, as the categories of criteria that impact on the TSM. These are referred to here as:

- *Mechanics of the subject* (instructional factors),
- *Learner and facilitator implications* (learner factors), and
- *Costs* (cost factors).

These criteria impact on the selection process and are described in the following sections.

The Mechanics of the Subject

The mechanics of the subject refers to the attributes that are necessary for the efficient and effective communication of the content and interactions of the subject. The attributes required are usually self-evident to the experienced facilitator or designer but as well they can be ascertained through answering questions such as the following. To efficiently and effectively achieve the desired learning objectives:

- Is text necessary or desirable?
- Are black and white graphics necessary or desirable?
- Are color graphics necessary or desirable?
- Is audio necessary or desirable?
- Is animation necessary or desirable?
- Are moving pictures (movie/video) necessary or desirable?

These fundamental decisions need to be made at the beginning of the selection process and they inform the selection of learning technologies by indicating the characteristics required by the content and interactions of the subject.

Learner Implications and Facilitator Implications

The use of technologies places demands on learners and facilitators that need to be taken into account during the selection process as the viability of learning technologies can depend on learners' access to them and their skills in using them. To ascertain learner implications questions such as the following need to be answered:

- What new skills will learners need to acquire?
- Will the technology cause learners to incur extra costs or buy equipment, and so forth?
- Will learners need access to extra equipment?
- Will learners need training in new study/learning skills?

Many of the learner implications apply to facilitators as well where facilitators are expected to design online learning events that will require training in the appropriate use of learning technologies and in the organizational and practical changes that accompany them.

Costs

It is obviously essential to ascertain the costs to develop learning technologies. Costs need to be considered in terms of training, production costs, and the facilitator's time. Some learning technologies require much greater preparation times compared to the techniques and technologies of traditional face-to-face learning events.

Table 8.1 is based on work by Sparkes (1984), Bates (1995), and on the author's experience in television, radio, videoconference, World Wide Web development, and other learning technologies. The units of the table are the amount of time taken to prepare a traditional one-hour presentation. Obviously some wide generalizations and assumptions have been made but Table 8.1 does serve to compare and highlight the magnitude of preparation times. The preparation times are indicated as ranges which reflect the wide variety of production values available. For example, putting notes from a presentation on the World Wide Web may add a small amount of time to preparation. However, if a complete, Web-based, learning management system was used, up to twenty times the preparation time could be anticipated. While this figure appears large it includes the time spent by Web programmers and graphic designers.

Table 8.1 indicates preparation times and while it is difficult to arrive at the very general figures in it, it is impossible to state figures for updating material as these vary with many criteria including the shelf-life of the subject area.

Table 8.1. Approximate preparation times

Approximate Preparation Time	
Technique or Technology	Time
Assume a conventional one–hour, face-to-face lecture takes	1 unit
Computer-mediated communications	2 - 5 units
Videoconference	5 – 10 units
World Wide Web	2 - 20 units
Radio/Audio cassette	5 – 10units
Print	2 - 10 units
Broadcast television	10 - 100 units
Multimedia	50 - 200 units

The TSM

As mentioned earlier the TSM is based on the process of matching technologies, as described by the LTM, to categories of the LAM. However, as the three groups of criteria: (1) mechanics of the subject, (2) learner and facilitator implications, and (3) costs will impact on the technologies selected, an iterative process is proposed that takes these groups of criteria into account. The selection method is based on the creation of a description of the proposed learning activities as categorized by the LAM. This description is then matched to all the available learning technologies,

Figure 8.1. Technology selection method

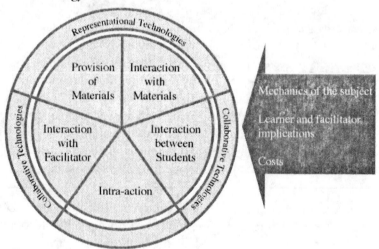

as described by the LTM, which are suited to each category of the LAM. Individual technologies are then removed from each category as the other two groups of criteria are considered.

This process is represented graphically in Figure 8.1. The LAM is shown at the center of the figure. The categories of the LAM are surrounded by representational or collaborative technologies, indicating the relationship between them and categories of the LAM. The groups of criteria, mechanics of the subject, learner and facilitator implications, and costs are located outside of the LAM and technologies to indicate that they impact on the process of technology selection.

The following steps are proposed as the iterative process by which the TSM is used for the selection of learning technologies that are appropriate for the learners, the material, the context, and the budget. While the proposed process consists of several iterations the TSM can be used in other ways. For example, it can be used to check a particular technology against an individual learning activity or group of them.

The TSM: The Process

In the first step a description of the learning event is created using the categories of the LAM. In the case of a learning event that is being converted from a traditional, face-to-face approach to online learning, the activities that occurred in the traditional event can be used to create the description. In the second step, a short-list of learning technologies is constructed using the list of available learning technologies as described in Chapter VII. Within each category of the description of the learning event, created in the first step, the learning technologies are short-listed according to the group of criteria: Mechanics of the Subject. In the third step, the short-list of the learning technologies is then refined, based on the two remaining groups of criteria:

- Learner implications and facilitator implications
- Costs

In the case of learning events that are being converted from traditional to online learning a fourth step is recommended in which the advantages and disadvantages of the new version of the learning event are compared with the old version.

The steps in the selection process are shown in Table 8.2 and the following fictitious examples are provided to illustrate and further explain the process of the TSM.

Table 8.2. The steps in the TSM

Step 1	Use the categories of the LAM to describe the event
Step 2	List all technologies appropriate for the mechanics of the subject within each category of the LAM
Step 3	Refine list of technologies based on learner and facilitator implications and costs
Step 4.	Compare advantages and disadvantages where possible

Example 1. Higher Education

An undergraduate humanities subject that has been taught on campus for some years is to be converted to online learning. The subject has been taught traditionally using a mixture of lectures and seminars. In the past learners were divided into 12 groups and each group selected a seminar topic and prepared and presented a paper on it. After the presentation of the seminar paper the whole class would discuss it. The assessment of the traditionally taught subject consisted of the group seminar paper, individual participation in the seminar discussions, a minor essay, and a major essay. It was decided to create an online learning version of the subject so that students who were dispersed geographically would be able to participate in it without traveling to campus, thus affording the subject some increased flexibility in terms of where and

Table 8.3. Example 1, technology selection method: Step 1

LAM Category	Description	Technologies	+/-
Provision of material	Textbook, lectures, overhead projector slides, handouts		
Interaction with material	Textbook, library books, lecture notes and handouts		
Interaction with the facilitator	Face-to-face in lectures and seminars, face-to-face consultation		
Interaction between learners	Face-to-face group work leading to presentation of seminar paper. Face-to-face discussion in seminars, informal on-campus or off-campus		
Intra-action			

when students study. A description of the traditionally taught subject was created using the categories of the LAM and is shown in Table 8.3.

At this stage, the *intra-action* category has intentionally been left empty as activities in this category cannot be prescribed and are dependent on factors controlled more by learners than the designer or facilitator of the learning event. However, the category is included as reminder to the designer that it is a salient category of learning activities and that the designed learning event should lead to activities in it.

In the second step a short-list of learning technologies was created from the list of available learning technologies, as described in Chapter VII, on the basis of the group of criteria: Mechanics of the Subject. In this example it was assumed that some limited color graphics were needed as well as text for activities in the LAM categories: provision of material and interaction with material. It was also assumed that some limited face-to-face interaction was preferable for activities in the LAM categories: interaction between learners and interaction with facilitator, although the majority of these interactions could occur effectively with text only (for example, by the collaborative technologies of Level 1 such as chat, online discussion, and e-mail).

The list of available learning technologies indicated that the technologies that were suited to the categories of provision of material, and interaction with material were print, video, and World Wide Web. Likewise, the list of available technologies indicated that the options for interactions between learners were videoconference and

Table 8.4. Example 1, technology selection method: Step 2

LAM Category	Description	Technologies	+/-
Provision of Material	Textbook, lectures, overhead projector slides, handouts	Print, video, World Wide Web	
Interaction with material	Textbook, library books, lecture notes and handouts	Print, video, World Wide Web	
Interaction with facilitator	Face-to-face in lectures and seminars, face-to-face consultation	E-mail, phone, fax, videoconference, listserver	
Interaction between learners	Face-to-face group work leading to presentation of seminar paper, face-to-face discussion in seminars, Informal on-campus or off-campus.	E-mail, videoconference, listserver	
Intra-action			

List server. For the category: interaction with facilitator, the options indicated were e-mail and phone. In addition, the videoconferences would provide opportunities for interaction with the facilitator. This step is shown in Table 8.4.

In the third step, the short-list of technologies was refined in consideration of the groups of criteria: learner and facilitator implications and costs. Technologies that have student or staff implications that cannot be met or options that are too expensive were ruled out. For example, it was found that video production was too expensive and as all students (in this example) had easy access to the Internet, the World Wide Web was chosen as the primary technology for the categories of provision of material and interaction with material in preference to video.

One of implications for the facilitator considered in this example was the change in consultation from face-to-face to e-mail and phone. Traditionally, the hours of the facilitator's availability for face-to-face consultation (without an appointment) were limited to those advertised (usually on their office door). Changing this to the phone and e-mail can make the imposition of time limitations difficult and has the potential to lead to changes in workload.

In the interaction between learners category it was decided to use videoconference on only one or two occasions during the course of the subject as it necessitated students meeting at the videoconference studio at a given time, hence reducing flexibility of time and place of learning. It was decided to use a listserver as the main technology for this category of the LAM. Opportunities for the group to interact with the facilitator were possible during the videoconferences however, as all learners in

Table 8.5. Example 1, technology selection method: Step 3

LAM Category	Description	Technologies	+/-
Provision of material	Textbook, lectures, overhead projector slides, handouts	World Wide Web	
Interaction with material	Textbook, library books, lecture notes and handouts	World Wide Web	
Interaction with facilitator	Face-to-face in lectures and seminars, face-to-face consultation	E-mail, phone, fax	
Interaction between learners	Face-to-face group work leading to presentation of seminar paper, face-to-face discussion in seminars, informal on-campus or off-campus	Listserver, videoconference	
Intra-action			

the example had ready access to the Internet, e-mail was selected as the primary technology for individual interaction with facilitator with phone being used as back up or for use in special instances.

The refined list of technologies is shown in Table 8.5. When the decisions about techniques and technologies for each category had been reached, the advantages and disadvantages were considered for each category of the LAM. It was considered that one disadvantage might be the lack of a human face, or the reduction in the attributes of the dialogue in the categories of interaction between learners and interaction with facilitator.

This arose as e-mail (Level 1 attributes) and phone (Level 2 attributes) were the main technologies in these categories and learners and the facilitator would only meet, face-to-face, by videoconference on one or two occasions. However, in this example this disadvantage could be adequately offset by the advantages of flexibility of time and place of learning. Often online learning subjects are characterized by comparisons or *trade-offs* like this. The advantages and disadvantages are shown in Table 8.6.

If the advantages and disadvantages are acceptable to the facilitator or designer the process of technology selection is complete. If not, another iteration of the last three steps needs to be undertaken.

Table 8.6. Example 1, technology selection method: Step 4

LAM Category	Description	Technologies	+/-
Provision of material	Textbook, lectures, overhead projector slides, handouts	World Wide Web	Color graphics available, hypertext available, face-to-face interaction removed
Interaction with material	Textbook, library books, lecture notes and handouts	World Wide Web	
Interaction with facilitator	Face-to-face in lectures, face-to-face in seminars, face-to-face consultation	E-mail, phone, fax	Face-to-face interaction limited
Interaction between learners	Face-to-face group work leading to presentation of seminar paper, face-to-face discussion in seminars, informal on-campus or off-campus	Listserver, videoconference	Face-to-face interaction limited
Intra-action			

Example 2. Human Resource Development

In the second example, employees of an organization, located at the head office and several branch offices, are required to become competent in a recently acquired software package. The branch offices are far apart and far from the head office making travel to a central location expensive in travel costs and time away. However, the branch offices are linked to each other and the head office by videoconference. To adequately train employees it is planned to use materials, demonstrations, discussions, group and individual work, and consultation with the facilitator.

The first step in the TSM is to create a description of the planned subject using the categories of the LAM. In this step it was considered that the activities in the provision of materials would be:

- A prescribed book supplied by the company and delivered to each trainee.
- Reference books held in the company library.
- A collection of information distilled from articles and books in the facilitator's own personal collection.

The facilitator was the designer of the learning event as well and considered that learners would interact with the materials and trial the software after reading sections of the text, references, and other information. This interaction could take place in the workplace or at home if learners have access to the necessary equipment. The designer considered the following activities for the category of the LAM: interaction with facilitator:

- Demonstration of the software
- Presentation of material
- Consultation
- Feedback given in respect of submitted assignments

In the interaction between learners category, the designer considered some group discussion as well as group work on projects to be desirable. The designer of the learning event also considered informal discussion between learners to be beneficial to the achievement of the desired learning outcomes. The first step in the TSM is the description of the subject and is shown in Table 8.7.

In the second step learning technologies were selected from the list of available technologies (see Chapter VII) on the basis of consideration of the group of criteria, mechanics of the subject. These are shown in the third column in Table 8.8. As the

Table 8.7. Example 2, technology selection method: Step 1

LAM Category	Description	Technologies	
Provision of material	Prescribed book, reference books, other information on the subject from the facilitator's own collection		
Interaction with material	Prescribed book, reference books, other information on the subject from the facilitator's own collection		
Interaction with the facilitator	Demonstrations of software, individual consultation, assessment		
Interaction between learners	Group work on project, group discussion, informal discussion		
Intra-action			

Table 8.8. Example 2, technology selection method: Step 2

LAM Category	Description	Technologies	
Provision of material	Prescribed book, reference books, other information on the subject from the facilitator's own collection	Print. video. World Wide Web	
Interaction with material	Prescribed book. reference books, other information on the subject from the facilitator's own collection	Print, video, World Wide Web	
Interaction with facilitator	Demonstrations of software, individual consultation, assessment	Videoconference, e-mail, fax phone.	
Interaction between learners	Group work on project, group discussion, informal discussion	Face-to-face videoconference, e-mail, fax, phone	
Intra-action			

facilitator was located at head office they could provide material through presentations to learners also at the head office. However, it was decided, where possible, to provide the same learning experiences at both the branch and the head offices. Apart from issues of equity this would be beneficial as all learners could be assessed using the same tests and communication between the groups could enhance the learning experience for all.

It was decided that learning technologies for provision of material and interaction with the material needed to be capable of displaying changing computer screens of the software, hence video and World Wide Web were considered in conjunction with print for the background material. Interaction between learners at the same location would be face-to-face while interactions between offices and interaction with facilitator would occur by videoconference, e-mail, phone, and fax.

In the third step the list of learning technologies was refined when the groups of criteria: learner and facilitator implications and costs were considered. As most reference material was located at the head office it was decided to prepare study guides and reprints of articles to distribute to learners. Along with the prescribed book these formed the print component of the provided materials. The facilitator/designer considered video too expensive for the provision of materials as it was known that the shelf-life of the material was limited with major updates to the software each year. It was decided to provide the dynamic display of software by the Internet as learners can access the Internet in the workplace. This would be achieved through still images of monitor screens in World Wide Web pages which would also be used for messages and as a directory for downloadable files.

As all the offices are connected by videoconference it was decided to use videoconference as the primary technology for interaction with facilitator, and interaction between learners. It was decided that individual contact with the facilitator would be by e-mail and that the facilitator would aim to reply to learners' messages within two working days. Formal, face-to-face interaction between learners would take place at each office and the videoconference would facilitate interaction between offices, thus permitting synchronous learning at all offices. As learners were required to complete a group project it was expected that groups would be formed at each office. However, it was anticipated that should the need arise, a group consisting of learners from a number of offices, facilitated by videoconference, could be considered. The third step of technology selection, using the TSM is shown in Table 8.9.

As intra-action was considered to depend in large part on the degree to which the other categories stimulated and encouraged learners to achieve the desired learning outcomes it is not shown. As the learning event was new there was no valid comparison event and hence the fourth step of the TSM in which advantages and disadvantages are listed could not be undertaken.

These two fictitious examples have been provided to assist in the description of the steps in the process of the selection of learning technologies using the TSM.

Table 8.9. Example 2, technology selection method: Step 3

LAM Category	Description	Technologies	
Provision of material	Prescribed book, reference books, other information on the sub-ject from the facilitator's own collection	Print, World Wide Web	
Interaction with material	Prescribed book, reference books, other information on the sub-ject from the facilitator's own collection	Print, World Wide Web	
Interaction with facilitator	Demonstrations of software, individual consultation, assessment	Videoconference, e-mail, fax, phone	
Interaction between learners	Group work on project, group discussion, informal discussion	Face-to-face, videoconference, e-mail	
Intra-action			

The TSM and Educational Philosophies

As mentioned earlier, the TSM has been developed for use by designers who do not have specialized instructional design knowledge or skills and as the designer of the learning events will often be the facilitator of the same events, several benefits are to be gained. Firstly, the process of technology selection is informed by the experience of facilitator/designer, as the knowledge they have gathered through prior facilita-tion experience can be used to inform the process. In this way some pitfalls can be avoided and effective approaches maintained. This experience would be incorporated into the first step in the TSM in which a description of the proposed learning event is created. Secondly, as the method is designed for use by facilitators there should be benefits from the proximity of the design process to the facilitation of the learning event. Hence, allowing facilitators to *own* the process of design. First-hand feedback is also available to refine the mix of technologies and activities.

The process of selecting learning technologies provides a natural opportunity for facilitators to reflect on their practice as well as their approach to the facilitation of learning. Within the higher education field there has recently been a groundswell of opinion among education theorists and commentators that constructivism is desirable as an educational approach or philosophy. In the field of human resource development constructivism is not as popular and sometimes a more instructive approach is advocated for reasons of cost and time constraints. Roblyer and Edwards (2000) describe constructivism and "Direct Instruction" as addressing different needs.

Needs Addressed by Direct Instruction

1. Individual pacing and remediation, especially when teacher time is limited.

2. Making learning paths more efficient (eg., faster), especially for instruction in skills that are prerequisite to higher-level skills.

3. Performing time-consuming and labor-intensive tasks (eg, skill practice), freeing teaching time for other, more complex student needs.

4. Supplying self instructional-sequences, especially when human teachers are not available, teacher time for structured review is limited, and/or students are already highly motivated to learn skills.

Needs Addressed by Constructivism

1. Making skills more relevant to students' backgrounds and experiences by anchoring learning in meaningful, authentic (e.g., real-life) highly visual situations.

2. Addressing motivation problems through interactive activities in which students must play active rather than passive roles.

3. Teaching students how to work together to solve problems through group-based cooperative learning activities.

4. Emphasizing engaging motivational activities that require higher-level skills and pre-requisite lower-level skills at the same time. (p. 51)

Clearly the approaches address different learning needs and contexts. In human resource development where management wishes to see a return on the investment the organization has made in training, the efficiencies associated with direct instruction could favor that approach. Conversely, in higher education where return in investment is not as high a priority, other motivating factors may take precedence. A full discussion of direct instruction, constructivism, and other approaches to learning is relevant to the selection of technologies but is beyond the scope of this book. However, a brief discussion of these approaches and the LAM and the TSM follows.

As well as in the first step of the TSM the LAM can be used as a means of unpacking a current learning event and to predict a new mix of activities if the event was to be moved to a different approach. It is likely that a learning event, characterized by direct instruction, would have many activities in the LAM categories of provision of material and interaction with material and fewer activities in the categories of interaction with facilitator and interaction between learners. As the categories provision of materials and interaction with materials are matched to representational learning technologies in the TSM it could reasonably be expected that direct instruction learning events would be characterized by more representational than dialogic technologies.

By contrast it is likely that a subject characterized by constructivism while having some activities in the LAM categories of provision of material and interaction with material would have a predomination of activities in the categories of interaction with facilitator and interaction between learners. As the categories interaction with the facilitator and interaction between learners are matched to dialogic learning technologies in the TSM it could reasonably be expected that constructivist learning events would be characterized by more dialogic than representational technologies.

The TSM presented here does not prescribe or proscribe any educational approach or philosophy. Rather the method allows the learning designer the freedom to use the approach or philosophy of their choice and provides an excellent and timely opportunity to move the learning experience they are designing towards or away from a particular approach.

TSM: Practical Context

The selection of learning technologies usually occurs as part of the wider process of the design of learning events. In Chapter IV, models of instructional design were discussed and the location of the selection of technology in the design process was indicated.

Often the first step in the design is a decision to offer a learning event. The next steps are the development of objectives of the learning event and the creation of a profile of the potential learners. While these three areas are shown one after the other in the flowchart (Figure 8.2), it is anticipated that there would be high levels of feedback between each step so that the learning event will meet the expectations of the institution or organization and learners. The selection of technologies is shown as occurring after the content has been decided upon and the outline of the learning event written. Like other components of the design process it is not suggested that once the technology decisions have been made, they are fixed and cannot be reviewed. It is suggested that as more information on the other elements of the design become available the selected technologies should be re-evaluated and changed if necessary.

Figure 8.2. A generic design flowchart

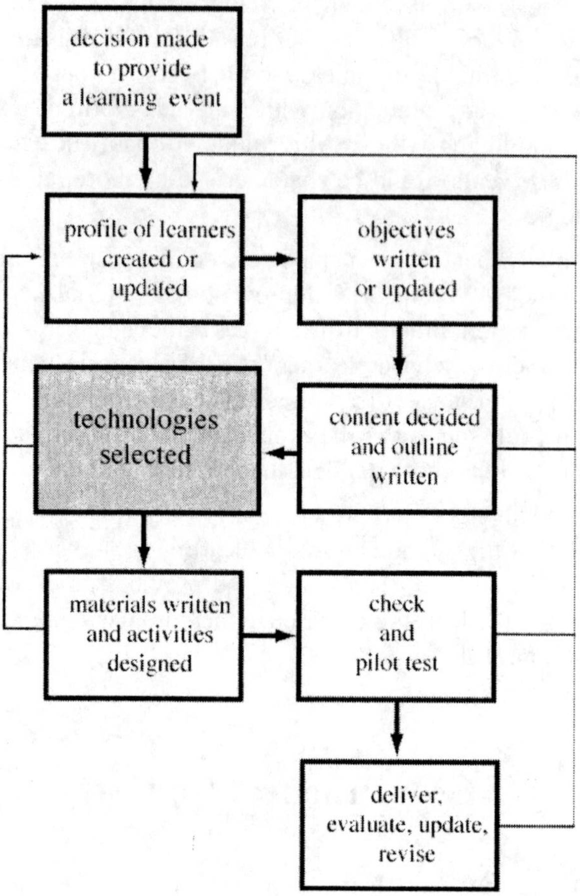

Conclusion

The TSM has been developed and is presented for use by students and academics in the instructional design field. However, the greatest use of the TSM is in the design of learning events in higher education and in human resource development. The TSM juxtaposes the two theoretical frameworks developed in earlier chapters: the LAM in Chapter VI and the LTM in Chapter VII. It is this juxtaposition that forms the basis of matching activities to technologies. The TSM is based on matching categories of the LAM to technologies as described by the LTM. The TSM is a four-step, decision-making process. The first step uses the LAM. The second and third steps consider the groups of criteria: mechanics of the subject, learner and facilitator implications, and costs to select learning technologies.

The TSM has been developed in response to the growing number of facilitators and designers of learning events in higher education and human resource development, who have little or no experience in the design of learning events that incorporate learning technologies, as central components of teaching and learning. To this end, the TSM is sufficiently simple to use to be accessible to learning event designers from other fields. Yet the TSM is robust enough to be effective in a wide number of subject areas. As well, the method has been developed to operate within the philosophy and approach of the designer of the learning event. It can be used in the design of constructivist learning, direct instruction (instructivism), or any other approach. The method can also be used as a tool to assist in the changing of the approach or philosophy used in a particular learning event.

The TSM does not simply prescribe technologies rather it allows designers to explore technological options and provides them with an insight to the characteristics of each technology. In this way, the potential to extend the use of technology in learning is fostered. The TSM is presented as a way to include learning technologies in learning events that are appropriate to the learners, the material, the context, and the budget.

In the next section of this book individual technologies are discussed. They are analyzed and described by the LTM. Features of the technologies are detailed and recommendations for their use in teaching and learning are presented. Several case studies are included that describe different aspects of selecting and implementing learning technologies and the use of simple and complex installations. The technologies covered all have the potential to enhance e-learning through media-rich content and interactions. The chapters on videoconference, video chat, and Access Grid describe how these technologies can be used to increase media-rich communications in e-learning while the chapters on video, podcasting, vodcasting, streaming, and recording lectures describe how these technologies can be used to enhance e-learning through media-rich content.

References

Bates, A. (1995). *Technology, open learning and distance education.* New York: Routledge.

Roblyer, M., & Edwards, J. (2000). *Integrating educational technology into teaching.* Upper Saddle River, NJ: Merrill Prentice Hall.

Sparkes, J. (1984). Pedagogic difference in the media. In A. Bates (Ed.), *The role of technology in distance education.* London: Croom Helm.

Chapter IX

Video

Introduction

Television and video have been used as teaching resources for almost as many years as they have been around. Some television programming and some video productions have been aimed directly at students, some have been partially intended for teaching and learning, and others have been not intended for this use at all. However, the intention of the maker of the program often has little correlation to the use of the program in teaching and learning. Television and video have provided opportunities for teachers to place moving images and sounds in front of students. The programs may have been of rare or dangerous events, interviews with people from other parts of the world, be they leaders, experts, or others. The benefits of the use of video in the classroom can be optimized through integration. Rather than simply screen a video or tune into a television broadcast, good teachers have always integrated these into the curriculum through devices such as worksheets, briefing, and debriefing activities.

There are many other uses of video and television that are appropriate for teaching and learning and as video capture and editing devices become cheaper and easier to use it is expected that the role of video in teaching and learning will increase. With a few notable exceptions, in the past video in education were generally stand-alone programs. In recent times this role has changed as video can be embedded in Web pages and hence contextualized. Thus short clips that would be incomplete by themselves can serve educational purposes. Today educational video ranges from very short clips of phenomena or objects through to multi-part programs that may total several hours of highly edited video. A 30-second clip of one subject may serve one learning need while a 4-hour series might serve another. Today, as video recording technology has evolved to such a high degree, it is rare to see television broadcasts being used in classroom. More often teachers use video recordings as they allow not only playback at a time that is appropriate to the teaching and learning but also afford the opportunity to pause, stop, and replay sections of the program. The recent advent of video distribution via the Internet has increased the ease with which video can be used in e-learning. As long as bandwidth is sufficient students can interact with online video from any networked computer.

Other technological innovations will also, or have already changed the way in which video is used in education. DVD technology has allowed teachers to depart from the linear access of videotape. They can now use the menu structure of a DVD to navigate, almost instantly, to the desired section of a program or to a particular clip. If the video resources are to be shared within an institution they can be placed into a content management system (CMS) and be made available in the same way as from a DVD. The advantage of the CMS is that metadata, or data about the data, can be stored along with the video file. The metadata can be used to foster sharing of the resource through the informing of the learning design process.

Originally the majority of video programs that were used in teaching and learning were produced by professionals and purchased by the institution. However, as mentioned previously, with the increased accessibility of video capture, editing, and distribution methods, it is now quite possible that teachers and students will produce video programs for educational purposes. Video technology is also improving in ways that make it easier to obtain pictures and sounds of high technical quality. These changes in the technology will possibly result in more resources made by teachers and students, which in turn could mean that programs are more closely tailored to the needs of the students and the subject. Perhaps the barriers to teacher-produced video are changing from ease of operation to time.

As mentioned earlier, the past few years have seen the advent and widespread adoption of the Internet as a way to store and share video files. It is predicted that in the near future a significant proportion of video will be delivered this way. This has implications for the producers of video programs as they will need to be compressed for Internet delivery and formatted to suit the video players on viewers' computers. In Chapter X the topic of streaming is discussed and expanded to describe some of the techniques for compression. Before compression and Internet delivery are discussed, general production methods will be covered and some time spent on the appropriate technical and pedagogical uses of the medium.

Definitions

Television has been around for long enough for it to need no introduction, let alone a definition. For our purposes here television refers to terrestrial or satellite broadcasts of moving pictures and sounds. Video refers to moving pictures and audio encapsulated in a medium or online.

Storage and Delivery of Video

The media that video programs are encapsulated in have changed over the years. At first all television broadcasts were live and moving pictures and sounds were broadcast by a system in which a television camera was pointed at the projected image of a film. Videotape was first demonstrated in the 1950s but it was not until the 1970s that domestic videotape players and recorders became commonplace. Today videotape is an obsolescent technology as the more robust and accessible storage systems of DVD, disc-based video, and hard drives gain preeminence. Technically, videotape was not a reliable medium as it has a limited life due to magnetic degradation.

Hard disc drives and disc-based video have the potential to provide rich learning materials as they can combine a menu structure with full screen, high quality video and unlike the linear videotape have the capability to replay different pieces of video in a seamless manner. Of course this means that the writing of programs for these media involves the writing of navigation systems. Writing for DVD is similar to writing for multimedia as they both can use a branched structure, typically accessed with a set of menus. However, DVD has some further unique attributes. Angles allow the user to select a particular camera shot, and non-contiguous scenes in the DVD can be played together seamlessly. Not only do these add another dimension to the experience but they also allow users to find their own way through the resource and hence customize their own learning experience.

Standard DVD is being displaced by high definition DVD media. The second generation of DVD has recently arrived and unfortunately there are two competing formats, Blu-Ray and HD DVD. Like DVD both of the new formats use the same principles of a laser and reflection. Both formats can store more information on a disc of the same diameter. The formats are not compatible but both have been introduced to deliver high definition video to the domestic market.

However, the disc-based media suffer from the problem of damage to the surface causing misreading and the more information on the disc the more susceptible it is. Perhaps the future will see portable hard disc drives such as those in portable music players, for example, iPods being used as media for the storage of video. The capacity of HD-DVD and Blu-ray discs is 30GB and 50GB respectively. The first iPods had 5GB or 10GB of memory, which had risen to the 80GB by 2007. So clearly hard disc drive technology has the capacity to store practical quantities of video, the prohibitive factor could be the cost. Further evidence of the future of hard disc drives and the storage of video is that some domestic video camcorders are being sold with hard disc drives.

While some storage media are moving to higher capacity, which leads to increased levels of definition and hence quality, other storage options that are gaining popularity are reducing resolution and hence technical quality. Online video has grown in popularity with remarkable speed. Online video sharing applications like YouTube and others see thousands of video files uploaded each week. Also, video can be incorporated into Web pages through use of formats like Flash, QuickTime, and Windows Media Format. Table 9.1 provides a comparison of picture quality between different storage media and sharing applications.

While the range of technical quality required by different storage media provides challenges to producers of video, it is emerging that the different storage media are used to serve different purposes. It appears from the volume of use that users' bring different expectations to the viewing of online video than those brought to viewing a high definition program. Of course this is in part due to the different screen sizes.

Television, Video, and Film Production Methods

Although these three media generally serve different purposes, there are many similarities in the production methods involved with each. Of course there are vast differences between producing a multi-million dollar feature length movie and a 10-minute home move but the differences are primarily ones of scale. Making

Table 9.1. A comparison of picture quality

Medium	Typical Picture Size (appprox. pixels)
VHS videotape	320 x 240
DVD	720 x 480
HD-DVD/Blu-ray	1920 x 1080
YouTube (recommended)	320 x 240

programs is generally divided into three stages: preproduction, production, and postproduction.

Preproduction

Preproduction refers to all aspects of planning, writing, and design that come before cameras are switched on. This includes things like deciding on either studio, location, or a mixture of both, selecting the locations or scenery, casting, organizing props, and a shooting schedule as well as researching and writing the script. Preproduction commences when the decision to make a program is made. For most programs it is the most important stage of production and attention to detail at this stage can save hours in production and postproduction.

At universities or colleges, scripts for educational television or video programs are generally written by academics and often with the assistance of instructional designers or video producers. The script may be an adaptation of lecture materials or it may be written specifically for the medium. In both cases the task is similar as the writer needs to covert text into a script that will communicate visually. For educational video programs that are more than a clip, one of the early decisions that will need to be made concerns the style of production.

Production Styles

Production styles range from the very expensive, complex, and time consuming to the quick and cheap. The choice of styles, and there is generally more than one in a program, will depend on the material, the audience, the way the program is intended to be used, and the budget. Typically a program might start with some pictures and some musical accompaniment that set the scene. These pictures are referred to as overlay footage. That is footage laid over the sounds. Of course there would usually be some opening titles and then the program might change to a talking head of a presenter. While the head is talking the picture might change to some other footage (overlay footage again) or a graphic of a diagram, chart, or graph (overlay graphic) to further exemplify or reinforce the message. Other production styles in the program could include interviews either recorded on location or in the studio. Table 9.2 provides an approximate correlation between production styles and their relative costs.

The Interview

A production style that is often used as part of an education film or video program is the interview. This is no surprise as it is widely used in television news and after

Table 9.2. Production styles and relative costs

Production Styles		
cheapest		Talking head
		Location interview
		Studio interview
		Panel discussion
Approximate increase in production time and costs		Overlay footage
		Overlay graphics
		Overlay animation
		Demonstration
most expensive		Role play
		Drama

all people have always talked with each other. However, not all interviews use the medium to its best advantage, and interviews are frequently misused or overused. Writers of scripts need to consider if the interview is the best way to convey the desired message. Sometimes there is great value in hearing from the source, and at other times other production styles are better ways to achieve this end. For example, a *piece to camera* or talking head of a presenter with overlay footage of the subject might be a better solution. Interviews can be used well and answering the following questions can help in the decision making process:

- Is an interview the best production style to convey the desired message?
- What is the purpose of the interview?
- What main points should emerge?
- Is a suitable person for the interview readily available?
- Who is the best person to be interviewed?
- Can they perform for the camera?
- If more than one person is to be interviewed should they be interviewed together or separately?
- Would a panel discussion be a better solution?
- Should the interview be on location or in an office or a studio?
- Is the interviewee fully briefed? Do they know what you want from them? Do they know who the intended audience is?

Writing the Script

The largest task in preproduction is often the writing of the script. Writing for educational video is more complex than writing a lecture or writing a script for general television, as it will need to result in an educationally sound and visually appealing program. While some scripts have been written by academics it is often worth consulting or working with an instructional designer at this stage. Before writing the script it is important to have a clear understanding of where the program will fit with the other components of the curriculum. For example, if it is to be screened in class the teacher can brief students on what to look out for and inform them of what they will be expected to do after viewing. This contrasts with the use of video for distance education, where links between the other components of the educational package need to be firmly in place so that the components come together as a cohesive whole. In e-learning this can be achieved by embedding the video in a Web page that contains contextual information in text or other media. Pace and timing are other elements that need to be considered in the early stages of writing. If the program is to be broadcast, the broadcaster will usually dictate the length of the program. If it not intended for broadcast, educational effectiveness is the criterion determining length. It is also important to get the right amount of material into the script. Although the old maxim is "a minute is a long time in television," it is also true that the amount students learn from the medium is limited. If the pace is right students will not feel bored by too little or swamped by information overload. Most programs work well with a three-stage structure that reflects the teachers' rule of three. The rule is to tell students what you are going to tell them, then tell them, and then tell them what you have told them. In video programs this is often reflected by an introduction that sets the scene, a middle that conveys the theme or body, and a conclusion that sums up and reinforces the main points.

One of the easiest ways to get the script written is to start with the basic idea and gradually expand it in stages. The stages could include an outline, visual treatment, storyboards, and the final script. The outline should be a brief collection of headings and constructed first. Each heading can correspond to a segment of the program and it is helpful to use the outline to divide up the estimated time of the final program. At this stage nothing is final and much may change during subsequent stages of script development. When the outline is complete it needs to be treated visually. At this stage it is customary to research the people and things that might appear in the program. In the visual treatment the people and things elicited by the research are connected to the headings in the outline. Preliminary decisions on all aspects of the production need to be made at this stage. However, as they are on paper they are inexpensive to change. Also at this stage production styles can be selected for each of the headings. In some cases more than one production style may be used for a single heading. As the treatment and other aspects of preproduction proceed, further research may need to be undertaken.

The following is an exemplification of the script writing process. To encourage academic staff at an Australian university to use video in teaching and learning, the author decided to develop a workshop on video making. A meaningful but innocuous topic was needed that could model the process. It was decided to make a short instructional video on how to open doors. The outline was written and is shown in Table 9.3.

The outline demonstrates a simple three-part structure consisting of an introduction, a middle, and a conclusion. The second stage in the script writing process is to treat the outline visually. The research undertaken was to locate doors, knobs, and handles of many different types. This was easy as the location was the local working environment. Through consultation of the list of production styles (see Table 9.2) the outline was treated visually. The visual treatment is shown in Table 9.4.

When the visual treatment has been completed the shooting script can be written. One way to keep a video shooting script organized is to use three columns—one for the shot number, one for the video, and one for the audio. The script for the example is shown as Table 9.5. Television, video, and film makers use a convention to calibrate shot sizes, as shown in Figure 9.1, which will provide the nomenclature to help minimize the details required in the script. The initials of shots sizes are sufficient to convey the details. This convention is the same as the one recommended for use with videoconference in Chapter XII.

When writing the shooting script a storyboard can help the visualization of a program. A storyboard uses rough sketches and a few lines of text to describe each shot. They are generally not intended to be artistic masterpieces, but can be an efficient way to communicate to the camera operator, the other members of the cast and crew, and to predict the success or otherwise of the visual treatment. They are particularly good at helping to visualize the transitions between shots. Television, film, and video are all dynamic media and if the material is not dynamic the chances are that the result will be less than satisfactory. For example, protracted talking heads usually

Table 9.3. Example of an outline

How to Open Doors
Introduction •   Importance of opening   doors

Steps in Opening Doors
 	
   1.   The approach
   2.   The grasp
   3.   Activation

Conclusion

Table 9.4. Example of a visual treatment

How to Open Doors

Introduction
* Importance of opening doors
* Overlay footage of many shots of doors, closing—audio of doors slamming
* Opening title "How to Open Doors"
* Overlay footage of many images of closed doors—audio of introduction perhaps talking head

Steps in Opening Doors

1. The approach—overlay footage of a person demonstrating the approach—audio of the approach instructions
2. The grasp—overlay footage of a person demonstrating the grasp—audio of the grasp instructions
3. Activation—overlay footage of a person demonstrating activation—audio of the activation instructions

Conclusion
* Overlay footage of many doors opening—audio restating how to open doors and the importance of it.

Figure 9.1. Shot size terminology

| Extreme Close Up (XCU) | Close Up (CU) | Close Mid Shot (CMS) | Mid Shot (MS) | Long Shot (LS) |

Table 9.5. An example of a shooting script

How to Open Doors		
#	Video	Audio
1	Introduction. Overlay footage of many doors closing	Doors closing
2	Opening Title "How to Open Doors"	Doors closing
3	CMS talking head	Doors are all around us and using them is part of daily life for most of us. As well as a variety of doors there is a variety of devices to open them.
4	Close up of door knob	The door knob
5	Close up of door handle	The door handle
6	CU of push plate	And some doors do not have either
7	MS talking head (as in 3)	If you do not know how to open a door access may be denied. There are three steps to opening a door.

continued on following page

Table 9.5. continued

8	Title "Step 1—The Approach"	The first step is to approach the door and stop when you are close enough to comfortably touch the opening device.
9	MS of someone approaching a door	
10	Title "Step 2—The Grasp"	In the second step the opening device is grasped with sufficient grip to activate it.
11	CU of someone grasping a door handle	
12	Title "Step 3 – Activation"	In the third step, the opening device is activated by turning the device. The door is then opened by pushing or pulling.
13	CU of activation	
14	Talking head	Opening doors is easy. When you know how to open doors access is no longer denied.
15	Doors opening	

do not make good programs and have been described, disparagingly as radio with pictures. It is suggested that for educational programs that talking heads make up no more than 20% of the program. Other rules of thumb are:

- It is a dynamic medium so use pictures rather than words.
- Do not start with a presenter, start with pictures.
- Keep 10% of the program free of speech.
- Use music to give the program some space to allow the audience to time to think.
- Use language that is simple and conversational.
- Use a variety of production styles.

From the examples of the three stages of script writing (see Tables 9.3, 9.4, and 9.5) it is easy to see how the script develops. Rather than trying to write the full shooting script from the outset, the three-stage process allows the development of visually oriented scripts that are suited to the medium. When the script is complete the camera work can commence. However, it is not unusual for minor changes to happen during the production stage.

Figure 9.2. Still image from the video "How to Open Doors"

Production

Production refers to the recording by a camera or similar device of the footage that will be converted into the finished program in the postproduction stage. In the preproduction stage a shooting schedule will have been developed that lists all the times, people, places, and equipment that are required. This may be a simple list in the head of a teacher in the case of a small production or a complex series of spreadsheets in a major production. As video camera equipment evolves it is becoming easier to obtain images that have high technical quality. If the camera work is to be undertaken by an amateur, there are a few guidelines that can help improve the result. First and most importantly, ample time needs to be scheduled for test recordings. They can then be reviewed and lessons learned from the shots that were successful and those that were not. Often newcomers to the medium of video move the camera too frequently and too quickly. Using a tripod is another way to minimize the movement of the camera, allowing viewers to concentrate on the essential message of the program rather than the camera work.

Video, film, and television are visual media and the visual image plays an important role in the communications. The way people appear on screen is worthy of consideration before putting them in front of a camera. For example, if the presenter is visible something as simple as combing one's hair can make the difference between a program that achieves the desired results and one in which the audience marvel at the presenter's hair. The style of clothing should also be appropriate to the material in the program. For example, news readers generally wear formal and conservative clothes. This clearly sends a message that many viewers do not consciously notice. However, if the newscasters were dressed informally the message would be different.

Cameras are often unkind to human faces, faithfully reproducing blemishes, spots, shine, and lines. In film and television production the use of make up is standard practice. However, it is not necessary to spend hours and a fortune on cosmetics and a make-up artist. Some powder and pancake make-up to even out skin tones and remove shine is often sufficient. As well as looking good, sounding good is also important. If you have to read from a script develop a reading style that does not sound like a person reading, rather a natural and conversational style. There can be a great difference between written and spoken language. Scripts should be written in simple conversational language unless there is an important production reason to do otherwise.

Postproduction

Postproduction refers to the activities that happen after the camera work or production. If adequate preproduction has been completed and if a log of what was recorded was kept, postproduction, while probably the most tedious part of the process, should be relatively simple.

The main task in postproduction is usually editing. After recording the pictures and the sounds, if a significant amount of editing is to be done, an edit decision list needs to be constructed. The edit decision list is just a rough idea on paper of the order in which the recorded scenes will appear in the finished program. For feature length movies edit decision lists are quite detailed spreadsheets. For educational video programs they are often much simpler. The basic transition between shots is the cut. In film this refers to one piece of film being physically cut and joined to another. In video the process is electronic but the effect is the same; that is, a direct transition from one picture to another. The combination of images using editing is one of the most powerful devices a film or video maker has access to. It allows them to tell a story by connecting things that are not physically proximate and this conjunction results in the viewer reaching a conclusion about what they are seeing. The discovery of this effect of editing or montage happened early in the 20th century. It has been reported that Lev Kuleshov (Uhde, 1995) was to first to report this effect. Kuleshov reported that a scene consisting of two shots provided viewers with an integrated message that added up to a greater amount than the sum of the two parts. This happens as viewers subconsciously connect the shots. For example, if a shot of a hand holding a gun is joined to a shot a person running away from the camera, the audience will interpret this as a person with a gun chasing the man even if the two are completely unrelated. This is sometimes referred to as the language of film. Much has been written on editing and film theory and there are many resources in libraries and online. These can be used to attain a deeper understanding of the process, which in turn allows users to employ the language of film.

The cut is only one of a number of transitions between shots that are readily available. Today video editing is usually performed by loading all the footage into a computer and then organizing the shots into order, trimming them for length, and establishing transitions between them. Not so many years ago videotape was edited by selectively copying from one videotape to another. The new method is much faster as it is non-linear. Shots can be selected from a gallery rather than by fast-forward or rewind searching of the tape. Also, the quality of the images has increased due to the digital technology employed. However, probably the greatest benefits of the new editing technology are the ease with which a novice can learn to edit and the low cost of the equipment. The video program mentioned previously, "How to Open Doors" was made by the author using a cheap, home movie style video camcorder. It was edited using an editing application that is included with the recent purchase of a personal computer.

As mentioned earlier the destination of the video program will often determine the required resolution. Like editing this task has been made easy by a function built into the editing software that allows the edited program to be configured for delivery in a number of ways ranging from standard DVD to highly compressed formats for streaming over the Internet. Compression will be discussed in greater detail later in this chapter.

There are many different types of video programs that can be easily produced by teachers for use online and in the classroom. They can range from fully produced and edited programs that are cohesive, complete, and can be used in isolation to simple single shot clips that can be used to illustrate a concept or phenomenon. Students can also create video programs that can be submitted instead of written work. Student produced video can be reused in later years as resources for the same and other subjects. In this way a collection of resources can be built up over a few terms. Further return on the time and effort invested in the production of educational video can be achieved through the sharing of video resources. One way to facilitate resource sharing is to use a CMS. A CMS is a way to attach metadata about the resource so that other teachers can access the data and make a decision based on them as to the suitability of the resource for their class. CMSs are briefly described in more detail in Chapter XVI, and much has been written about them elsewhere.

Educational Use

Television and video have been used in learning contexts for many years as useful adjuncts to learning and have been used to provide educational course material, especially in distance, open, and flexible learning programs. Video is a convenient way to bring images of dangerous, rare, or distant objects or phenomena into the virtual space of e-learning. While it is not the same as being there it might be cheaper and safer to include a video of an erupting volcano or a working coal mine than to transport the class to one.

It is generally known that television and video are suited to the display of action, objects, color, and motion. If action or movement is not required then still photograph may be cheaper and probably have more clarity or resolution. Television is suited to the display of moving things and three-dimensional objects, for example: the training of sales staff in new product knowledge. Berge (2001) suggests television can be used to train large audiences in things such as product knowledge and do so in a short period of time. Berge suggests the use of television for this kind of training should have high production values and works well for the transfer of knowledge.

Learning Technologies Model: Television and Video

Clearly when television or video is used in e-learning, it is an asynchronous, one-way technology and can be described by the learning technologies model (LTM) as a representational technology. As it conveys pictures and sounds it has level three attributes. As interaction with television is rather limited and interaction with video is limited to pause and replay, it is suited to the category of learning activities model (LAM) of *provision of materials*. Learners can interact with the material on videotape, online file, disc, or DVD through stopping and reviewing sections of the material.

This mechanical type of interaction can lead to clarification and the desired learning outcomes and hence video is suited to the *interaction with materials* category at this level. The analysis of the learning technology, television and video by the LTM is shown in Table 9.6.

Examples of Video in E-Learning

Television, film, and video can be used for many subjects. In the past it has had many uses including the evaluation of the performance of student teachers or for the evaluation of student presentations. When video files are placed online they can be

Table 9.6. The LTM: Television and video

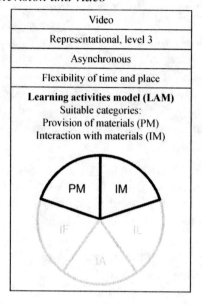

Video
Representational, level 3
Asynchronous
Flexibility of time and place
Learning activities model (LAM) Suitable categories: Provision of materials (PM) Interaction with materials (IM)

evaluated by a wide audience if the video site is public, or a restricted audience if the file is uploaded to a subject in a learning management system. Video is also a good way to record student sentiment or opinion. Students with access to video recorders can record themselves and upload the files to a private or public Web page.

Video is unique from other media as not only can it capture and display motion, it can display the progressive development of a phenomenon. For example, time-lapse effects can illustrate the development of storms and other meteorological phenomena or any development that occurs at a rate not apparent in real time. Similarly a camera mounted on a stand can capture the development of a diagram or solution to a mathematical or scientific problem. For these reasons video can be a powerful tool in e-learning and to maximize the value of video in this context students need to be coached to become active viewers. In the classroom teachers would usually brief students before they screened a video program and the same holds true for online learning. One idea is to give the students a task to complete before they watch the video. They might be asked to note their ideas or opinions about the topic and after watching the video they can be directed to revisit what they wrote to see what changes have occurred. During the viewing if students have a task to complete they will watch with this purpose in mind. Tasks might be complex or as simple as a question that can be answered by the material on the video. In some cases it may be appropriate to ask students to undertake some deconstruction of the video. They may be asked questions about production values such as the editing techniques, camera angles, shot choices, music, and so forth and asked to prepare comments on how these techniques impact the message of the program. After watching the video students can be directed to undertake any of a number of tasks. Depending on their locations these tasks may be undertaken by individuals or by groups. Students may be asked to solve a problem using the material covered in the video. They could be asked to brainstorm a solution. Other post-video activities include creating conceptual maps, categorizing and classifying, and comparing and contrasting to name a few.

Special Uses of Video

One special use of video for online learning concerns the display of mathematical and scientific symbols on Web pages. In 2006 a project at an Australian university investigated ways in which mathematics symbols could be placed on Web pages. The following case study contains details of the project.

Case Study

Online Solutions to Mathematical Problems: Combining Video, Audio and Stills on the Web.

The Problem

For several years students enrolled at the university in computer science, engineering, and science degrees have performed poorly in mathematical subjects. These subjects are the building blocks of the degrees and are co-requisites or prerequisites for the subjects delivered by the departments they are enrolled in. The mismatch between the mathematic skill levels that students arrive at the university with and those required for them to successfully complete their degrees is well documented in the literature (Artigue, 2001; Fadali, Johnson, Mortensen, & McGough, 2001; Kajander & Lovric, 2005; Robinson & Croft, 2003).

The science and engineering syllabi are subject to external review and are very full. There was little space for revision of high school mathematics. So to help students acquire the skills needed quickly, learning resources were created and made available through the learning management system. This enabled students to access the resources at times that suited them. The material that required revision was broken down into concepts, and for each concept, definitions and trial questions were developed. Each question was linked to a worked solution, a video worked solution, and an answer.

Displaying mathematical symbols on Web pages is technically difficult as many of the symbols are not included in the character set of the language of the Web, that is, HTML. The available options included a number of translation software applications like MathML. However MathML was not used for two reasons. MathML can be used to display mathematical symbols on Web pages in two ways. Firstly, the software can be used to output graphics of mathematical expressions in formats that are compatible with the Web. This option was not adopted as it was deemed that a still image of a complete solution was not as pedagogically effective as a method that let students clearly see the line-by-line development of a solution. The second way in which MathML and similar software can be used required a viewing application to be installed on users' computers.

Options like Math ML were considered but not used as students would be required to install reader software. It was decided that asking students to install software on their home computers would create more problems. It should be noted that a previous investigation determined that 65% of students used online learning at home. The use of graphics output from MathML (JPEG) was investigated but did not meet the pedagogical requirements that students needed to see the line-by-line development of the solution as well as hear an explanation.

Video was seen as one way to deliver line-by-line solutions and if it would replay from a Web page in the computer's media player, students would not have to install further software. Early in the project experiments were conducted with recording teachers working out problems on a whiteboard. However these proved not to be as successful as anticipated due to several problems. Light reflecting off the whiteboard (even a *non-reflective* one) made recording high quality video difficult, cameras struggled to resolve the fine lines of the whiteboard markers and often the body of the teacher would mask the solution. Two other methods of video capture were then investigated. The first used a pen stroke capture device. There are a number of devices on the market that enable pen strokes to be captured from a whiteboard. The device used consisted of a receiver placed in the corner of the whiteboard and sheaths into which whiteboard markers are placed. The sheaths emit ultrasonic radiation that is detected by the receiver. In this way the technology can detect the position of the pen on the whiteboard. The technology is shown in Figure 9.3.

The second method of video capture used a consumer (design for domestic use) video camera mounted on a copy stand as shown in Figure 9.4. The solution to each mathematic problem was written on paper under the camera on the platen of the camera stand. The output of the camera was captured by the computer via a firewire connection directly from the camera. In this way no videotape was needed.

Figure 9.3. Pen stroke capture apparatus

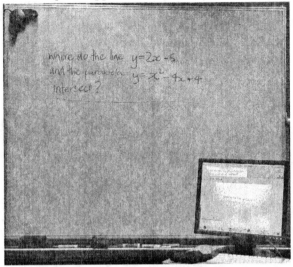

Figure 9.4. Video camera and copy stand capture apparatus

Production Methods

In both methods the video was captured and edited before recording the audio commentary. The writing of the question was edited out and replaced with a still image of the question for sufficient time for it to be easily read. In most cases the writing of the solution was sped up through the removal of footage in which little or no action took place.

The pen stroke capture files were exported into the editing software and edited. Both were then exported as audio video interleave (AVI) and QuickTime files for online playback.

After editing the video an audio commentary was added. This was recorded as the vocal artist watched the edited video of the worked solution. For some solutions a detailed audio commentary was added, while in others only the key points were recorded. The audio track was captured directly into the editing software package. The combined video and audio file was then edited to ensure that the audio was synchronized with the video. The same audio was used for both the video from the pen stroke capture device and from the camera stand. Screen images of both video methods are shown in Figure 9.5.

After editing, the video files were exported from the editing software. Two versions were exported: one in Windows Media Format and one in QuickTime. This enabled playback on both Windows and Apple computers. For video to be played over the Internet the files need to be reduced in size so that playback can be undertaken in real time and download times are minimized.

The Product

A Web site was developed that used three frames. Across the top of the Web page one frame contained the banner which was also a link to the home page of the resources. Down the left hand side another frame listed the topics or concepts, and from each were links to definitional statements with examples and questions. When students clicked on a link to a definition or question, the files would be loaded into the main section of the Web page. The Web page layout is shown in Figure 9.6.

Figure 9.5. Screen captures of both video capture methods (pen stroke capture is on the left camera stand, the right)

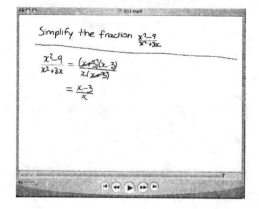 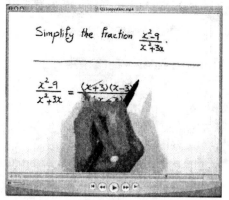

Figure 9.6. Web page layout

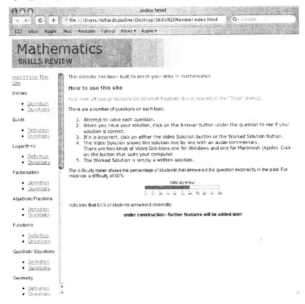

When students clicked on a *definition* link, a page is opened that displayed hand-written definitions and rules relating to the concept. When students clicked on the *question* link a list of questions would be loaded into the main section of the page as shown in Figure 9.7.

Each question was followed by a difficulty meter and button styled links to the answer, video solutions for Windows and Apple computers, and a still image of the complete worked solution. These were labeled, Answer, Video Solution—Windows, Video Solution—Mac, and Worked Solution.

The difficulty meter was included to provide students with a guide to the relative difficulty of each question. It consisted of a red bar and a scale of zero to one hundred percent and is shown in Figure 9.8.

The difficulty was calculated as the percentage of students, from previous years, who answered the question incorrectly in a test. So if 60% of the students answered the question incorrectly the difficulty meter would indicate 60%.

Students were instructed to try to answer the question and then check their answer by clicking on the Answer button. This produced a pop-up widow that displayed the answer. If their answer was not correct they then could select one of the video solutions or the still version by clicking on the appropriate button. Figure 9.9 shows a screen captured image of a video solution.

Early evaluations have been conducted and to date the results have been anecdotal but very positive. At the time of writing it is too early to present empirical evidence

Figure 9.7. A typical questions page

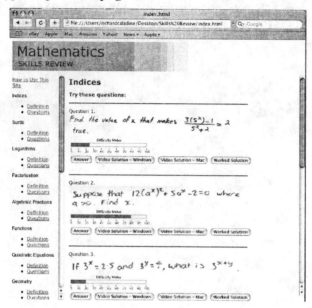

Figure 9.8. The difficulty meter

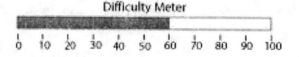

Figure 9.9. Video solution

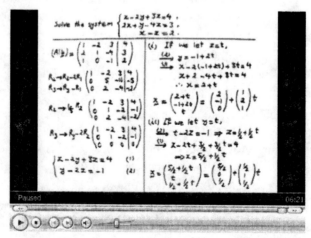

that the resources are assisting in the raising of students' basic mathematics skills. However, it has been decided to continue the project for the next two years and during that time an exhaustive evaluation will be undertaken. The system of capturing mathematical symbols by a video camera has created a moderate level in interest from teachers in other faculties, and it is expected that the use of this technology in chemistry and other science subjects will ensue.

Conclusion

For many decades academic work has been centered on writing. Academics write articles, theses, journals, books, papers, and they deliver lectures from notes. For some years the notion of submitting work for assessment by means other than writing has been entertained but has not resulted in widespread adoption. Online learning provides a vehicle through which a change from text-rich to media-rich is possible. In the early days of online learning the Web pages were text-rich and the discussion forums were text-based. If online learning follows the trends of other online experiences, activities, and applications, this will change. As video production becomes easier and the equipment cheaper, more people will create video. The Internet is emerging as a popular way to share video. Earlier the phenomenon of video sharing Web sites was mentioned and usage indicates that these will remain and that the numbers of uploaded video programs will increase. Students who have witnessed online sharing of video and who may have produced and shared video online bring to their online learning experience the expectation that video will be part of it. This will be discussed in further detail in the last chapter.

Access to video production technology is not the only technology that has become cheaper and easier. The current trend is that access to the Internet will continue to increase in bandwidth and decrease in cost. This will make sharing of video on sites like YouTube even more attractive than they currently are. However, to ensure the protection of intellectual property in some video products, and to manage the flow of revenue generated by the sale or licensing of them, repositories are expected to be used by institutions to provide access to legitimate users. Repositories, or CMSs not only allow and manage access, they also allow metadata to be attached to the media files. The metadata can include a wide range of information, ranging from the details of ownership and distribution, levels of copyright material in the file as well as usage details, and comments on the quality and suitability of the file to particular subjects and cohorts of students. In this way designers of subjects can accelerate the process of selecting resources. Typically they make decisions to preview the media or not based on the material in the metadata. In addition, the metadata provide record of where the file was used and hence minimize the chances of inadvertently providing the same file to the same students on multiple occasions. Further developments of video production will allow for automation in the positioning of chapter marks in the finished program. Chapter marks allow viewers to jump, more or less, instantly to a particular section of the file such as in the scene selection option in many DVDs. For educational purposes this has great potential when combined with CMSs. At the basic level teachers and designers will be able to select a scene from a program, by linking to a chapter mark. In this way students will click on a link in the online subject and access a scene from a program, rather than the complete program. Expanding the concept, it is not technologically difficult to provide some rudimentary editing functions in the interface to the CMS that will allow teachers and designers to select scenes from different programs and organize for them to be replayed in a seamless fashion. Of course organizing the copyright interests will provide somewhat of a challenge to this.

For many years television, film, and video have allowed teachers and designers of subjects to bring color and movement to learning. As access to the production and sharing of video becomes easier, students are increasing their skills in interpreting and producing video. Providing video content and encouraging students to produce video content as part of their online learning appears not only timely but inevitable.

References

Aminifar, E., Caladine, R., Porter, A., & Nelson, M. (2006). *Online solutions to mathematical problems: Combining video, audio, and stills on the Web.* Accepted for E-Learning Conference, Oct. 13-17, Hawaii.

Aminifar, E., Porter, A., Caladine, R., & Nelson, M. (2007). *Creating mathematical learning resources: Combining audio and visual components.*

Artigue, M. (2001). The teaching and learning of mathematics at university level: An ICMI study. In D. Holton (Ed.), *Proceedings of the Ninth International Congress on Mathematical Education.* Dordrecht, The Netherlands: Kluwer.

Berge, Z. (2001). *Sustaining distance training: Integrating learning technologies into the fabric of the enterprise.* San Francisco: Jossey-Bass.

Caladine, R. (2001). Learning environments of the future: Narrow to broadband via DVD. In G. Kennedy et al. (Eds.), *Meeting at the Crossroads: Proceedings of the 18th Annual Conference of the Australasian Society for Computers in Learning in Tertiary Education (ASCILITE).* The University of Melbourne: Australia.

Fadali, S., Johnson, J., Mortensen, J., & McGough, J. (2001). Preliminary results of an online mathematics testing program for engineers. *Electronic Proceedings of the Fourteenth Annual International Conference on Technology in*

Collegiate Mathematics. Retrieved September 2, 2006, from http://archives.
math.utk.edu/ICTCM/EP-14/C1/pdf/paper.pdf

Kajander, A., & Lovric, M. (2005). Transition from secondary to tertiary mathematics: McMaster University experience. *International Journal of Mathematical Education in Science and Technology, 35,* 2-3.

Robinson, C. L., & Croft, A. C. (2003). Engineering students—Diagnostic testing and follow up. *Teaching Mathematics and its Applications, 22*(4).

Settel, I. (1983). *A pictorial history of television.* New York: Frederick Ungar.

Uhde, J. (1995). *Films illusions: Kuleshov revisited.* Retrieved March 6, 2007, from http://www.kinema.uwaterloo.ca/ju-952.htm

Chapter X

Recording Lectures, Streaming, Downloading, Podcasting, Vodcasting, and Webcasting

Introduction

There can be a range of reasons to record lectures or presentations, from the creation of resources to meeting the needs of distant students. Of course recordings are one-way. The information in them flows from the recorded file to students and student interaction with recordings is generally limited to interacting with the controls of the player, that is, they can pause, stop, and replay the recording in part or in its entirety. It can be argued that this interaction adds another level of access to educational presentations. While this low level of interaction can have positive educational outcomes it cannot be equated with interactions between students and teachers. Clearly the person-to-person interactions have the potential for far greater educational outcomes ranging from the answering of questions to the exploration and extension of the subject area. In cases where students are distant from teachers and interact with recorded resources other technologies and techniques are need to provide viable two-way communications channels between them. All learning technologies impose on teaching and learning activities and recordings of presentations are no exception. It is argued that recordings by themselves seldom, if ever, are sufficient for effective and efficient learning in higher education. However, it is suggested that recordings when used in conjunction with other learning technologies and techniques can be a fundamental part of the learning experience.

The recording of lectures in higher education is not a new phenomenon. Lectures have been recorded in print for many years and in recent decades audio recording technology has been used. Audio and video recordings are also being used in the development of human resources as they are seen by some managers as a way to increase the return on their training dollars.

Just as there are a number of reasons to record presentations there are a number of technologies that perform this task. They range from simple technologies totally controlled by the presenter through to institution-wide systems that automatically record, process, and deliver recordings. The technologies are popular and many new terms have entered our language to describe them. Before they are explored definitions of them are provided for the sake of clarity.

Definitions

Streaming

Streaming is the playing of video or audio files as they are downloaded from the Internet. Most computers are sold today with software that will play audio and video streams. Downloaded files that are of the appropriate format can be played on these as well. For example MP3 audio and MP4 video can be played on most readily available computers.

Webcasting

Streaming can be of prerecorded materials or of live events. Generally recorded lectures are not streamed live due to the increase in technology and expertise required. However, sometimes circumstances warrant live streaming. The occasion might be a media-worthy event or perhaps is a visit by an important subject expert. Streaming of live events is called Webcasting.

Podcasting and Vodcasting

Streaming and Webcasting can be of audio or audio and video files. In the past few years with the increasing popularity of MP3 players a process was developed to make downloading of media files more simple. The process is called *podcasting* (or *vodcasting* for video) and first became popular in 2004. Podcasting and vodcasting are systems that use software on a user's computer to automatically download media files. For example, for a student to subscribe to a podcast of lectures for a subject, they copy a URL from the recording Web site to their podcasting software. When they next connect to the Internet the software automatically interrogates the server and downloads any new files. The software then may alert the user. In this way podcasting (or vodcasting in the case of video) is an automated downloading of media files.

Changing technologies and changing practices characterize the background of recording lectures. The history of recording lectures at an Australian university is provided as it is probably typical of that at other institutions in Australia and other nations.

A Case Study of Recording Lectures at an Australian University

Recording of lectures is not a new phenomenon. In the early 1980s, there was an audio recording system in place at the university. The system was rudimentary by today's standards and consisted of portable audiocassette recorders that were placed on the lectern and recorded whatever sound was in the vicinity. The tapes were duplicated with a high-speed copier and made available to students. Access to the tapes was limited to students who were ill or had a timetable clash. The system did not have the capacity, nor did the university have the resources, to make copies available to all students.

This service was canceled in the early 1990s for several reasons. Academics were becoming more concerned over the intellectual property in the recordings. The system was not secure as students could borrow the tapes and take them away. Also, the student demographic was changing to one where a much higher percentage of students needed to undertake part-time work. This increased the demand on the system to an untenable level. In the late 1990s online learning was becoming a major resource for face-to-face students and a number of university managers agreed that if lectures could be recorded in an efficient manner the recordings would provide useful learning resources. At about the same time the Internet was increasing as a network through which resources could potentially be distributed and the local university network was increasing in capacity. The Internet provided an opportunity to disseminate resources to a geographically dispersed student body in a cost-effective way.

The early 2000s saw the popularization of streaming media across the Internet. In 2003 the university recommenced the recording of lectures. However, as they were recorded to computer, compressed, and distributed via the Internet it was possible to make the recordings available to the entire cohort of students. At first the recordings were only available as streams from the university's streaming server. It was considered that downloadable files posed an unacceptable risk to the intellectual property in the recordings. However, it soon became clear that streaming provided an extremely light layer of security as reports of many breaches came to light. At the same time a large percentage of students who lived in rural areas complained that their connections to the Internet were insufficient to support streaming. While a range of compression levels was used to provide bandwidth choices to students, a number of students could not access the recordings as the bandwidth of their connections was less than that required by the minimum stream, which was 14kbps. An investigation of this problem revealed that being tens or hundreds of kilometers from the telephone exchange compromised many rural connections. Thus they were well out of the range of broadband asymmetric digital subscriber line (ADSL) and in many cases the phone lines were in close proximity to electric fences and reservoirs. All these factors led to the establishment of another model of distribution which was a logistic rather than a technological solution.

While the students at the university were scattered over several thousand square kilometers, they were expected to attend an *access center* on a weekly basis during term. The university had five access centers as well as its main campus. The distance between the furthest campuses was significant and equated to about five hours driving time.

In 2003 the campuses and access centers were connected to the main campus by connections of varying bandwidth. As the connections to the outlying access centers were limited to 256kbps, streaming servers were installed at each center and every night after the office hour's traffic on the network had ceased the recordings were delivered from the campus where they were recorded to the server at each center. In this way students could access the recordings at the access centers the day after they were recorded at the main campus. The files could be streamed or downloaded so that students could copy them to their laptop, CD, MP3 player, USB drive, or other device and take them away. Each academic who used the system to record their lectures was made very aware of the security issues of the system, and while they were cautious, none to date has declined to record for this reason. A small layer of security is achieved through not distributing URLs of the links to the recordings. Rather the links are embedded in the learning management system (LMS) behind the student sign on.

The system for recording and distributing lectures has grown in usage and today in excess of 140 hours per week are recorded. The system uses a commercially available software system to schedule and automate the recording, processing, and distribution, thus making the system cost effective. Files are delivered to students in formats that play on either QuickTime or Windows Media Player so that students do not have to install extra software. Also, the system supports MP3 and podcasting.

Learning Technologies Model:
Streaming, Podcasting, Vodcasting, And Webcasting

Streaming, podcasting, vodcasting, and Webcasting all concern the delivery of media (audio or audio and video) files to users. When considering their use in teaching and learning it must be remembered that these are resources that are being made available to students. The files are delivered to students and the delivery processes do not facilitate interaction with the teacher or interaction between students. Therefore the technologies, when described by the learning technologies model (LTM) are one-way or *representational*. If the files are audio only they are of level two and if video they are of level three. The LTM for these technologies is shown in Figures 10.1 and 10.2. Streaming, podcasting, and vodcasting are by their nature asynchronous as the files are downloaded and accessed after they are recorded. On the other hand Webcasting is defined as live. That is, occurring at the time of the event and is therefore synchronous. Webcasting therefore does not facilitate the flexibility of time. However, often Webcasts are archived and made available to users after the event as streams.

What to Record

Obviously the first recordings of lectures or presentations were in print and hence confined to text. The LTM describes text as having level one communicative attri-

Table 10.1. The LTM: Streaming, podcasting, vodcasting

Streaming/Podcasting/Vodcasting
Representational, level 2 or 3
Asynchronous
Flexibility of place Flexibility of time
Learning activities model (LAM) Suitable categories: Provision of materials (PM) Interaction with materials (IM)

Table 10.2. The LTM: Webcasting

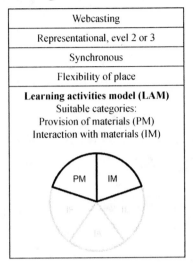

Webcasting
Representational, evel 2 or 3
Synchronous
Flexibility of place

Learning activities model (LAM)
Suitable categories:
Provision of materials (PM)
Interaction with materials (IM)

butes. When the technology to record audio became readily available many lectures were recorded to audiotape and audiotape is described by the LTM as having level two communicative attributes. Level two combines the text of the presentation with the vocal characteristics such as emphasis, pace, timbre, volume, and so forth. Today the options for recording are:

- Audio only
- Audio plus video
- Audio plus PowerPoint or presentation
- Audio plus video plus PowerPoint or presentation

Many institutions that have installed systems for recording have standardized on recording audio plus PowerPoint slides. It can be argued that video of the lecturer does not convey significant pedagogical value when compared to the costs of extra bandwidth. This is particularly true for compressed video where quality is reduced in order to reduce file size. However, there are instances when seeing the video does carry sufficient worth to warrant the increased files sizes and bandwidth, for example, where there is a renowned guest speaker or some visual element to the event. In some instances anecdotal evidence has suggested that even a very small video image of the presenter serves to reinforce the presence of a real person and thus adds value to the recording. Clearly, as bandwidth becomes cheaper and more readily available it is reasonable to expect video to become the norm for recorded presentations.

Reasons for, and Approaches to, Recording

There are a number of reasons to record presentations or lectures. In many cases they are recorded so that students at other locations can have access to them. They can also be used for a number of purposes:

- Clarification of lecture notes, either taken by or provided to students.
- The removal of the pressure students often feel to write everything down. If they know that the recording will be available they have greater opportunities to engage with what the presenter is saying and hence an opportunity to increase the effectiveness of learning.
- Revision prior to examinations or assessments.
- The resolution of timetable clashes.
- Covering missed lectures. If students cannot attend lectures due to illness or other constraints the recording can be used in the place of the lecture. In the case where a lecturer is called away or ill they can use the recording of a previous year's lecture if it is appropriate.
- International students for whom the language of the lecturer is not their first language can find recordings helpful in understanding the language as well as the topic.
- Students with some disabilities (e.g., sight impaired or unable to write) can find recordings to be helpful learning tools.
- To create resources that can be reused in later or other classes
- To create briefing or pre-class materials to assist students in preparing themselves and hence lead to increases in effectiveness.
- Student presentations, when recorded, provide rich opportunities for self assessment and provide examiners with the opportunity to either revisit the presentation or examine afterwards.
- Often the chance to hear one's performance after the event provides a powerful professional development opportunity.

The author has been involved with systems for the recording of lectures for many years. In recent years, as the popularity of recording has increased, a number of typical views or approaches to the recording of lectures or presentations has emerged. The following five fictitious scenarios exemplify these views.

1. **First year economics:** The subject has a large enrollment and is an introduction to the principles of economics. The lecturer is friendly and approachable. As the student numbers in the class are comparatively large (approximately 400) there is little scope for group activities in lectures. Group activities take place in the many tutorials in the subject. The lectures are generally content rich and lend themselves to encapsulation in a recording. The lecturer is aware of many reasons that make it difficult for students to attend his/her lectures. They may need to work or have other commitments. So he/she is happy for them to use the recordings as an alternative to attendance at lectures. The vast majority of students use the recordings rather than attend lectures and to date no negative impact on their performance has been noted.

2. **Third year management:** The subject has a relatively small enrollment (approximately 50) and explores the principles and practices of international management. The lecturer is friendly and takes this area of expertise very seriously. He/she expects his/her students to engage with the material that is presented in lectures and seeks their feedback during lectures. The lecturer used a system to record lectures during one term and attendance at lectures dropped. The lecturer believed that there was a correlation between the decrease in attendance and the decrease that occurred in student performance. He/she no longer records lectures.

3. **Second year statistics:** The subject has a medium-sized enrollment (approximately 120) and is a service course in statistics for engineering students. A statistician teaches the course. As many students do not see the direct application of the statistical principles to engineering their motivation is not as high as it might be. While the lecturer's teaching style is primarily presentational he/she does try to encourage interaction but most students are reluctant to do so and often cause disruption to the class rather than having positive input. The lecturer warmly embraces the idea of recording lectures and encourages the disruptive students to use the recordings. In this way he/she has increased the effectiveness of learning for those who attend as well as those who do not.

4. **Second-year nursing:** The subject has a medium sized enrolment (approximately 150) and covers rehabilitation and palliative care for nurses. The lecturer recently redesigned the subject as he/she was of the mind that the original 13 lectures per term were not appropriate for this topic and he/she wanted to adopt a more discussion-based approach. He/she also wanted to increase the amount of group work in the subject to reflect the team approach taken in many care centers. The redesigned subject consists of five *power lectures* and while they are recorded he/she emphasizes to students that they must attend. During the

power lectures students are discouraged from taking notes in favor of engaging with the presentation. Student performance in the subject has increased.

5. **Second-year information technology—Offshore:** Offshore teaching is very important to the cultural and fiscal well-being of many universities. This subject on the management of information technology used to be taught in an intensive block. The lecturer would travel to the nation and deliver 20 hours of lectures in a five-day intensive teaching block. Cultural and fiscal issues aside, this was not a good way for him/her to teach or for students to learn. As he/she teaches a similar subject at his/her home university he/she now records the lectures and makes them available to the offshore students prior to his/her visit. He/she also chooses not to make them generally available to his/her local students. He/she uses videoconference technology and printed materials to brief the offshore students. He/she still travels to the nation but rather than delivering 20 lectures in five days, the time is spent in discussions, group work, and other activities. Student satisfaction and the effectiveness of learning have increased markedly.

Technologies

Earlier in this chapter we saw that there are different reasons to record lectures and presentations. In addition, there are a number of technologies available with differing levels of functionality and requiring different levels of investment. At a basic level, one can use the annotation tool in PowerPoint to add audio to slides. While this system works, the resulting files can be very large and hence can be difficult to distribute. Over the years many institutions have used video and/or audiotape to distribute recordings. However both of these have unit cost implications, that is, the cost to produce and distribute individual tapes. These implications also can increase the time between recording the presentation and student use of it.

Streaming, Podcasting, and Vodcasting

Clearly if the Internet can be used to distribute recordings, the individual production costs are removed and the distribution costs either reduced or offset. There are several technologies that takes advantage of the Internet and can be described as systems for presentation capture, publication, and management solution for the enterprise or automated recording and delivery systems. The systems generally consist of scheduling, capturing, processing, monitoring, and distribution components.

The processing and monitoring components of these systems consist typically of a cluster of computers that perform a number of tasks. In the cluster there is typically a computer with a large hard disc capacity. This computer, often referred to as an FTP server, holds the raw files after they have been transferred from the capture computer and before they are processed and delivered. The cluster also contains the scheduling computer, or database, that not only delivers the schedule of recordings to each of the capture computers but also serves the index pages that list the available recordings for each subject or course. The processing computers take the original recordings and compress them so that file size is reduced. For example a raw 50-minute audio file can be 50MB in size. These are reduced to approximately 15MB for the MP3 format and much less for the small streams. When the files have been processed they are delivered to streaming and media servers and hence are available to students. The equipment layout is shown in Figures 10.3 and 10.4. After the files have been processed they are delivered to streaming servers and hence made available to students.

The capture components are located in lecture theatres and consist of a recording computer, microphone, and in the case of video recording, a camera or VGA capture device. Audio alone is recorded for the majority of lectures. These audio files are then connected to the PowerPoint slides used in the presentation. In some cases video is recorded but this is generally of the document camera and is only used in cases where most of the presentation is conducted using it.

Teachers use a Web interface in recording software to upload the PowerPoint slides for each lecture. The PowerPoint processing computer in the cluster then converts the slides to appropriate formats and associates them with the audio files. Slides are generally also available as downloadable PDF files.

The system is sufficiently developed to capture everything that happens on the presentation computer screen, synchronized with the presenter's voice, compress and format the files, and deliver them to students. However, capturing the audio only and connecting the audio to the PowerPoint slides requires students to click on a link to see each slide. This low level of interaction can change the way in which students use the files. Even though the interaction is mechanical and simple it changes the experience from one of passive reception to one in which there is a degree of interaction. As the slides are linked from the lecture viewer students can look at slides that are yet to be spoken about and thus preempt what is coming in the presentation. Also, they can go back and look at previous slides to remind themselves of what was said earlier.

Student Interaction with Recordings

Streaming and media servers are located in each of the university's access centers and campuses. Students have a number of options of where and how they interact with

Figure 10.3. Equipment layout for capturing presentations

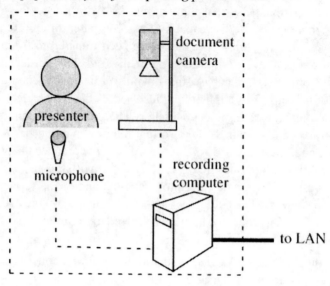

Figure 10.4. Equipment layout for the processing and monitoring of recordings

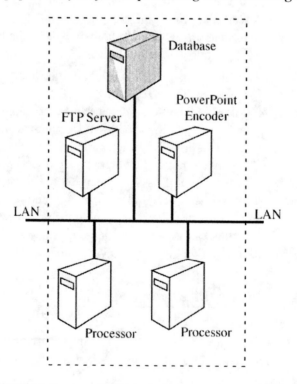

the recordings. They can stream them at home or on campus or they can subscribe to podcasts and vodcasts. If students do not have access to the Internet at home or if their connection is slow (that is less than 14kbps) they can elect to copy the files from the servers at their closest access center or campus and take them away on their laptop, MP3 player, USB drive, CD, or other device. Students generally connect to the recordings for their subject through a link on the subject page of the LMS. This places access to recordings behind their sign on for the LMS and hence delivers a marginal level of security. Having a level of integration with the LMS also has benefits in linking other activities and resources to the recordings and the grade book.

Recordings other than Lectures

Systems for the automated recording have been specifically designed to record live events such as lectures and for most institutions this is their main function. However, the system can be used to record other events and presentations. At least one Australian university has used such a system to record the audio and video of videoconferences. The system has also been used to record student presentations. Plans are in place to connect a series of television tuners to recording computers and in this way scheduled recording of television programs will be undertaken. In Australia the copyright law provides for such recording through a system where institutions pay. It is recommended that local laws be consulted before such systems are installed.

Automated recording systems can also be used for public relations purposes. Like many institutions the university has a range of lectures that are open to the public. With permission these are recorded and made available on the public area of the university Web site. Automated recording systems have also been used to deliver oral defenses of doctoral dissertations to overseas examiners and to provide hospitalized students with access to their lectures.

Webcasting Technology

Earlier Webcasting was described as live streaming of audio or video and audio. The video and audio files are compressed in real time so that they are delivered to listeners or viewers as soon after they happen as possible (generally a few seconds). Typically a Webcasting system consists of three sections. The capture section of the system consists of microphones and cameras to capture the audio and the video. At the simplest level this can be a video camera with an on-board microphone. More complex systems can have multiple cameras with vision switchers and multiple microphones with audio mixing. The capture section of the system delivers a single raw, or uncompressed, video and a single raw audio stream to the encoding or processing section of the system. The encoder compresses the video and audio streams so that they can be transmitted across the Internet. The encoder also converts the files to one or more of the streaming media standards. The third section of a Webcasting system is the server. The server receives the compressed streams from the encoder and makes them available to users. The greater the number of connected users the greater the server power required.

Equipping Teaching Spaces for Webcasting

Webcasting can be used for many purposes. In the higher education context it is most often used for education and for communicating university news to the community. Educational Webcasting can be as simple as a fixed camera on a presenter or complex with several cameras and microphones. Teaching spaces can be configured for Webcasting through the installation of cameras and microphones.

Figure 10.5 shows a plan view of a teaching space that has been equipped for Webcasting. The room has a large screen and lectern at the front and two ceiling mounted cameras. In Figure 10.5 these are camera A and camera B. They are equipped with pan, tilt, zoom, and focus and are remotely controlled. In some circumstances an operated camera, camera C in Figure 10.5 can be added to the system.

The technology controls in the room have been programmed so that three different modes of operation can be used. In the simplest mode only camera A is used.

Figure 10.5. Webcasting equipment layout

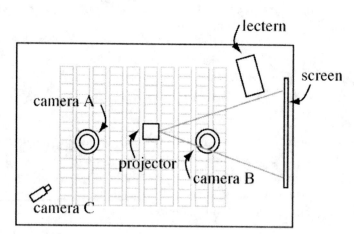

Generally this camera would be orientated so that an image of the speaker and the screen would be streamed. In the second mode of operation camera A and camera B are used as well as the image from the screen. Camera A captures the image of the speaker and camera B captures the image of the audience. These three video signals (camera A, camera B, and the projected display) are then switched by the speaker through a touch screen panel on the lectern.

The third mode of operation requires extra personnel and is generally reserved for guest speakers or special occasions. The room has been wired so that a video camera can be connected into the Webcasting system via a panel on the back wall of the room. This is camera C in Figure 10.5. In this mode of operation a camera operator controls camera C following the speaker as they move about the room. Also, a vision switcher is connected to the panel at the rear of the room and is operated by a staff member. The vision switcher reflects the one on the lectern and allows switching between all three cameras and the images displayed on the screen. The images on the screen are from the presentation computer and projected as shown.

The three levels of operation allow for a range of presentations to be Webcast. As the two lower levels do not require extra staff they are cost effective. However, as the presenter has to switch between cameras and the projected image in the middle level, this extra skill is required of the presenter. The top level is the most expensive in that two extra personnel are required. However, from a technical point of view the visual variety of these Webcasts provides them with a professional appearance.

Adding a Return Channel to Webcasting

Webcasts are generally used in preference to asynchronous streaming when there is a sense of occasion, for example, a media worthy event or a famous presenter. Often in cases where the event is an educational one, responses from the public can add a further dimension and dynamic to the Webcast. This can be achieved technically in a number of ways. If appropriate, a telephone number can be published and viewers of the Webcast can phone in. However, this can become untenable with large audiences and requires extra telephony technology. Another approach is to use an e-mail address or an Internet chat room. Listeners can send an e-mail or a chat message with a comment or question. If the recipient of the messages is in the room they can coordinate the comments and questions, passing them to the speaker when there is a critical number of similar questions or when a salient point is made. Webcasting systems like this have been used in the past for public lectures on topics where the social impact is significant and thus reflected in high levels of public interest and involvement.

Archiving Webcasts

To increase the return on investment from Webcasting, most Webcasters archive Webcasts and make them available as streams. In this way Webcasts can become reusable learning objects, for example, presentation by guest experts can often be used many times. It is suggested that where an asynchronous system for recording lectures exists, it can be used to deliver archived Webcasts as well. Management of large numbers of recordings can become a challenge that can be met through the use of content management systems (CMSs). Such systems use metadata to identify recordings to potential users. In the last two chapters the use of Webcasts and other media in CMSs is discussed.

Teaching with Recordings

While there are often rigorous discussions between academics about the merits or otherwise of using systems to record presentations, there is very little in the literature.

Pedagogical Dilemma

Many academics and teachers have resisted the push to record lectures on the grounds that it reinforces a one-way or transmission style of teaching. It is felt by many of these that this approach is not appropriate for effective learning in higher education.

Such points of view are often arrived at without considering the details of recording lectures. Many make the decision not to record based on the misconception that the only option is to record a complete 50-minute lecture. This is far from the reality. Modern recording equipment and systems are flexible and in most cases the academic or teacher has control of the microphone switch. It is argued that the majority of courses have an element or elements of content that can be more effectively and efficiently transferred to students through recording. In fact it is also argued that providing a recording of the *content* section of a lecture can increase the effectiveness of learning as students do not feel pressured to write it all down. In addition the recordings can be reused in later years as resources outside of class time thus creating opportunities for further interactions. Also, it has been argued (Fardon, 2003) that recording lectures provides opportunities for students whose "preferred learning style does not match that of a traditional lecture well." In the management of human resources, where often the focus is more on the transfer of information or the acquisition of skills, recordings can be used to provide training at times and places that best suit the trainee and the tasks they are faced with.

Another misconception is that if the lecture or presentation is recorded, no local interaction can take place as it does not translate to the recording. It is argued that some interactions can translate effectively to the recording so long as students listening to the recording are kept apprised of what was happening in the lecture room. Interactions can be simple or complex, for example, often a teacher or lecturer will ask students to share an idea, experience, or opinion with the person sitting next to them. If a sentence or two are added to the recording, interactions can be retained in the lecture without degrading the educational effectiveness of the recording. Further, by adding a sentence or two of instruction to students two further things are achieved: Firstly, local students are reminded that recording is happening, which can increase the felt sense of importance of the material. Secondly the recording can be enriched through the translated activity. For example, when local students are briefed to share with the person sitting next to them, a directive to students listening to the recording can also be added. They could be asked to pause the recording and share an opinion, idea, or experience with someone nearby at home, in the workplace, or where ever they are listening.

For longer activities such as group work or break outs the recording should be stopped unless the technology has the capacity to record all the required audio and video, if it is required. When stopping recording to undertake an activity, informing the students listening to the recording will serve to retain the context. For example, the lecturer may say that the presentation part of the class is about to end, local students will be briefed on the group work required of them and students working with the recording will undertake the group work through other means. This could be through another collaborative technology or at another class meeting.

Using Recordings in Teaching and Learning

Further to the pedagogical discussion of recordings and their propensity to reinforce a transmission style of teaching and learning several commentators suggest that the opposite can be the case. Thornhill, Asensio, and Young (2004) and Donnan, Kiley, and McCormack (2004) both argue that when recordings are integrated into the curriculum in a pedagogically sound way, the potential is to change the pedagogical paradigm from one of transmission to one of constructivism. Donnan et al. sum up by saying that if there is a systematic and strategic focus on initiatives that develop staff and the pedagogical approaches they take, streaming technology can considerably enhance lectures. Baez-Franceshi, Dinshaw, Evans, and Van Nieuwenhuise (2006) concur that streaming lectures can greatly enhance teaching and learning through the creation of a new channel of communications between teachers and students. It appears that while using recordings by themselves may have a positive impact on learning the full pedagogical potential of recordings is more likely to be attained if they are integrated with other resources and activities. In this way the teaching and learning package is only partly made up of the recordings.

In many cases automated recording systems are used to record and distribute lectures. However there are many other possible uses of this technology. Almost any video or audio resource can be delivered to students using the technologies of streaming, podcasting, and vodcasting. For example, audio resources that introduce students to a new subject, course, or topic can add value to the learning experience as students interact with them prior to class meetings in which they are discussed. Often resources like these can be created from previously recorded lectures. For example, if the lecturer believes that part of a recorded lecture is particularly well delivered then it can be appropriate to edit the other parts of the recording out creating an audio or video learning resource for future classes.

Of course student created content can also be delivered to teachers and other students using these technologies. As mentioned earlier, creating records of student presentations can be very useful in that they provide rich opportunities for self-assessment and provide examiners with the opportunity to either revisit the presentation or to examine it afterwards. If student presentations are appropriate the recordings can be reused as guides to students who are required to prepare presentations or, in some cases, as resources themselves. Anzai (2006) found that over half the students surveyed use podcasting, among other technologies, to send large amounts of information using Internet-based mass media. However, many of the students surveyed were happier receiving podcast material than sending it. Perhaps this will change as personal podcasting, vodcasting, and audio and video blogging grow in popularity.

Recordings for Students with Disabilities and Non-Native Speakers

A discussion of the pedagogical advantages of streaming, podcasting, vodcasting, and Webcasting is not complete without the inclusion of two significant uses of the technology. These are for students with disabilities and students who do not speak the language of the lecturer as their first language. In both cases it can be easily seen that the technology can enhance learning. Obviously, sight-impaired students will find access to an audio recording of the lectures of immense benefit. When this access can be provided via the Internet and hence be available at home or wherever a networked computer is available another level of convenience is attained. Also, recordings of lectures are of immense benefit for those students who cannot, or find it difficult, to write or to take notes. Also, by listening to the recordings they can be used as a source for note takers rather than employing them to attend lectures.

Many universities and colleges have growing numbers of students who for one reason or another are not native speakers of the language in which the lectures are delivered. Recordings are particularly valuable to these students allowing them to replay the lecture as many times as they like. This can serve two purposes: The primary purpose is to assist learning and the secondary one is to help them to increase their skills with the new language.

For some time, the idea of connecting voice to text conversion with recordings has been explored. This would create very powerful learning resources, particularly for non-native speakers and for the hearing impaired. While software for voice recognition exists, the level of accuracy at the time of writing, while improving, is not quite sufficient to make audio to text translation of recordings viable. It is hoped that in the near future it will be. Often the flexibility of when and where students listen to or watch recordings can provide benefits of inclusion. Recordings can be used by students who are ill or hospitalized and hence help to reduce the impact on their studies.

Webcast, Stream, Podcast, or Download?

Streaming, podcasting, vodcasting, and Webcasting are all similar in that they deliver either video and/or audio to the user via the Internet. Webcasting is streaming, that for practical purposes, is close enough to happening in real time and podcasting and vodcasting are automated ways to download media streams. Of course some Web sites contain media files that are simply downloaded and then played by users. One advantage of downloading over streaming is that when the files have been downloaded they can be transferred to mobile devices such as MP3 players or video players, thus enabling mobile learning or *m-learning*. The literature of m-learning is particularly young and just a little younger that the technology itself. Early reports on m-learning, while favorable, indicate that there are barriers to m-learning that need to be investigated and overcome before it becomes widespread. For example Lee and McLoughlin (2006) believe that:

Although learners may be comfortable with the technology and use it ubiquitously for entertainment and other purposes, to engage with deep learning while simultaneously performing other tasks requires the development of new skills/competencies, or at the very least a different mindset.

Webcasting can be considered to be live streaming, and there are key criteria that can be used to decide when to use Webcasting and when to use asynchronous streaming. As mentioned earlier often the criterion can be loosely defined as "a sense of occasion." For example, in the scenarios described earlier in this chapter, the power lectures in scenario 4 could be adapted to Webcasting if students were located too far from the campus to easily travel. Other examples of appropriate use of Webcasting include, guest lectures and public lectures where a return communications channel can be used for audience feedback.

Conclusion

Recording lectures can enhance learning in a number of ways. At the very least, removing the pressure to take copious notes provides opportunities for students to think about and engage with what is being said in the lecture. Also, recorded lectures can be used as resources to cater to students studying at a distance or for students in later semesters or in related courses.

The LTM, which was discussed in Chapter VII, describes three levels of communicative attributes in learning technologies. When streaming, podcasting, vodcasting, and Webcasting are evaluated by the LTM clearly audio recordings or streams have level two attributes as they contain the text of the presentation in the speaker's words as well as vocal attributes such as emphasis, pace, volume, timbre, and so forth. When video is used with these technologies the LTM, the attributes of communication are level three as they include the text, the vocal attributes, and the non-verbal attributes such as body language and the ability to display other images.

The technologies can also be used to benefit students with disabilities. The sight impaired and those who cannot take notes can obviously benefit from audio recordings and students too ill to attend can keep up by connecting to a recording or Webcast.

The technologies of streaming, Webcasting, podcasting, and vodcasting can be used for more than recording lectures. They can be used to provide pre-class briefing materials. They can be used for self-assessment of student presentations. Indeed some teachers have used them for the professional development of their teaching style. There are other educational uses that the technology can serve such as resource creation. As video production technology becomes simpler and easier it will not be surprising to see increasing numbers of academics and teachers using Webcasting, streaming, podcasting, and vodcasting to deliver the audio and video resources that they have created.

The Internet has provided a most cost-effective way to distribute media files. However, while there are students who live in areas where broadband access is not available or prohibitively expensive, other means of delivering the files to them will need to be found. In this way a level of equity of educational experience must be ensured.

When downloaded files are copied to an MP3 players or other devices it is possible for students to learn while mobile, or to undertake, m-learning. It is too early in the history of m-learning to comment on its effectiveness and the literature is not conclusive that this is an effective and efficient route to deep learning. More research needs to be undertaken in this area. Another area for further work is in the development of voice recognition software that can be integrated with streamed files so that students see the video, hear the audio, and can read the text.

The leaning activities model categorizes the appropriate uses of recordings as *providing materials* and *interaction with materials*. Further the LTM describes them as one-way and representational. Therefore to ensure a rich e-learning experience they need to be integrated into the wider course, connecting them to other activities. In this way e-learning experiences can be created where media-rich resources are connected with ample opportunities for interaction with other students, with the facilitator of learning and for reflection; connections with experiences and other resources; and for deep learning.

References

Anzai, Y. (2006, October). Podcasting and Japanese university students. In *Proceedings of E-Learn World Conference on E-Learning,* Hawaii.

Baez-Franceshi, S., Dinshaw, A., Evans, I., & Van Nieuwenhuise, D. (2006, October). Drag and drop streaming: An inexpensive method for recording and delivering lectures is becoming the next revolution in e-learning. In *Proceedings of E-Learn World Conference on E-Learning,* Hawaii.

Donnan, P., Kiley, M., & McCormack, C. (2004, November). *Lecture streaming: Getting the pedagogy right.* Paper presented at the Online Learning and Teaching Conference 2004: Exploring Integrated Learning Environments, Brisbane, Australia.

Fardon, M. (2003). Internet streaming of lectures: A matter of style. In *Proceedings of ASCILITE (Australasian Society for Computers In Learning In Tertiary Education) Conference.* Adelaide, Australia.

Lee, M., & McLouglin, C. (2006, October). Educational podcasting using the Charles Sturt university flexible publishing platform. In *Proceedings of E-Learn World Conference on E-Learning,* Hawaii.

Ogawa, M., & Nickles, D. (2006, October). Improving students' perceptions in large-enrollment courses through podcasting. In *Proceedings of E-Learn World Conference on E-Learning,* Hawaii.

Smeaton, A., & Keogh, G. (1999). An analysis of the use of virtual delivery of undergraduate lectures. *Computers and Education, 32,* 83-94.

Thornhill, S., Asensio, M., & Young, C. (2004). *Video streaming: A guide for educational development.* Retrieved November 25, 2006, from http://www.ClickandGoVideo.ac.uk

Chapter XI

Teaching with Real Time Communications Technologies

Introduction

Real time communications technologies are just that: technologies that facilitate real time or synchronous communications. An example that springs rapidly to mind is the telephone. The real time communications technologies (RTCs) that are commonly found in educational contexts include text-based examples such as text chat, and rich media examples such as video chat, videoconference, and Access Grid. Teaching with RTCs is not the same as face-to-face teaching due to the imposition the technology makes on the learning, thus limiting some activities. Full definitions of videoconference and video chat and recommendations for teaching with videoconference and video chat are discussed in detail in Chapter XIII. Likewise, teaching with Access Grid plus a description and a definition of it are provided in Chapter XIV. In this chapter some general approaches to teaching that are common to all RTCs are discussed and contrasts are drawn between other approaches that clearly highlight the differences in the RTCs.

In Chapter VII the learning technologies model (LTM) was introduced as a theoretical framework that classified learning technologies in two dimensions. The first dimension classified technologies as one-way or two-way and referred to them as *representational* and *collaborative*. The second dimension introduced three levels of communicative attributes. The LTM is shown in Figure 11.1.

Video chat, videoconference, and Access Grid are all collaborative technologies and of level 3 attributes when classified by the LTM. These RTCs are important in education as they provide cost effective communications channels between students and between students and teachers. Their importance to e-learning and their future role is increased by the:

- Global trends of increasing bandwidth.
- Increasing availability of free or low cost video communications software.
- Yhe trend towards cameras, microphones, and speakers as standard computer features.

As video chat increases in popularity it is reasonable to expect that students will use it to communicate with their peers, and it is not unreasonable that they will expect it to be part of their online learning experience.

Technologies often impose restrictions on teaching and learning activities and there are tasks they perform well and other tasks for which they are not suited and do not perform well at all. In Chapter VIII the technology selection method was introduced and takes as part of its basis the notion that different technologies are appropriate for different categories of learning activities. For this reason technologies are seldom used singularly in e-learning. Learning management systems are good examples of

Figure 11.1. The LTM

	Learning Technologies		
	Representational	Collaborative	
		Dialogic	Productive
1	text	text	text
2	voice	voice	voice
3	voice and image	voice and image	voice and image

this as they bring together several technological elements. Some elements provide communications between students, for example, chat or discussion forums. Others are used for the posting of content as Web pages or downloadable files and linking to podcasts of recorded materials. Different technologies serve different educational purposes by supporting different learning activities.

The literature concurs (Caladine, 1999; Daunt, 1997; Kobayashi, Tanaka, Yamaji, & Otsuka, 1997; Mitchell, 1993) that videoconference and by extension other RTCs are best used as interactive technologies in teaching and learning. Of course videoconferences are often combined with images from computers that can add to the visual richness while introducing visual variety to the participants. Other RTCs bring other technological elements to the communicative process such as the rich multimedia experience of a room-based node on the Access Grid. However, generally when the technology is used in an interactive fashion the technological interface becomes transparent and the focus of students' and teachers' attention is on the interactions.

Changing Mindsets

At their simplest, RTCs can be thought of as resembling television as the participants see pictures on what appears to be a television screen and hear sounds from its speakers. From the early days of videoconference one of the challenges to proponents was to change the mindset of participants from one of passive viewing to one of active participation. It is not surprising that new participants react this way to videoconference as they have had many hours of unintentional training in watching television in a passive, relaxed fashion. Later in this chapter and in Chapter XIII methods of changing this mindset are discussed.

The LTM and the learning activities model (LAM) are designed to provide designers and teachers with a deeper understanding of learning technologies and are used in conjunction in the process where technologies are selected that are appropriate for the subject, the students, and the learning objectives.

As their goals are for students to achieve the learning objectives, teachers prefer to match technologies to education rather than the other way around. In this way the meeting of educational needs is paramount. However, often the reality is that existing technologies are the best choice for teaching students at a distance. For example, if the institution has invested in a videoconference system or Access Grid, the amount invested in the technology is significant enough for there to be institutional pressure to use it. Also, in cases where the technology is institution wide students may be used to it and may have the metacognitive skills to learn with it effectively and efficiently. So in such instances learning is designed to suit the technology. Even within these constraints designers and teachers can create mixtures of learning activities, resources, and technologies that can lead to effective and efficient learning.

One-Way and Two-Way Technologies and the Learning Activities Model

The LAM clearly divides learning activities in to those that are one-way and those that are two-way. Also, learning technologies can be broadly aligned to these categories as shown in Figure 11.2. The center of the figure is the LAM as discussed in Chapter VI. The outer circles indicate the technologies that broadly fit the categories and whether they are one-way or two-way. However, it can be argued that this approach could benefit from a more detailed approach to ensure the most appropriate use of technologies and that this will yield learning events and designs that result in better learning outcomes.

While much has been said about the innate differences between one-way and two-way technologies, the difference between one-way and two-way activities can be more subtle and in some cases it is indeed difficult to differentiate between them. For example, a 50-minute presentation in which there are no opportunities for feedback from students is clearly one-way. Just as a student listening to a broadcast cannot ask a question or interact with the broadcaster is another example of a one-way activity. However, a lecture in which short presentations are interspersed with two-way activities (such as questions and answers, student activities, etc.) is clearly not completely one-way or two-way. Rather is a combination of both. Also, when considering two-way activities what exactly is meant? Is there no presentation of information that flows from one person to another? Even when chatting informally material is being presented. This is a one-way activity albeit generally only a few moments or minutes long. So it could be argued that two-way activities are a collection of one-way activities and whether it is classified as one-way or two-way depends on the level of granularity. Perhaps the concept of pure two-way activities exists only as a theoretical extension in which the one-way sections of the two-way activity approach the infinitely small.

Returning the example of the 50-minute presentation, when there was no opportunity for feedback obviously the activity was one-way. If the presenter decided to change their approach and introduced 5-minute opportunities in the middle and at the end of the presentation for students to question or comment this would introduce an element of the two-way. However, 10 minutes of interaction with students and 40 minutes of presentation still equates to a predominantly one-way activity. If the presenter changed their approach yet again and used the 50 minutes to deliver five short presentations of 5 minutes each and between them allowed five interactive sessions of 5 minutes each, many would suggest that the activity is predominantly two-way. However, half of the time was still taken up by one-way presentations. Rather than continue into this challenging area, perhaps it will serve the needs of teachers and designers better, to consider a continuum of one-way and two-way learning activities.

Figure 11.2. The LAM and learning technologies

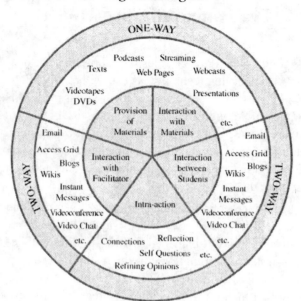

The One-Way/Two-Way Learning Activities Continuum

A *continuum of learning activities* with completely one-way activities at one pole and completely two-way activities at the other pole is suggested as the starting point for the consideration of the factors that contribute to the effectiveness of teaching and learning with RTCs. The continuum could be for a class or for a course or for a section of a class, the level of granularity is variable. The continuum is represented in Figure 11.3. Most teaching and learning could be represented on a section of the continuum. As shown in Figure 11.3 the extremes of the continuum have been omitted from the zone of most teaching and learning. This does not imply that teaching does not or cannot happen at the poles, rather it focuses our attention on the areas of the continuum in which there is a mixture of one-way and two-way activities.

As mentioned previously there is concurrence in the literature that can be extended to argue that an interactive approach works best in teaching with RTCs. However, the question is: What degree of two-way activities will be necessary to ensure effective and efficient learning takes place? Effective learning can be defined, for the purpose of this chapter, as occurring when the learning objectives of a subject, course, or lesson are achieved by a majority of students. Rather than quantify the majority here, which would be far too general to be useful, it is left to individual designers and teachers to establish the degree of the majority for their own courses,

Figure 11.3. A continuum of one-way and two-way learning activities

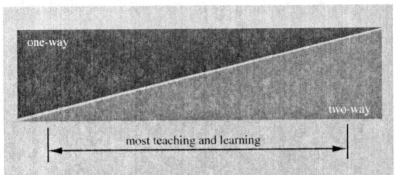

subjects, and lessons. Efficient learning is defined for the purpose of this chapter as effective learning within the designed time frame.

Threshold Of Effective and Efficient Learning

For each teaching event (course, subject, or lesson) there exists a threshold on the continuum above which learning can be expected to be effective and efficient. Conversely, it is reasonable to expect that below the threshold learning would not be effective, not be efficient, or both. This is based on the premise extrapolated from the literature that RTCs are best used as interactive technologies in teaching and learning or are best suited to two-way learning activities.

The *threshold of effective and efficient learning* is shown on the continuum of learning activities in Figure 11.4—Figures 11.5 and 11.6 show high and low thresholds respectively. While it is suggested that moving the threshold to the right will improve effectiveness and efficiency this cannot be adopted in isolation from other elements of the learning event. In fact it is suggested that there are a number of factors that determine the location of the threshold on the continuum for any given learning event. It is argued that if these factors determine the location of the threshold then there is a good chance that they can be used in the design of teaching and learning with RTCs that will result in effective and efficient learning.

Criteria for the Location of the Threshold

At the time of writing the criteria that effect the location of the threshold are based on observations of numerous videoconferences. However, as the other RTCs, Access

Figure 11.4. The continuum of learning activities and the threshold.

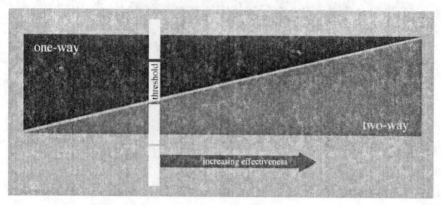

Figure 11.5. A high threshold on the continuum of learning activities

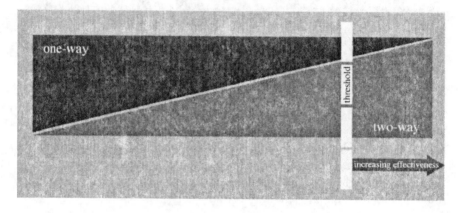

Figure 11.6. A low threshold on the continuum of learning activities

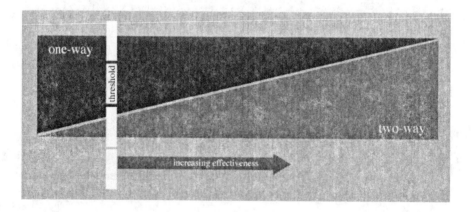

Grid and video chat are relatively new to teaching and learning in higher education or in the development of human resources. The experience with them is limited. Anecdotal evidence and limited experience suggests that while there will be some common criteria, there will be others that are specific to, and based on, the features of the different technologies.

There are numerous criteria that determine the location of the threshold. These include but are not limited to the:

- Mix of one-way and two-way activities
- Nature of the activities
- Media richness of the experience
- Notoriety or fame of the presenter
- Presentation skills of the presenter
- Motivation of students

Mix of One-way and Two-way Activities

Clearly the first criterion is that of the degree of interaction, or two-way learning activities. For example, when lectures are translated from face-to-face to videoconference delivery with no concession to the technology now being used, teachers often report that students do not engage as readily when the videoconference is compared to the face-to-face lecture. It is not strange to hear teachers say in such situations that students go to sleep in their videoconferences. In these examples the learning event would be located to the left, or below the threshold on the continuum. As mentioned earlier it is possible that if the RTC looks like television, participants will bring a television viewing mindset to it. The television viewing mindset is usually passive and there is nothing innately wrong with it for viewing television. However, when it is brought to a videoconference, for other RTCs, the result can be less than satisfactory. RTCs such as videoconference do not have the same production values as most television. Television typically uses numerous edit points and different images combined with a variety of sounds to communicate its message. Videoconferences, on the other hand, usually have lower production values, with fewer edit points (or their equivalents), and less variety of images and sounds. In fact a videoconference if viewed as a one-way technology can be seen as very low quality television. This could be one reason why students go to sleep in one-way presentations delivered by videoconference. Clearly two-way activities in which participants communicate with each other via the videoconference will change this mindset and be more likely to keep students awake.

Nature of the Activities

Another way to change this mindset is to give participants something to do that is actively different to viewing television. In this way the experience is taken beyond "talking to a television." Activities such as brainstorming, debates, buzz groups, role plays, and case studies as detailed in Chapter XIII can be used to achieve this. The resulting learning event would then have a high threshold on the continuum of learning activities.

Media Richness of the Experience

While the technology of videoconference can be likened to television, this is not the case for Access Grid and video chat. The experience with Access Grid differs with the nature of the Access Grid installation. In room-based nodes on the Access Grid, participants see a multi-projector image containing windows of participants and shared applications, documents, and presentations. Visually it is quite different to television. While this difference is significant, the effectiveness and efficiency of teaching and learning can be increased through the addition of two-way activities, for example, if students have access to a sharable electronic whiteboard as part of the Access Grid, when they use it to develop, clarify, discuss, and debate, this rich and interactive style of experience is then far removed from passive watching. Smaller installations of the Access Grid, while lacking the awe-inspiring *wall of video* appear as scaled down versions of room-based nodes and as such are still quite different in appearance to television. It would then appear that due to their inherent media richness, Access Grid sessions can result in effective and efficient learning with a threshold on the learning activities continuum that is higher (that is containing a higher proportion of one-way activities) than that for videoconferences and video chat.

There is some degree of media richness available with videoconference and video chat as well. Most videoconference suites are set up with at least three inputs: main camera, document camera, and computer. Switching between these inputs can create a level of visual variety that when combined with interaction result in an experience far removed from that of passively watching television. While video chat is a relatively new technology it is clear that future versions of the technology will have the facility to transmit images from a number of sources. The logical sources are those that can be found on the computer hosting the video chat and could be presentations such as PowerPoint, digital photos, audio, or video. Of course video chat has the potential to approach the smaller installations of Access Grid in functionality when it is coupled to applications that allow the sharing of desktops and electronic canvases.

Expert Presentation

Just as more viewers will tolerate poor quality video if the person speaking is some one they want to hear, participants will tolerate a higher degree of one-way activities on an RTC if this is the case. For example, if a teacher uses videoconference to connect to a world expert in the topic area, chances are students will engage with what the expert is saying to a greater degree than they would with the teacher (unless of course the teacher is in fact the world expert). Thus the expert presentation could result in an effective and efficient learning event in spite of a low threshold on the learning activities continuum, such as that shown in Figure 11.6.

Presentation Skills

Just as an audience may be more prepared to watch a poor quality television program of a world expert, they generally will put up with poor production values if the presenter is well skilled in the art and science of presentation. Being a good presenter or speaker can involve many things and there are numerous sources available to develop these skills. It is suggested that the better the presentation skills the lower the threshold can be on the learning activities continuum.

Student Motivation

Conversely, to the expert presenter or the well skilled presenter, it is no surprise that effectiveness and efficiency of learning are strongly linked to student motivation. Just as highly motivated students will learn in spite of a poor teacher, they are more likely to learn from an RTC learning session in which the threshold is low.

No doubt there are many other factors that have roles to play in the location of the threshold and the effectiveness and efficiency of learning. The challenge for the future is to define these and to test the level of their impact on the location. As mentioned earlier Access Grid and video chat are relatively new to learning and hence their use needs to be observed and analyzed before a definitive theory of teaching and learning with RTCs can be developed. In the meantime however, the concept of the continuum and the factors that determine the location of the threshold on it can be used as a guide for the design of learning events that use RTCs.

How the Continuum is Used in Designing Learning Events

The concept of the continuum of learning activities and the threshold of effective and efficient learning has been introduced with designers of learning events in mind. It is intended to provide a deeper understanding of the nature of learning activities that are suitable for RTCs and hence assist in the design of effective and efficient learning events.

The continuum and the position of the threshold on it, at the most basic level, serve to inform teachers and designers about the proposed learning event. To design effective and efficient learning events, a procedure is suggested in which all of the criteria that determine the location of the threshold on the continuum, with the exception of the mix of one-way and two-way activities, are considered and a location of the threshold thus achieved. At this stage it is recommended that the threshold location is only a guide as several of the determining criteria are approximate. The location of the threshold then can be used to determine the mix of activities. For example, if the threshold is located in the middle of the continuum, the minimum level of two-way activities for effective learning is one half of the learning event.

Returning to the example mentioned earlier in this chapter, consider the conversion of the 50-minute presentation for a learning event that uses RTCs. When the criteria that determine the location of the threshold are considered (except the mix of one-way and two-way activities), for this example it is assumed that the teacher is not a leading expert in the field, that their presentation skills are neither high nor low, that student motivation is likewise of a middle level, and that the media richness of the event is low. These factors combine to indicate a central location of the threshold as shown in Figure 11.7.

If the teacher planned to simply deliver the 50-minute presentation with no opportunities for student interaction, the mix of one-way and two-way learning activities would be well below the threshold, at the extreme left hand end of the continuum as shown in Figure 11.7. The addition of two, 5-minute opportunities for interaction and the concomitant reduction of the presentation to 40 minutes locates the planned event further to the right on the continuum but still below the threshold. When the planned structure is changed to five, 5-minute presentations interspersed with five, 5-minute opportunities for interaction the event is collocated with the threshold in the middle of the continuum. This suggests that the last mixture of one-way and two-way activities could result in effective learning and that increasing the amount of two-way activities could lead to more effective and efficient learning.

The Importance of Granularity

In the learning event in the example, rather than have half the lesson presentation followed by a single block of interaction, the structure of interspersing presentation and interaction was selected. While quantitatively equal, there can be a vast difference in the effectiveness of learning between these two approaches. Earlier, the need to change student mindsets from passive reception to active engagement was discussed as central to the achievement of effective and efficient learning with RTCs. It is also necessary to maintain this change. To do so opportunities for interaction must be provided at regular intervals and the length of time between opportunities is critical. Like the threshold this time between opportunities differs with the same criteria and a maximum time between opportunities exists for any given learning event. Perhaps the continuum could be reinterpreted as a scale of time to the next opportunity for interaction as shown in Figure 11.8.

At the left hand end of the scale the figure of 100% indicates that there are no opportunities for interaction as the learning activities are all one-way. One-hundred percent is chosen to represent all of the time taken for the learning event or the length of the lesson. At the other end of the scale the time is shown as zero indicating that there are continuing opportunities for interaction during the lesson. As with the one-way and two-way continuum perhaps the poles are theoretical and most teaching and learning occurs in a broad central section as shown in Figure 11.8.

Figure 11.7. Examples and threshold

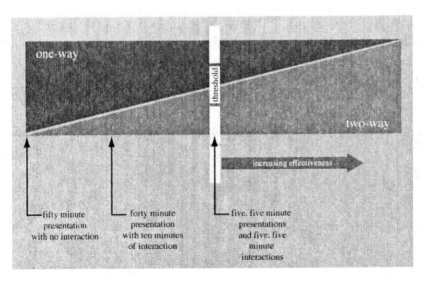

Figure 11.8. The continuum of learning activities and the time to interaction scale

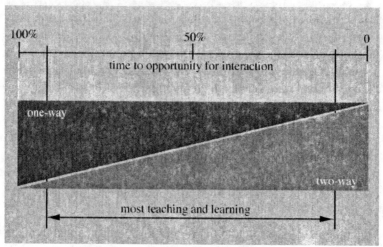

Conclusion

The use of RTCs in distance learning and e-learning is trending upwards due to the availability of increased bandwidth, the increases in availability of the technology, and accessibility of the software. However, RTCs impose restrictions on the learning activities and changes to the design of learning are needed to result in effective and efficient learning as participants bring mindsets to the RTC experience that have been acquired with other technologies such as television. One way to change mindsets of passive reception to ones of active engagement is to provide regular opportunities for interaction. This is the challenge presented to designers and teachers who use RTCs. The continuum of learning activities and the threshold of effective and efficient learning were introduced as hypothetical devices to assist designers come to terms with and meet this challenge.

It is anticipated that with further refinement, observation of learning activities with RTCs, and data collection that the continuum and threshold will grow in to a theory of teaching and learning with RTCs that will be suitable for the guidance of designers in the future. For the present, the bottom line is that generally speaking interaction is necessary for these technologies to be used in effective and efficient learning events.

References

Caladine, R. (1999). *Teaching for flexible learning: Learning to apply the technology.* Monmouthshire, Wales: GSSE.

Daunt, C. (1997). Is teleteaching different? In J. Osborne et al. (Eds.), *Open, flexible and distance learning: Education and training for the 21st century.* Proceedings of the 13th Biennial Forum of ODLAA, Launceston, Australia.

Kobayashi, T., Tanaka, K., Yamaji, H., & Otsuka Y. (1997). Crosscultural joint classes between Japan and Australia using ISDN. In J. Osborne et al. (Eds.), *Open, flexible and distance learning: Education and training for the 21st century.* Proceedings of the 13th Biennial Forum of ODLAA, Launceston, Australia.

Mitchell, J. (1993). *Video-conferencing in higher education in Australia: An evaluation of the use and potential of video-conferencing facilities in the higher education sector in Australia.* Occasional Papers Series. Canberra, Australia: Department of Education, Employment and Training, Higher Education Division. Australian Government Printing Service.

Chapter XII

Videoconference, Audioconference, and Video Chat

Introduction

Videoconference and audioconference have been used for communications in businesses for many years. In teaching and learning videoconference has been used for at least the last 15 years and possibly longer. Videoconference and audioconference technologies have been used in education, especially in distance education where students and teachers are in different locations. Like all educational technologies, videoconference and audioconference are suited to some and not all teaching and learning activities. Before these established real time communications technologies (RTCs) and the newer technology video chat are explored they need to be carefully defined to eliminate or minimize confusion.

Definitions

Videoconference, sometimes referred to as video-teleconference is a technology that allows two-way video and audio communications between remote parties. In videoconference parlance the parties or locations are referred to as *points* or *endpoints*. Audioconference is the technology that allows two-way audio communications between remote parties. By this definition a person-to-person phone call is an audioconference, so to differentiate, audioconferences are defined as the technology that allows two-way communications between at least three remote parties. The newer technology of video chat is defined as an application of computer technology that allows two-way audio and video communications between remote parties. Thus video chat can be thought of as videoconference on a computer.

Video chat is gaining acceptance as a videoconference tool and is developing into *enhanced video chat* (as discussed later in this chapter) and it is clear that enhanced video chat poses a threat to the market traditionally held by videoconference technology suppliers. Perhaps, for this reason several videoconference hardware manufacturers have recently initiated strategies to reposition themselves in the marketplace. For example, two of the world's leading suppliers, Tandberg and Polycom have introduced and prioritized high definition videoconference endpoint technology. Also, both suppliers have also introduced a range of telepresence technologies that use high definition videoconference to emulate a real meeting by creating a closer-to-reality experiences through an "immersive multimedia experience" (Polycom, 2006).

Another similar technology is Web conference. To differentiate between videoconference and Web conferencing, videoconference is defined here as not being hosted by a World Wide Web browser. While this difference might seem trivial and the functionality of both technologies is very similar, the differentiation is significant when used to describe the practices concerning videoconference equipment that is installed into teaching spaces with multiple cameras, screens, and microphones. On the other hand, Web conference technology is often designed for a majority of single user endpoints, as Web cams and headsets are the basic technology used.

Background

In essence videoconference has been around for as long as television, as videoconference can be thought of as two parallel, counter directional, closed-circuit television systems. However it was not until the 1980s that dedicated videoconference technology appeared on the market. The systems took advantage of the then new digital telecommunications networks such as integrated, services digital network (ISDN).

Typically ISDN lines were designed, and hence the term *integrated*, to carry two separate connections on the one line with a data rate of 64 kbps(for an explanation of bit rates, bandwidth, and file sizes see Appendix 2). So it is no surprise that the first ISDN videoconferences had a bit rate of 128 kbps as two ISDN lines were used. Unfortunately the compression needed to reduce the video and audio to 128kbps was so great that the resulting audio and video looked and sounded significantly degraded. Today organizations that use videoconference generally connect at a higher bandwidth so that the degradation of pictures and sound quality are not as great. This can be achieved through the use of several ISDN lines or through the use of the Internet. This increase in bandwidth combined with the new and more effective compression methods makes possible high quality videoconferences. Today many organizations, universities, and colleges around the world use videoconferences of 384 kbps, 768 kbps, and up to 2Mbps (in the case of high definition).

Compression and Quality

Raw video and audio files are extremely large and to transfer them in real time across a network would require extremely large bandwidth. To get around this videoconference signals are compressed before they are transmitted and decompressed on arrival at their destination. Compression uses one or more algorithms to reduce the amount of information sent and results in some degradation of the quality of the pictures and sound. High levels of compression can cause movements to look jerky and for images to appear grainy or less clear. Generally, the greater the level of compression the greater is the degradation. This relationship is represented in Figure 12.1 as either a straight line or a curve.

In the early days of videoconference it was often difficult to see an image in which the movement of the mouth was synchronized to the sound. Today with advances in compression hardware and software, and with the increases in available bandwidth, much higher quality is available.

While the videoconference technology may not appear to have changed greatly in the past 15 to 20 years, and the configurations of room-based videoconference facilities look very similar, many changes have happened behind the scenes improving not only compression methods but also in organization, management, and user-friendliness of the technology. However, other factors play a part in determining the effectiveness of the communications. For example, the degree to which the images of participants can enhance the communication, in large part, will be determined by how they are framed on the videoconference camera.

Figure 12.1. Technical quality of a videoconference decreases as compression levels increase

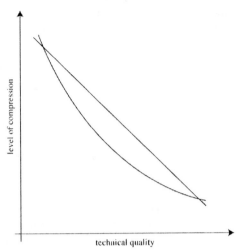

Figure 12.2. Shot size terminology

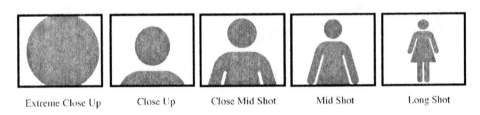

| Extreme Close Up | Close Up | Close Mid Shot | Mid Shot | Long Shot |

Shot Sizes

In a videoconference users often have control of the camera that sends their image to the other participants. While this is democratic it often results in poor quality videoconference images due primarily to the shyness of the camera operator. Television and filmmakers use a convention to calibrate shot sizes, as shown in Figure 12.2 and discussed in Chapter IX, which will provide the nomenclature to help overcome or at least accurately describe the problem.

Most participants are shy about transmitting an image of themselves that is larger than a Mid Shot and often closer to a Long Shot. While they may feel comfortable with this it can really defeat the purpose of the videoconference. If the image appears far away and facial cues are too small to recognize, the communicative purpose of the images can be questioned. Strategies to overcome shyness need to be found and it is suggested that if the presenter or participant is seated the preferred shot size is the Close Up in which all of the head is visible and just the top of the shoulders. This shot size provides the other participants with an image that conveys non-verbal information.

Return on Investment

Videoconferences have been used by organizations in business as well as education to increase efficiencies and decrease travel times and expenses. While it is not suggested that a videoconference is communicatively equivalent to a face-to-face meeting, judicious use of this technology can provide a solution in which a reduction in travel time and costs can be traded off against the reduction in communication. The case for videoconferencing is gaining further strength as the costs of travel to the environment and the rising costs of fuel are increasingly drawn to our attention by the media. Two examples highlight this. Many universities have access centers and campuses located some distance away. Rather than teachers traveling between campuses they can use videoconference to teach at both (or several) locations concurrently, thus saving time. Many universities also send their teachers overseas to teach in intensive blocks. While it is not suggested that videoconference should replace

Figure 12.3. Point-to-point videoconferences

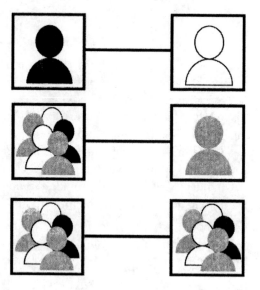

these blocks it can be used to extend the contact the teacher has with the overseas students. Further, the videoconference technology could be used to connect local and overseas students thus providing a new level of cultural richness.

Point-to-Point or Multipoint

The first videoconferences were point-to-point as they connected one videoconference location with one other and many point-to-point conferences are still used today. For example a company in New York may wish to communicate with a branch office in Chicago and at each location there could be a single or several participants. Examples of point-to-point videoconferences are shown in Figure 12.3.

However, often participants at more than two locations need to communicate at the same time. To do this a further piece of equipment is required if all locations are to see and hear each other. In the early days this device could only support one conference at a time and was called a *videoconference bridge*. Today they are called multi conference units (MCU) as they can host several concurrent, multipoint conferences. For example, an organization may use its MCU to connect its New York, Chicago, Los Angeles, and Seattle offices in one videoconference, and at the same time as a conference connecting Washington DC, Detroit, San Francisco, and New Orleans. While the number of conferences and connections is only limited by the capacity of

Figure 12.4. Multipoint videoconference

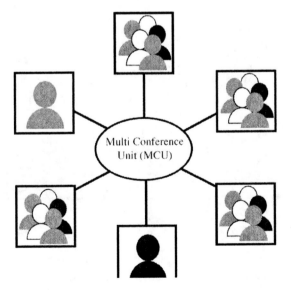

the MCU and the bandwidth of the network there are human factors that can limit the effectiveness of a videoconference with a large number of participants. A schematic diagram of a multipoint conference and the MCU is shown in Figure 12.4.

Other important features of the newer bridging technologies or MCUs include enhanced conference management and screen layout options. Conference management includes the ability to assign configurations to endpoints, scheduling, archiving, monitoring, and maintenance. Initially, the screen of multipoint conferences displayed only one other endpoint at a time. If there was an endpoint connected to the conference at which the participants were passive, as they were not seen, they could soon be overlooked by the other more active endpoints. A solution to this is termed *continuous presence* and refers to a screen configuration or layout in which all endpoints are always visible. There are many variations of the layout; however, perhaps the most popular consists of a large image of the endpoint that is speaking surrounded by smaller images of the endpoints that are listening. In Figure 12.5 the screen is divided into six windows. The endpoint shown as the largest window is the one speaking and is surrounded by images from the other connected endpoints.

Switching Between Endpoints

In many multipoint videoconferences the switching between endpoints is voice activated. When the participants at one endpoint talk their image is placed in the

Figure 12.5. Continuous presence of endpoints connected to a multipoint video-conference

large window (as shown in Figure 12.5) and the images of the listening endpoints appear in the smaller windows. Most MCUs allow the administrator to set a delay so that the voice activated switch is not inadvertently triggered by a cough or some other arbitrary noise. While this works well for many conferences it can result in the truncation of the first syllable or word spoken. Experienced multipoint participants soon get used to this and often start by announcing themselves twice. In comparison to voice-activated switching, switching between endpoints can be directed. In directed or chairperson switching one endpoint has control and manually switches between endpoints.

Technology

Videoconference uses devices at each endpoint to compress the video and audio it sends and to decompress the audio and video signals it receives. This compressor/decompressor is called a *codec.* Some people refer to these as coders and decoders. Either way the term codec works. In the early days of videoconference this device was generally a black box to which cameras, monitors, microphones, and speakers were connected. Today it is often integrated into the camera unit that sits on top of the screen or screens.

Videoconference installations can range from small units designed for use by one or two people to large installations consisting of multiple cameras, microphones, and screens at each endpoint. In universities and colleges the installations tend to fall into four categories: *large installations, designated videoconference rooms, medium-sized rooms,* and *personal installations.* The most expensive category is where large installations, mentioned previously, are put into lecture theaters.

Large Installations

Typically these installations are used for teaching local and distant students at the same time and the equipment could consist of:

- Presentation camera
- Presentation microphone
- Student camera or cameras
- Student microphones
- Presentation computer

- Presentation projector
- Far endpoint projectors

The presentation camera and microphone are generally used to capture the image and voice of the presenter and likewise the student camera(s) and microphone(s) capture the images and sounds of the students. In locations where there are a large number of participating students a technology that links the camera positioning equipment to individual microphone switches can deliver large images of the speaking student. Press-to-talk switches on microphones have been used for many years to minimize the amount of ambient noise captured. If the camera positioning equipment is connected to the system, when a speaker holds down the press-to-talk button to activate the microphone the camera repositions to frame the speaker. In this way student cameras can automatically capture large images of each speaking student. The presenter uses the presentation computer to display computer images such as PowerPoint slides and Web pages to the local audience. As it is connected to the videoconference codec the computer images can be transmitted to the other endpoints. The presenter generally switches between the computer and images of themselves or the local audience to send to the connected endpoints. The presentation projector displays the computer images to the local audience and far end projectors display images of students at the connected endpoints. Often two far endpoint projectors are used. One located at the front of the lecture theater and another at the rear. The rear one allows the presenter to keep local and far-end students easily within their view. Local students view two projector screens at the front of the room. One displays the computer images and the other students at far endpoints.

Designated Videoconference Rooms

Many institutions and organizations have one or more rooms that are specifically designed for teaching and learning with videoconference. While these rooms are usually designed to hold a number of local students, they are often used to connect learners in different locations with one presenter. Generally they contain a limited number of cameras and microphones and the distant participants provide a change in emphasis for the presenter. In large installations the presenter is generally more aware of the large number of local students, and while it is not recommended, the reality is that students at the endpoints often simply observe the interactions between the teacher and the local students (this will be discussed in detail in Chapter XIII). This compares to the designated videoconference room in which the focus, starting with the name of the room, is on the students who are connected by videoconference rather than the local students. This shift in emphasis is often reflected in the organization of the room in that generally the presenter sits with the local students and they all face the far endpoint students through the videoconference equipment.

Medium Installations

As well as designated videoconference rooms many institutions now have portable or semi-portable equipment that can be rolled into a medium-sized classroom. The equipment is generally self-contained and after connecting to the power the network can be used to connect students and teachers. One use of this level of technology is for tutorials or seminars between several campuses or updates between offices of an organization. The teacher and some students are usually located at one location and other students located at other campuses or locations.

Personal Installations

With the advent of desktop or computer-based videoconferences many teachers now choose to connect to remote students by videoconference from their offices. This can have a number of benefits to the organization. When teachers videoconference from their offices they save the time it would have taken to walk to the videoconference room and, more importantly, it frees up the videoconference room for other uses. Also, in their offices teachers have ready access to their resources and if access to the equipment permits they are more likely to use it for other purposes such as meetings with tutors, consultation with remote students, off-shore teaching, and research collaborations.

Standards

As videoconference technology has been used for some time, international standards have been developed to ensure equipment at one organization will operate effectively with equipment at another organization. This interoperability is an important feature of any videoconference equipment purchase and technology datasheets are often full of numbers, initials, and acronyms that need interpretation. Videoconference technology standards have been developed and are recommended by the International Telecommunications Union (ITU), which is based in Geneva, Switzerland and is within the United Nations system. The ITU works with governments and the private sector to coordinate global telecommunication networks and services. The videoconference family of standards that covers videoconference typically are designated H.3xx. H.323 is a standard that describes the protocols, services, and equipment necessary for multimedia communications including video, audio, and data on networks with protocols such as Internet protocol (IP) (Tandberg, 2006b). The H.320 standard describes an umbrella standard for ISDN videoconferences and has been adopted by many manufacturers thus ensuring a fair degree of interoperability and interconnectivity. There are other standards that need to be considered when designing a videoconference installation or purchasing equipment. One of these is the video standard, H.261. H.261 is a standard that describes the resolution of the video image and frames per second. In videoconference, screen resolution is a significant issue as while a lower resolution can render acceptable pictures of the participants, generally higher resolutions are required to render clear images from computer files. In videoconference standards, resolution is defined by the common interface format (CIF) as a number of frames per second and 352 x 288 pixels. Other resolutions are quarter CIF (QCIF) at 176 x 144 pixels, 4CIF at 704 x 576, and 16CIF at 1408 x 1152 (Tandberg, 2006b).

IP or ISDN?

It was mentioned earlier that early videoconferences used ISDN lines. These are typically owned by telecommunications companies and even though the cost of the lines can be quite high, a positive business case could be made in favor of videoconferences when the time and costs of travel were taken into account. However, videoconferencing can also be carried out over the Internet and as mentioned earlier a standard for videoconference over IP has been developed. In recent years the Internet has increased in reliability and become a central part of organizational communications. Higher bandwidth connections are replacing dial-up as the norm and making possible initiatives such as Internet telephony (often referred to as voice over IP or VoIP). These factors coupled with the cost benefits of IP over ISDN have made videoconference over IP attractive. Typically ISDN cost structures are similar to long distance telephony with cost increasing with distance between parties. Internet pricing structures, while varying from country to country are typically based on the quantity of information received (and/or sent). Thus for the same duration and data rate, a videoconference between New York and Washington DC should cost the same as one between New York and Sydney (Australia). The business case is even more attractive for videoconferences between offices of an organization as often the organization will own the network. In the case of a medium-sized Australian university the change from ISDN to IP videoconferencing resulted in a net annual saving of $80,000 AUD in ISDN charges.

A further disadvantage of ISDN is that connections generally need to be installed by the providing telecommunications company and are very expensive. With IP videoconferencing all that is needed is a connection to the network of sufficient bandwidth. This results in the change from centralized, purpose-built videoconference facilities to videoconferences from almost anywhere in the organization.

While a strong case is put here for IP videoconferencing, one consideration that must be taken into account at the planning stage is the load that will be placed on the network. When the organization owns the network, it can be expected that videoconference operators and users will increase the bandwidth of connections to increase the quality of the pictures and sound. At first the bandwidth requirements of a videoconference may seem insignificant when compared to the capacity of the network. However, when videoconference from multiple venues has been installed and the bandwidth of each increased, the load can impact on the network and a range of technologies and practices is available to manage the load on the network.

Gateways and Gatekeepers

As well as the MCU most modern videoconference installations also include a gateway and a gatekeeper. Some suppliers include these functions in the MCU or they can be performed by stand-alone machines. Gatekeepers control access to the MCU, and log and manage the calls. Gateways allow transcoding between different protocols. Transcoding refers to the ability to connect endpoint equipment with different protocols or standards. For example, an ISDN connection can be transcoded to an IP connection, individually or as part of a conference. Also, transcoding can be between different videoconference over IP standards.

Setting Up Rooms

As the Internet replaces ISDN as the network of choice for videoconferences, universities and colleges will take advantage of the lower costs of connection, which will in turn enable them to change from a model of centralized to distributed videoconference facilities. However, some large spaces and some designated videoconference spaces will still be required for some teaching and learning activities.

Videoconference Facilities in Large Teaching Spaces

A schematic diagram of one way to set up videoconference in a large teaching space is shown in Figure 12.6. In installations of this kind there are usually two projectors projecting images onto two screens at the front of the room. Screens are used to ensure images of sufficient size to be seen easily by students at the rear of the room. Typically one screen will show the students at the other locations while the second screen will show the presentation (for example PowerPoint slides or a Web page). A third projector may be used to project a duplicate image of the students

Figure 12.6. Equipment arrangement for videoconference in a large teaching space

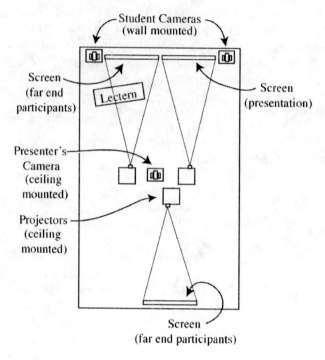

Figure 12.7. Equipment arrangement for a designated videoconference space

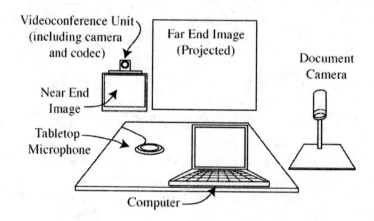

at other locations, hence allowing the presenter to see local and videoconference students within similar sight lines. Alternatively, a small monitor of the students at the other locations may be located on the lectern. The lectern can also contain a monitor displaying the image that is being sent to the students in other locations. The importance of this monitor should not be underestimated as it reminds presenters to change the image being sent rather than transmitting the last presentation slide long after the presentation has moved on. The lectern (or equipment rack is space is limited) is also a good place to locate any other equipment that may be used as a source of video and audio during a videoconference, for example, a VHS videotape player or DVD player, as it is from the lectern that the presenter controls the images and sounds that are being transmitted.

The videoconference unit containing the codec can be located in the lectern or in the equipment rack. Cameras to capture images of the local students are generally mounted on the front wall and the presenter's camera can be on the rear wall or mounted on the ceiling. While some presenters prefer microphones that are attached to the lectern, it is probably more practical to use a clip-on, wireless microphone so that the presenter is free to move around the room. Of course this will require the presenter's camera to be zoomed out wide enough to keep them in shot. Capturing sound from students in large teaching spaces presents somewhat of a challenge. Often it is not possible or affordable to supply each student or every second student with a microphone. In teaching spaces where tablets are used rather than desks installing student microphones can be difficult. Other approaches are to have a handheld wireless microphone that is passed from student to student, but the time taken can interrupt the flow of the class. Similarly having students move to a microphone can also slow things down. A better approach, although one that it more expensive, may be to install boundary microphones suspended from the ceiling along with technology to eliminate ambient noise.

Designated Videoconference Spaces

Small- to medium-sized videoconference spaces have roles in many institutions. They can be used for distance teaching as well as many other purposes such as student consultation, small group training, postgraduate supervision, and staff and administrative meetings. A possible configuration is shown in Figure 12.7. As in the large teaching space two screens are located in the front of the room. They can be both flat screen monitors or projected (or a mixture as shown in Figure 12.7) to suit the size of the room. Generally an integrated videoconference unit is used in smaller spaces and it can be located on top of one of the screens. A computer and document camera should be connected to the unit so that inputs can be switched between them and the main camera. If the number of participants is small a tabletop, boundary-type microphone should suffice.

A Case Study of the Migration of Videoconference from ISDN to IP at a Medium-Sized Australian University

The university is typical of many medium-sized universities as it has five satellite campuses situated up to five hours' drive from the main campus. Videoconferences have been used at the university for teaching and learning for approximately 15 years. Today the videoconference service is a central element of university's core business as it is used in teaching and learning to the satellite campuses. The service is also used for videoconferences to locations outside of the university. For example, personnel services use videoconference on an ad hoc basis for job interviews with overseas applicants. The majority of teaching and learning videoconferences are multipoint, that is more than two locations are connected (generally three, four, or five sites) as part of the one conference. To manage the connection of more than two endpoints an ISDN bridge was used from 1998 to 2005.

Prior to 2006 videoconferences used Telstra (Australia's Telecommunications company) provided ISDN lines for connections between the main and regional campuses. In 2006 a project was initiated with the goal to use IP over the university network for videoconference connections instead of ISDN, which will save an estimated $80,000 AUD in Telstra charges per annum. To do this the ISDN bridge was replaced with technology that will allow connections between locations using IP. As not all locations initially had network connections that could support videoconference over the Internet, the technology had, in the short to medium term, to manage a mixture of ISDN and IP connections. It was anticipated that within 12 to 18 months all endpoints would be capable of videoconference over IP.

Apart from the reduction in the charges for ISDN, the benefits of upgrading the multipoint technology and changing to the use of IP also include:

- The ability to host multiple concurrent multipoint conferences.
- The ability to connect videoconference endpoint equipment to any network connection of sufficient bandwidth.
- A cost structure based on volume rather than distance which makes international videoconferences more affordable than ISDN.

A project outline was written that stated the objectives of the project as:

- To replace the ISDN videoconference bridge with an IP MCU and gatekeeper that will provide and manage videoconference connections between main campus and the five satellite campuses at, or above, the current standard videoconference transmission rate of 384Kbps.

- To manage point-to-point and multipoint videoconferences between university and other locations both national and international.

- The replacement videoconference bridge will be so sized as to have the capacity to allow for the planned expansion.

- The replacement videoconference bridge will have both traditional ISDN capability and new IP-based capability to allow conferencing using existing network bandwidth.

- Satellite videoconference units at all campuses will be upgraded to be able to participate in network based conference sessions.

- Equip seven teaching rooms and academic offices at the main campus to take advantage of videoconferencing over IP.

Project Coordination

As the project had significant implications for the network the unit responsible for managing videoconference technology in teaching and learning worked closely with the unit responsible for managing the organization's network. Network support personnel were responsible for the installation, maintenance, and support of the MCU and gateway (bridging device) and collaborated with videoconference support personnel on the purchase of the equipment. Videoconference support personnel organized the purchase, installation, maintenance, and support of videoconference equipment in teaching and learning venues. In 2005 this was two locations: one was a lecture theater seating 98 and the other a designated videoconference room. Videoconference personnel were also responsible for scheduling, monitoring, and operation of videoconference equipment.

Project Organization

A two-stage approach to the development of videoconferencing over IP was taken and Figures 12.8, 12.9, and 12.10 are schematic representations of the previous, current, and future videoconference configurations. Figure 12.9 reflects the technology and the limitations of single conference capability of the previous, ISDN, bridge.

Figure 12.8. Old videoconference schematic

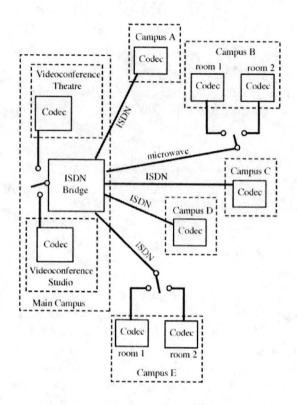

Previous Network Load

While previous videoconferences used ISDN as the transmission protocol, conferences between the main campus and campus (as shown in Figure 12.8) made use
of the, 100Mbps microwave link owned and operated by the organization. As all
endpoints were limited to transmit 384Kbps this resulted in a maximum contribution
to the load on the microwave link of 786Kbps (2 x 384Kbps) for videoconferences
that include campus B, typically this was about 30 hours per week.

Stage 1

Figure 12.9 illustrates the first stage of the videoconference over IP implementation.
In this stage two new devices were installed: a gatekeeper and an MCU. Network
support personnel maintained and supported the MCU and gatekeeper technology.

Figure 12.9. Videoconference schematic Stage 2

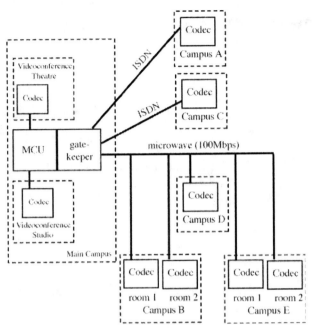

Videoconference support personnel operated the MCU and scheduled and monitored videoconferences. During stage 1 of the project, videoconferences were only being sourced from the existing venues on the main campus. This restricted the number of concurrent conferences to two for the period of this stage.

Until sufficient bandwidth is available at Campus A and Campus B as shown in the figures, ISDN will remain the transmission protocol between the main campus and those sites. This was changed to IP as soon as the network infrastructure was installed. This had an impact on the replacement MCU and gatekeeper technology in that for the short term it will need to manage conferences that are a mix of IP and ISDN connections.

Network Load

From Figure 12.9, based on the number of rooms, it is clear that a maximum of five concurrent videoconferences would use the 100Mbps microwave link. At the standard videoconference rate of 384Kbps (in each direction) this would result in a maximum contribution to the load on the microwave link of 3.84Mbps (5 x 2 x 384Kbps). However, in the quest for better quality videoconferences the endpoint technology was reconfigured to transmit 786Kbps which then elevated the load on the microwave link to 7.86Mbps

At some stage in the future the videoconferences facilities at Campus A, C, and D will be duplicated. This will then result in an extra contribution to the load on the links to those campuses. Of course videoconference over IP has a high definition standard that allows much higher bandwidth connections which would impose further load on the network. This will need to be managed to ensure continuity and quality of all network services. For example, if the bandwidth of all endpoint equipment was increased to 2Mbps the load on the 100Mbps microwave link would be 24Mbps (2Mbps x 2 x 6 endpoints).

Stage 2

In this stage of the development of videoconference over IP (see Figure 12.10) further venues at the main campus were equipped for videoconference capability. Where a department, school, or faculty was a high user, a teaching room in that area was equipped and small units were made available for use in academic's offices.

Also during this stage of the project it some users took advantage of the different cost structure and undertook international videoconferences. While ISDN charges are related to distance between locations (or videoconference endpoints) the charging structure for IP is based on the amount of information received. Preliminary calculations indicate that a videoconference at 788Kbps and of one-hour duration will attract approximately $8 AUD (based on Australian Academic and Research Network off net schedule). This compares with approximately $1,000 AUD for an hour of ISDN.

Network Load

The maximum load on the network is very difficult to determine for this stage of the project as there are no firm indicators of usage levels for new uses. During the final stage of the project, seven further, central videoconference facilities were installed at the main campus as well as equipment for use in academic offices. When all eight central facilities host concurrent videoconferences, the load on the network between the facilities and the MCU/gateway would be a total of 6.144Mbps (8 x 768Kbps). As there are a limited number of videoconference facilities at the satellite campuses the total network load can be calculated and is 4.608Mbps (6 x 768Kbps). As the number and frequency of conferences to locations outside of the university cannot

Figure 12.10. Videoconference schematic Stage 3

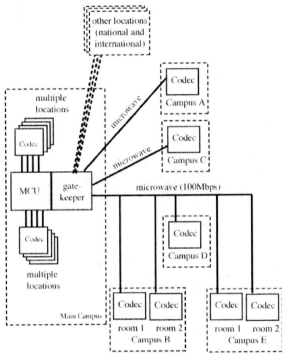

be determined accurately it is impossible to estimate a realistic figure of the load on the network. While the impact such new initiatives will have on network load is difficult or impossible to estimate with any accuracy, it should be noted that new compression technology is on the horizon that could reduce the network load of each videoconference.

As videoconferences are part of the core business of the university (i.e., teaching and learning) it is essential that the service is reliable. During the implementation and first year of videoconference over IP some ISDN capacity was retained for use in the event of failure.

Equipment List

The list shown in Table 12.1 contains details of the equipment that was acquired and installed as part of the project.

Table 12.1

	Multi Conference Unit
	Codian MCU (40 ports up to 4Mbps each)
1	MCU-4220 40 port enterprise MCU
1	HRO-4220 High Resolution Option (4CIF)
1	GWP-3210 1 PRI IP-ISDN Gateway
	Maintenance - next business day - year 1
	installation and freight
	IP Coordination unit (H323 Gatekeeper)
1	Sun Netra server
1	Linux software (public domain)
	Monitoring
1	Polycom PVX Videoconference software
1	Logitech Quickcam 4000 camera USB
1	Allowance for rack, leads and cables
	Replacement Endpoint Equipment
8	Tandberg 880MXP
8	Tandberg 1000MXP
2	Tandberg 2000MXP
1	Tandberg 3000MXP
20	Polycom PVX

Audioconferences

As mentioned earlier audioconferencing can be defined as a conference telephone call with three or more participants. In the last decades of the 20th century, audioconference was used in higher education as a tool for discussion and is still used today, although its main use is for meetings rather than education. This probably reflects a trend in learning technology in higher education that has taken place over the last 15 years in which overhead projectors have been replaced, in the main, by PowerPoint presentations. Hence, raising the importance placed on the visual elements of presentations.

Figure 12.12. Equipment for basic video chat

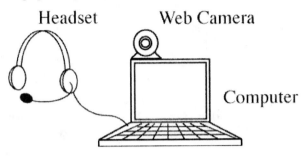

Figure 12.13. Equipment for advanced video chat

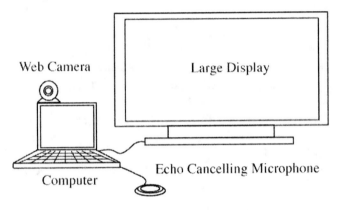

Video Chat and the Future of Videoconference

Video chat is gaining acceptance as an alternative to videoconferencing and has the singular benefit of being very cheap to use. Services such as Skype video, Windows Live, AOL Instant Messenger Video, MSN Video, and Apple's iChat AV all provide point-to-point, computer-based, video communications. Recent developments in Video chat have included multipoint (e.g., Apple iChatAV and Sightspeed) and the ability to include other files in the transmission. Clearly when the technology has been developed further and these functions are readily available, this enhanced video chat will pose a threat to the market traditionally held by videoconference technology suppliers.

Video chat is rather simple and inexpensive to set up as all that is needed is a computer, a Web camera, and a headset. Of course the Internet connection will need to be of sufficient bandwidth to support video chat and most broadband connections are ample for this. If video chat is to replace videoconference a few additions to the basic configuration mentioned previously will need to be made. For example, a larger screen may be needed that is large enough for all local participants to see, and some audio equipment will be needed to enable all to hear and be heard. Figure 12.12 and 12.13 show the different equipment required for single-user video chat as opposed to multi-user video chat.

Conclusion

Videoconference technology has been used in teaching and learning for quite some time and the technology has improved in reliability and in the quality of pictures and sounds. Perhaps the change that has had the greatest impact on the way in which videoconference is used and organized is the change from ISDN to the Internet. Using the Internet has increased the affordability of connection and hence the number of possible points in an organization from which videoconferences can be sourced. This has also reduced the need for designated videoconference studios that require participants to relocate to this environment that may not always have been relevant to the subject matter of the conference. The change is certainly a great opportunity to initiate new practices that enhance the way videoconferences are conducted.

Video chat appears to be poised to take over the market traditionally held by videoconference hardware manufacturers who are trying to reposition themselves by offering new features such as high definition videoconferences and telepresence. However, outside of specialized uses such as medical imaging, microscopy, and motional analysis, high definition has a natural upper limit being the limit of our ability to resolve reasonable levels of detail. In addition, telepresence currently comes with a price tag that is sufficiently high to limit its implementation in educational institutions.

Video chat developed as an enhancement of instant messaging and is expected to become as ubiquitous as its text forebear. The challenge then to educators is to design and implement learning events in which the technology is used in ways that are appropriate to the subject material and the participants and their preferred methods of learning. In the next chapter several basic principles for teaching and learning with videoconference and video chat are discussed. Also, practical guides to activities suited to these technologies are provided.

References

Polycom. (2006). *Real presence experience (RPX)*. Retrieved September 25, 2006, from http://www.polycom.com/solutions/0,1694,pw-15772-15773,00.html

Tandberg. (2006a). *HD videoconferencing at your desktop.* Retrieved September 25, 2006, from http://www.tandberg.net/

Tandberg. (2006b). *Videoconferencing standards. D10740 Rev 2.3.* Retrieved September 27, 2006, from http://www.tandberg.net/collateral/documentation/White_Papers/Whitepaper_Video-Conferencing_Standards.pdf

Chapter XIII

Teaching and Learning with Videoconference and Video Chat

Introduction

In the last chapter, videoconference and video chat were defined as technologies that allow two-way video and audio communications between remote parties. Definitions of the technologies were provided and they were differentiated. Video chat was computer-based while videoconference was appliance-based. Functionally and for teaching and learning the technologies are very similar. The single greatest logistical difference is generally the number of participants possible at each location.

Background

While much has been written on the technical details of videoconferences, only a limited amount has been written on the use of this technology for teaching and learning. However, the literature concurs on a correlation between interaction and the success of videoconference and by extension video chat. The literature concurs that for effective teaching and learning interaction is paramount.

Latchem (in Mitchell, 1993) suggests that videoconferences work best with small- to medium-sized groups of students at each site who are encouraged to interact with each other as well as trainers, tutors, or teachers. He further suggests that video-conferences are excellent in the support of learning activities such as simulations, role plays, case studies, brainstorming, problem solving, and in general cognition building. Daunt (1997) reinforces the importance of interaction in videoconferences and describes facilitators of videoconferences in learning as "teleteachers."

Most teleteachers agree that interaction is an important element in their teaching - after all it is the only thing that distinguishes teleteaching from a video tape! Interactivity takes many forms; it is not just limited to audio and video, or just teacher-student interactions. It represents the connectivity students feel with the teacher, the local tutors and their peers. (p. 109)

Laurillard (1993) describes videoconferences as a discursive media and suggests that they are not suited to the transmission of presentations or lectures. She continues to argue that video would be more appropriate for this. Kobayashi, Tanaka, Yamaji, and Otsuka (1997) reflect on their experience with videoconferences in higher educa-tion and argue that the least effective forms of discourse for this technology were those characterized by presentations—monologues where the sole purpose was the one-way transfer of information. The author's experience with videoconference in learning is congruent with the view that they are suited to interaction rather than presentation. Many times he has been faced with teachers who ask why the students go to sleep in their videoconferences. The answer is usually that one-way lectures are not suitable for videoconferences. Videoconferences rely on interaction to be effective and there are a range of technologies that are more suited to the encapsula-tion and delivery of one-way materials.

The author's experience with videoconference in learning is congruent with the view that they are suited to interaction rather than presentation. One-way presentations such as lectures are not appropriate for videoconferences and it is probably cheaper, as well as more educationally effective, to use a one-way technology for these kinds of teaching and learning activities such as text, audio, or video recordings.

Videoconference and the Learning Technologies Model

The literature concurs that videoconference is best used as an interactive technol-ogy in learning. Hence in the learning technologies model (LTM), as described in

Chapter VII, is a collaborative technology and as it supports voice and image, has level three attributes. Of course videoconferences are often combined with images from computers which can add to the visual complexity of the conference. Students and/or staff can use videoconferences as an adjunct to the production of teaching objects. However, the technology plays only a communicative role rather than hosting the objects produced and as such the classification of videoconference in the LTM is collaborative-dialogic.

On the basis of videoconference being best suited to two-way communications, it is clear that this technology is suitable for the categories of the learning activities model (LAM) that concern interactions between humans: *interaction between learners* and *interaction with facilitator*. As it is assumed that all parties will be connected to the videoconference at the same time, it is a synchronous technology. The description of the learning technology, videoconference—by the LTM—is shown in Table 13.1.

Teaching with Two-Way Technologies

There are a number of ways in which teaching and learning with two-way technologies differs from face-to-face. Perhaps most obvious is that students and teachers are in different physical locations, often separated by great distances. This different

Table 13.1. The LTM: Videoconference

Videoconference
Collaborative - dialogic, level 3
Synchronous
Flexibility of place (some)
Learning activities model (LAM) Suitable categories: Interaction between learners (IL) Interaction with facilitator (IF)

context can impede communications between locations. Even though students and teachers may use the videoconference technology to interact in real time, the interactions are quite different to their face-to-face equivalents. In the pervious chapter the technology of videoconference was discussed and the need for compression to transmit the video and audio signals. The downside of compression is that the quality of the signals can suffer. Compression can make the picture look slightly out of focus or grainy and movements can look strange. Fast movements in particular can result in a jerky picture as the codec struggles to keep up with the action. This jerky motion is sometimes referred to as *stutter vision*. The degradation of pictures and sounds caused by compression make videoconference images harder to watch in comparison to television.

Even high definition videoconferences with their clear pictures are not as easy to watch as television as there is much less visual variety. In television, edit points provide the viewer with regular new visual information such as angles and scenes. This is very difficult if not impossible to achieve with videoconference. For these reasons videoconference is best used as a two-way technology with high levels of interaction between as many participants as possible. In this way participants are pushed into a psychological approach to the videoconference that is more akin to interacting with another person rather than passively viewing television. In the last chapter the relationship between compression and technical quality was discussed.

While there is no empirical evidence, anecdotal evidence abounds to suggest a correlation between effective videoconferences, technical quality, and the degree of interactivity. It is suggested that videoconferences that have high technical quality can be effective with less interactivity than videoconferences with low technical quality. However, a word of warning indicates that even with high technical quality, there is a minimum level of interaction that is necessary. Below this level, videoconferences of even the highest technical quality can be ineffective. (This is discussed in further detail in Chapter XI). In Figure 13.1 the straight line or the curve represents the relationship between the level of interactivity necessary for an effective videoconference and technical quality of the videoconference. Whether the curve or the line is the best fit for this relationship cannot be determined until further empirical research has been conducted. The area to the left of the dashed line in Figure 13.1 represents the region where no matter how high the technical quality of the videoconference, the level of interactivity is too low for the conference to be effective. A level of interactivity is necessary if students are to change their cognitive processes from passive reception, similar to that used when viewing television. This could well be the single biggest challenge to teachers using videoconferences.

While it is not always easy to determine if a videoconference is effective or not, there are some cues that provide an indication. When a teacher complains that he or she does not know why students always go to sleep in their videoconferences, it would be reasonable to assume that the videoconference could be more effective. High levels of active and passive engagement by students characterize effective

Figure 13.1. Relationship of technical quality and interactivity for effective video-conferences

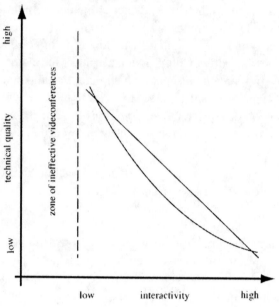

Figure 13.2. Matrix of videoconference effectiveness

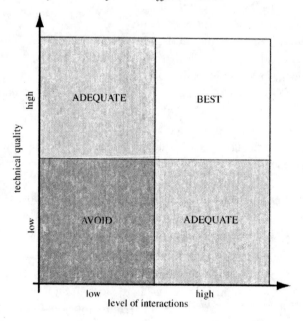

videoconferences. This can range from attentive listening at the passive end of the scale through to dialogue at the other end. An alternative graphical representation of this relationship is shown in Figure 13.2.

Figure 13.2 illustrates that the combination of high technical quality with high levels of interactivity is best for effective videoconferences. From the relationship between technical quality, interactivity and effectiveness of videoconferences in teaching and learning, it is clear that some teaching activities are less suited to videoconference than others. A reductionist, but general view is that one-way activities such as presentations are among the least suited activities, while two-way activities are more suited. However, the reality is not as simple. Effective videoconferences can consist of presentations, for example, if the presenter is a world authority, an expert, or someone who commands attention. This and other criteria are discussed further in Chapter XI. Alternatively, presentations can be effective if they are broken up with interactive sessions. Figure 13.3 suggests a hierarchy of broad categories of activities suitable for effective videoconferences.

Earlier, the LTM was used to describe videoconference as a collaborative-dialogic technology. At the lowest level of the hierarchy are teaching activities that are one-way or representational activities and hence usually not suited for videoconference unless integrated with discussion. At the higher levels of the hierarchy two-way communications predominate. In the top two levels of the hierarchy, videoconference is used to provide the communications channel for students to undertake productive collaborations. The technology does not host the collaboration just the communication. Videoconferences can be used in conjunction with other technologies to facilitate the collaborative production of content. For example, virtual network computing (VNC) can be used with videoconference to enable students to work on shared applications such as documents, spreadsheets, and eWhiteboards.

Planning for Teaching with Videoconference

Due to the limitations imposed by the technology, planning a videoconference teaching session takes on a few further dimensions. A variety of activities need to be included and also a variety of different inputs, including the document camera, student and presenter cameras, video sources, and a computer should be used. Elements of a videoconference class may include opening interactions, closing interactions, student-led discussion, group discussions, presentations, question and answer sessions, demonstrations, and individual and group projects. A more detailed list of activities is discussed later in this chapter.

Figure 13.3. A hierarchy of activities suitable for videoconferences (adapted from Cole et al 2004)

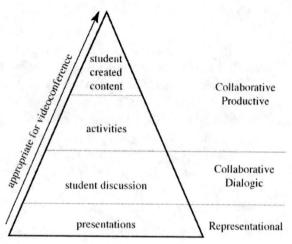

The Document Camera

The document camera can be used for many things, for example, illustrations from books; cartoons; diagrams and charts; photos; semantic maps/concept maps; and slates (develop a graph, chart, or diagram). Although they are called document cameras they can be used to capture images of small objects such as samples of rocks, chemicals, circuit boards, or small demonstrations. The document camera can also be used as a clock to let students know how much time is left for a group or individual activity. Preparing documents that will be successfully displayed by the document camera differs from preparing handouts. Possibly the biggest difference is that, although the camera can capture a full document in portrait, or vertical orientation, this is not an effective or efficient use of the camera (see Figure 13.4). A better approach is to prepare documents in landscape, or horizontal format, which is closer to the aspect ratio of the screens on which it will be viewed. There are a number of sources that advise of minimum fonts sizes to deliver readable text at the endpoints. Rather than prescribe a minimum font size, as methods of compression improve and resolution increases, a better solution is to run some tests with the equipment you will be using.

Video Sources

While video can obviously be played and transmitted via videoconference there are a few considerations that must be remembered if it is to be used effectively. Com-

Figure 13.4. Preparing documents for the document camera

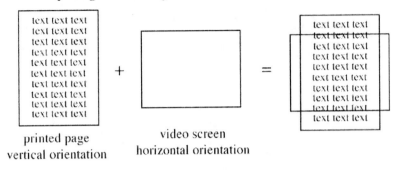

printed page
vertical orientation

video screen
horizontal orientation

mercially produced, or DIY video can be valuable media for learning resources. However, transmitting video via videoconference can be problematic for technical or legal reasons. Often commercially produced video has fast moving action, camera movement, and fast edits. All of which cause the compression process to work extremely hard. If the movements exceed the ability of the compression software and hardware the result can be that the transmitted video will be distorted, consist of still frames or a blank screen. Always use a test transmission of the video prior to the teaching session. In some countries it is illegal to transmit commercially produced video via videoconference. Where this is the case some teachers purchase multiple copies of the video and distribute them to students through their library extension programs.

The Computer

With a computer connected to the videoconference technology a wide range of images can be transmitted. For example, PowerPoint slides, photos, charts, tables, and spreadsheets (note about resolution at the far end being less than at near end—test beforehand to check it will work).

Planning for a Videoconference

Careful preparation can often determine the success of a videoconference. There are a number of practical details that are best organized well in advance of the scheduled conference. The contact details, such as who is going to call whom; the address or number and protocol of the other party; or the MCU need to be readily available. Also, it is a good idea to know where the local technical support staff will be and to have phone numbers for the technical support people at the other end or ends. For first time connections a test before the videoconference is highly recommended. Through testing issues like firewall traversal and mismatches of quality can be resolved.

The Agenda

Effective teaching and learning videoconferences often include a variety of activities and inputs. To keep the conference on track it may be a good idea to write and distribute an agenda. Students' names can be added to agenda items that they will conduct and in this way all know beforehand what will happen. The agenda can then serve the purpose of an advance organizer and thus increase the efficiency of videoconferences by:

- Announcing the aims and objectives of the videoconference
- Outlining the structure and designate who is responsible for each item
- Grouping material into points or chunks
- Indicating the relative importance of the points
- Providing bridges and links between the points
- Providing sample questions
- Summarizing

As well as an agenda, prepare a handout that explains the protocols for the activities that will be undertaken and the limitations videoconference puts on communications.

Preparing Students

Students who are new to videoconference often bring to the videoconference a television viewing mindset. These expectations need to be changed if learning is to be effective. To do this the teacher must clearly communicate the learning objectives to students and the proposed ways in which they will be achieved. This can be reinforced by the agenda, however, statements to students at beginning such as "you will be expected to…" make it clear that students are expected to actively participate in the videoconference activities rather than passively receive it. If students are opened up to the best ways to use the technology it can become clear that this is not television and should be approached differently.

Challenge students to optimize the camera settings (zoom, pan tilt) for the best communications. Explain that the image is compressed and hence not the same as television. Further the differences between television and videoconference can be highlighted through reminding students of the high costs of television which fosters production values that are not achievable in videoconference. These serve to emphasize the difference between the two technologies. Television is a one-way technology and videoconference is two-way and its purpose is to facilitate communications between participants. A good way to prepare students is with a test videoconference. This will give them opportunities to get used to the camera and the microphone, to see and hear what other participants look and sound like and by extension understand what they will look like to the other participants. Ask students to use the remote control to set up preset shots of themselves. In the previous chapter the relationship between shot sizes and communications was discussed. Draw this relationship to students' attention and be ready to advise them on appropriate shot size. Where possible arrange for students to see the compressed images that they are sending. Sometimes fast movements pose a problem for the codec and result in jerky movements referred to as stutter vision. You may need to modify your movements and ask student to modify theirs if stutter vision is a problem. Ask them to consider how they can move on camera to minimize distraction.

Another way to help students get used to the communicative nature of videoconference is to use it for purposes other than just class times. If the videoconference is used for student consultation or *office hours* students quickly become familiar with the conversational, two-way style that works so well with videoconference.

The test videoconference will also prepare participants for the audio component. In high bandwidth videoconferences with high quality codec audio is generally fully duplex. Fully duplex refers to the capacity for audio to be delivered in both directions at once. If audio is not duplex, only one person can speak at a time, and if two parties speak at once no one is heard. Some cell phones do not support full duplex. During the test videoconference a number of organizational details can be tested. Nametags can be tested for legibility, different arrangements of the room can be tried out, and students can experiment with use of the mute button on the microphone as a way to manage activities and reduce the amount of background noise sent to the other participants.

Videoconference in Large, Medium, and Small Teaching Spaces

In the previous chapter when the technology of videoconference was discussed, different configurations of the technology were suggested for large and medium teaching spaces. In large videoconference teaching spaces the presenter is generally very much more aware of the large number of local students and while it is not recommended the reality is that the experience of students at the videoconference endpoints is often limited to the simple observation of the interactions between the teacher and the local students. This compares to the small spaces such as designated videoconference rooms in which the focus, starting with the name of the room is on the students who are connected by videoconference. Medium-sized spaces often present the greatest opportunities for teaching with videoconference as they often can be easily configured to suit a range of activities. If the furniture can be moved around, different work areas can be established for small groups including groups made up of students at different endpoints and hosted by the videoconference.

Videoconference Activities for Large Teaching Spaces

There are many learning activities or teaching methods that are suitable for videoconference. All of them either rely on, or are adapted to the two-way nature of the technology and hence contain high levels of interaction between the connected parties. Some of them are described hereafter.

The Lecture

In the age of constructivism and post-constructivism many teachers have reconsidered the role of the lecture in higher education. However, a well prepared and delivered lecture can be an effective learning activity to deliver a large amount of material in a short period of time. Lectures can be a good way to introduce a new subject or topic and work well with highly motivated students who are used to learning this way. However, lectures are predominantly one-way and videoconference is a two-way technology. So it would appear that lectures are not an appropriate learning activity for videoconference. However, if they are broken down into small chunks with opportunities for interaction in between, lectures can be appropriate learning activities for videoconference. The activities that can be used in conjunction with lectures are many. Things that ask students to connect to what has been said with their own experience or to contrast it to their own opinions work well when undertaken in small groups. An example could be as simple as asking students to compare their own attitudes, beliefs, or ideas with the person sitting next to them. Of course questioning is the time-honored method of breaking up presentations. In a lecture theater often eye contact and body language provide feedback to the teacher on the degree to which students are engaged with what is being presented. In a videoconference this visual feedback is often less clear or unavailable. Directing questions to students at other endpoints can not only elicit the feedback needed but can help those students to feel part of the larger, local class. Open questions serve little purpose in this context and can often lead to no response, so rather than blanket statements of "any questions?" direct specific questions to key students in the videoconference audience. For example, "Mary at Springfield can you tell me of an experience you've had that relates to ....?" Directing questions to individuals also lets the other participants know that a question might be directed to them and hence puts then on notice. Of course all the attributes that make a face-to-face lecture better, enthusiasm, pacing, variety, and so forth also make a videoconference better.

Expert Presentations

Lectures can also be used for expert presentations. In the previous chapter the reduction in costs of international videoconferences was mentioned as videoconferences change from ISDN to the Internet. With ISDN the costs were such that it was only rarely affordable to bring an international or external expert into the classroom with videoconference. With the Internet this is now more easily afforded and the challenge has generally changed from affordability to one of time zones. The experts or celebrities in the area being taught may be those who are undertaking groundbreaking research or who have international reputations. These experts can make an impact on learning and motivate students even though they are busy and the budget may be limited. They can bring the latest developments or special skills into the classroom through videoconference. Prepare the expert presenter as much as possible beforehand. As well as organizing the technical details and the time, provide them with information about the students or the audience and the learning objectives. A demonstration of the videoconference technology will reduce their apprehension if they are not familiar with it and agree on a format for the videoconference. For example, if they are not comfortable with presenting about their work suggest an interview style. Develop a rapport with the guest who may not be used to talking to large groups of students and make them as comfortable as possible. Also agree with them beforehand on how and when questions from students will be handled. Ask the guest if they are happy to take questions from students during the videoconference or if they would prefer to have them beforehand. Ask them also if they would prefer the teacher to act as chairperson or will students ask their questions directly to the guest?

As well as preparing the guest, to optimize the session, also prepare the students. Give them salient biographical information about the celebrity guest and outline how they and their work connect with the course being studied. This may be best done as a handout or e-mail message to the class. Ask students and maybe guide them in the preparation of questions to put to the guest. If there are students connecting to the lecture by videoconference, asking one at each endpoint to act as speaker for the group can create the role of coordinator at each location and make for smooth interactions.

Two Can Be Better Than One

While an expert guest can connect the course to new and real events having two (or more) experts in the one session can create a rich interaction for students. Having two presenters not only shares the load but also can present to students differing views and approaches. Hence it is possible for students to hear and see more than one point of view. Whether the experts agree or disagree does not matter so long as students have the opportunity to interact with both guests. An alternative to an informal structure is to use a debate format if the guests disagree. Clearly if the guests disagree vehemently having them separated by videoconference can provide an incentive for them to develop very precise arguments. With multiple guests a conversational approach can work well by providing variety as the speaker changes from one guest to the other and to the teacher. However, it must be remembered to clearly identify each guest and the position they are taking so that confusion is avoided.

In the previous chapter, the technologies videoconference and video chat were compared. While they are functionally similar the low cost of video chat makes it even easier to connect to guests as they do not have to travel to a designated video-conference room. They can connect from a computer. Most multipoint videoconference technology is capable of connecting videoconferences and video chat so long as the video chat software complies with the appropriate standard.

Other Activities and Student Representatives

Other activities that are suitable for large teaching spaces include student presentations, debates, interviews, panel discussions, and games. In very large classes, where it is not feasible to get microphones to each student, it is often practical to have student representatives act as speakers for groups of students who share the same point of view or attitude. In this way students serve as audience representatives. The representatives do not need to be in the same location as those they represent so long as sufficient time and access to the technology has been previously allocated for briefing purposes. A session that includes student representatives can be structured in the following way. Firstly, the teacher sets up the topic or question to be discussed and ascertains the rough split of attitudes and opinions. Student representatives are then appointed or volunteer. Next, time is needed for students to brief their representatives. This part of the session will take some management. If more than one videoconference can be held at the same time then each group can brief its representative at the same time. However, this is often not possible and in cases like these setting up the briefing before hand can be a good idea. Student representatives can then either give short presentations, engage in a debate, or other activities

Videoconference in Medium and Small Teaching Spaces

Teaching with videoconference in small and medium spaces can be significantly different to large spaces as there is often more opportunity for group and individual activities. There are a number of configurations that can occur with small and medium spaces. For example:

- Multipoint or point to point?
- Are there local students or is the teacher by themselves?
- What are the student numbers at the other endpoints?
- What technology is available?

As mentioned earlier videoconference is a two-way technology, so it is no surprise that two-way activities are best suited to it. With students at endpoints it is possible to structure the dynamics between students so as to have two dimensions of interaction. Figure 13.5 illustrates these dimensions as interactivity between the whole class and interactivity between students at an endpoint.

Activities

There is a range of activities that can be undertaken with videoconference and lead to effective teaching and learning. As mentioned earlier presentations or lectures can be successful with videoconference if they are broken up by other activities. However, just as smaller face-to-face classes often have more flexibility for group and individual activities, videoconferences between small to medium groups can benefit from a range of group activities as well. In addition individual activities can be effective in small and medium settings.

Organizing Group Activities

Group activities have been used in teaching and learning for many years, and the principles that guide face-to-face group work, generally apply to videoconference group work. Depending on student numbers, each endpoint of the videoconference

Figure 13.5. Two dimensions of interactivity

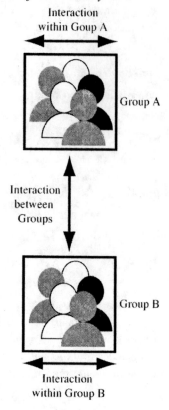

can be a group. In multipoint videoconferences individual groups can be formed at each location. However, if there are endpoints with only one or two participants a strategy to include them can be to use the videoconference link for one of the groups.

Group work needs to be carefully designed and planned so that students have a clear idea of what is required of them and have the skills to work cohesively. Group work also needs to be situated within the context of the course so that clear links between the activities and the learning objectives are available to all. Robust briefing and debriefing will go a long way towards successful group activities. In activities where groups produce materials, motivation levels can be increased through the announcement of plans to use the student-created materials as reference content for the course. Further, if students know that the materials they are creating will have a use other than assessment and be used by subsequent classes they are more likely to perform well as the work takes on a greater importance in their eyes.

Buzz Groups

Buzz groups are not new to teaching and learning. They have been used for many years in adult education and training. Buzz groups are generally small groups of students discussing or *buzzing* an aspect of a topic and are a good way to get them talking, sharing, thinking, and participating. For buzz groups to work well in videoconference clear instructions need to be given. The instructions need to cover the time limits, the report back time and, as the degree of lurking supervision is limited by the videoconference, specific instructions for the assignment to be undertaken by the buzz group need to be given and probably repeated. The instructions should preempt the deliverables that each buzz group is to develop. For example groups may be asked to:

- Develop one question,
- Make two suggestions, or
- List one advantage and one disadvantage of …

The instructions must also ask each group to allocate a recorder and a reporter so that both roles are prepared and the reporting of all groups can be as seamless as possible. If needed, each group can use the document camera to share points made during the reporting process. A typical structure of a buzz group session consists of the following steps:

- Explain the process—hand out instructions
- Form small groups
- Select or ask each group to select recorders and reporters (these can be the same person)
- Buzz for the designated time
- Ask reporter to report
- Debrief

Brainstorming

Another teaching and learning activity that transfers well to videoconference is brainstorming. Basically brainstorming is a method of solving a problem through the pooling of ideas. The quality of the ideas is not an issue during the brainstorm so quantity rather than quality is the driving force. The central concept of brainstorming is that the ideas suggested should not be evaluated until later. In this way ideas that on later analysis would be disregarded are available to stimulate other useful ideas. Participants need to be briefed to not evaluate ideas but to keep the flow of ideas as uninterrupted as possible. In face-to-face brainstorms, the ideas are written on a whiteboard, flipchart, or overhead projector slide so that all can see them. In videoconference brainstorms, the document camera can be used as the tool to record the ideas. Alternatively, a camera can be pointed at a whiteboard or a flipchart can serve the same purpose. In video chat a sharable electronic whiteboard such as those found in learning management systems can be used to record ideas.

Brainstorming may require some direction by the teacher to reduce the evaluation of ideas during the process of the brainstorm. An open and supportive atmosphere needs to be created with the teacher reminding participants not to evaluate ideas until the end of the session. Keep the brainstorming session short and if possible do not evaluate the ideas straight away so that there is no expectation of evaluation during the process. Brainstorming is good way to stimulate creativity and participation within a dispersed group, connected by videoconference.

Case Studies

Case studies can be effective ways for students to apply what they have learned to real life. A case study should describe a problem in sufficient detail so that the group can work together to analyze the problem and recommend a suitable remedy. In fact case studies can be used to evaluate different solutions to the same problem. Case studies usually have three elements: a scenario, supporting materials, and the problem. The scenario is the statement of the real world problem. Sometimes the problem may be simplified and usually the names of individuals and/or organizations are removed. The supporting materials are often documents but can be Web pages, media files, or tables of data. Where possible they should be authentic. The problem should be an open-ended one in which students develop a solution as well as a supporting argument. Case studies scenarios are usually paper based and case studies can be conducted with videoconferences if the materials are distributed beforehand. Alternatively, the scenario can be delivered verbally via the videoconference link and students then divided into to groups to use the (previously distributed) supporting materials to come up with a solution and supporting argument. Reporters from each group can then use the videoconference to share their group's response with the whole class. While the process of a case study is a worthwhile learning activity it is also a starting point for what can be a rich discussion of the problem and the proposed solutions. The discussion can involve the whole class again linked by videoconference.

Role Plays

Role plays provide opportunities for students to explore new behaviors in an environment where the consequences of mistakes are limited. The outcomes of a successful role play can range from a solution to a real world problem through to a deep understanding of those with different beliefs, mores, knowledge, and attitudes. Role plays are short dramatic enactments of interactions between humans in which students take on the role of some one different to them. They are challenged to consider how the role they are playing would react in the described scenario. As such role plays are good techniques for the development students' interpersonal skills. Typically there are three parts to role plays in teaching and learning. Firstly the students need to be briefed. The goals and objectives must be set, the rules of the role play made clear, the roles need to be assigned, and time limits set. Secondly the role play is conducted. Thirdly the debriefing session involving the whole group evaluates what was successful and what was not and connections are made to the learning objectives. Videoconference and video chat can be used in a number of ways to host role plays. Roles may be preassigned to individuals or to small groups of individuals. Successful role plays have been conducted with the group at each endpoint jointly playing one role. It is possible to assign roles at the beginning of the teaching term and have a number of role plays through the term. While the roles are preassigned, the scenario for each role play can be provided verbally on the spot or delivered beforehand to suit the learning objectives.

Debates

Debating is a time-honored method for teaching and learning about controversy. Students taking part in the debate as well as those observing can acquire critical thinking and analysis skills and an appreciation of conflicting viewpoints. As the debating process is firmly based on argumentation, it is an excellent opportunity to develop reasoning skills, communication skills, analysis of multiple relationships, and consideration of multiple perspectives. Debating involves the use of arguments to put and defend a position and as such is best applied to topical or controversial subjects, dilemmas, legal, or ethical problems. Traditionally debating in teaching and learning has three distinct phases. Firstly, before the debate, teams of usually two or three students are formed. The teams select, or are assigned, a side of an argument to prepare. As they will need to articulate their position and argue against the other team they need to be prepared on both sides and all aspects of the argument. Where appropriate, students can prepare visual materials to supplement their arguments. This preparation must be done before the debating session except in special classes where the prime learning objective is to teach students how to think on their feet, for example, in preparing students for court room practice. When the debate happens the teams must be given a set time in which to present the three elements of the debate. The elements are the opening argument, the rebuttal of the opposing team's opening argument, and closing summary. Debates work best when a timekeeper enforces strict time limits. Like several other activities mentioned earlier, the learning opportunities of the debate are shared between the process itself and the discussion or other activities that follow. A post debate activity can explore not only the topic argued but also the process and quality of the arguments. Debates can work very well with videoconference and video chat. Like role plays and case studies, debating teams can be located at different endpoints or can consist of students at different endpoints. The timekeeper, teacher, and other students can be at any endpoint. Of course, departure from the traditional format of the debate can provide further opportunities, for example, allowing questions from students in the audience or stopping the clock to draw students' attention to a particular element of a presentation.

Individual Activities

Just as there are many individual activities that students can undertake in a classroom, there are similar activities that work well with videoconferences. Many of these activities involve a component of student presentation. Presentations by single students or groups of students are great ways to share the teaching of the subject while providing students with an opportunity to present to their peers. Presenting gives students an opportunity to practice their communications and presentation skills, to become familiar with presentation software such as PowerPoint, and to become generally more at ease with the idea of speaking in public. As many jobs for graduates require them to give presentations to their colleagues and superiors, presenting to fellow students is a valuable activity. Also, many businesses use videoconference, and video chat is becoming an important business communications tool, so the experience is worthwhile. For students to be successful they will need the time and opportunity to test videoconference communications, their slides, and the other materials they prepare.

If possible student presentations should be recorded. A recording of a presentation provides students with the chance to review and self-evaluate. The teacher can view their own presentations for the same purpose and viewing recorded student presentations is often a better way to assess them. Also, if the recorded material is satisfactory it can be stored in a content management system and reused as a teaching resource for later classes.

Electronic Field Trips

Electronic field trips have been used in K-12 education for a number of years. They generally link the classroom to experts in the field via a videoconference. While benefits in reducing travel time, avoiding dangerous environments, and impacting negatively on them are clear, they are yet to have a large role in higher education. Another type of videoconference field trip can be achieved through connecting with another videoconference class at another institution. This can provide richer and more diverse interactions and when used between cultures is a cost-effective cultural exchange tool.

During the Videoconference

There are a number of things a teacher can do during a videoconference to increase effectiveness. Just as a teacher often needs to encourage participation in face-to-face discussions and activities, the same can be true of videoconferences. The teacher needs to find ways to engage students and to encourage them to engage and communicate with each other. Videoconference sessions should be structured with ample opportunities for students to talk formally and informally. If there is a break in the class leave the conference link connected and suggest to students that they use it. Where possible involve as many participants as possible in the first five minutes of the conference even in an ice-breaking activity. This can serve to create the feeling of inclusion, particularly of students at the remote endpoints. As mentioned earlier, the use of questions directed to particular students can ensure that even the quietest student has a role in the videoconference. Also asking a particular student if they have a question can elicit a question that others in the class may have as well. When answering questions there is a trick about how to appear to give eye contact to the students as in a classroom. While it is natural to look at the image of the students on the screen if you look into the camera it will appear to them that you are looking into their eyes. When the question has been answered ask the student if there is anything else and then bring the session back to the whole group by throwing it open, ask another question, or ask other students to elaborate or comment.

If the numbers of students at each endpoint are not too great ask the students to introduce themselves. While they do this draw a simple map of each endpoint, including the students' names. The resulting *mud map* can be used later in the class to direct questions to and seek comments from particular students. An alternative is to use nametags. As mentioned earlier another role the teacher needs to undertake is the management of the videoconference activities. Draw students' attention to the agenda and be clear in handing over from one activity to the next. In this way the videoconference will appear more cohesive and seamless. Also, student activities need managing. Often student activities can be noisy and the mute buttons on microphones may need to be used to keep audio to a reasonable level.

Recording Videoconferences

Today the technology exists to record videoconferences and make the recordings available via the Internet. No longer do videoconferences have to be ephemeral. They can be used for review and for students who missed the session. However recordings of videoconferences do not equate to being there and certainly do not come close to the experience of participating in an effective videoconference. It is recommended that the use and availability of recordings of videoconferences be carefully monitored so that recordings are not viewed as an alternative to attending. A logical but absurd outcome could be the recording of a videoconference with no participants.

Conclusion

Videoconference and video chat are both two-way technologies that can, if used appropriately bring rich discussions and interactions to distance and e-learning by reducing transactional distance. There are many educational uses of videoconference and now that the Internet can be used, the costs of connection have fallen significantly. Videoconference can be used to connect classrooms in different countries and enrich interactions through cultural diversity and as a way to continue the cultural richness of international exchange programs long after the students have returned home. They can also be used to bring experts in the field into the classroom from around the world. Videoconference and video chat can also be used for teaching activities that do not take place in a classroom. For example, students can collaborate on group projects outside of class times and thus complete projects in geographically dispersed groups. They can also be used for student consultation or office hours and for the supervision of honors, postgraduate, and research students. Videoconferences can be combined with face-to-face and other technologies to provide a rich and continuing learning experience for offshore classes

Video chat appears to be about to replace videoconference due to the simplicity of its hardware and its low cost. As business and private users embrace video chat as the prime technology for communications, and as video chat develops into enhanced video chat, the scope for two-way technology-mediated communications will increase. The near future will probably see video chat functionality added to learning management systems, which will pave the way for a range of activity templates which in turn will reduce the preparation load.

Videoconference and video chat are two-way learning technologies that can be used in many ways to achieve educational objectives. A newer and related technology is the Access Grid which is just entering the education arena. The technical aspects and the use of the Access Grid are discussed in the next chapter. With planning and some limited changes to the approach taken, these technologies can be rich and rewarding learning technologies for e-learning.

References

Caladine, R. (1999). *Teaching for flexible learning: Learning to apply the technology.* Monmouthshire, Wales: GSSE.

Cole, C., Ray, K., & Zanetis, J. (2004). *Videoconference for K-12 classrooms: A program development guide.* ISTE: Washington.

Daunt, C. (1997). Is teleteaching different? In J. Osborne et al. (Eds.), *Open, flexible and distance learning: Education and training for the 21st century.* Proceedings of the 13th Biennial Forum of ODLAA, Launceston, Australia.

Kobayashi, T., Tanaka, K., Yamaji, H., & Otsuka, Y. (1997). Crosscultural joint classes between Japan and Australia using ISDN. In J. Osborne et al. (Eds.), *Open, flexible and distance learning: Education and training for the 21st century.* Proceedings of the 13th Biennial Forum of ODLAA, Launceston, Australia.

Laurillard, D. (1993). *Rethinking university teaching: A framework for the effective use of learning technologies.* London: Routledge.

Mitchell, J. (1993). *Video-conferencing in higher education in Australia: An evaluation of the use and potential of video-conferencing facilities in the higher education sector in Australia.* Occasional Papers Series. Canberra, Australia: Department of Education, Employment and Training, Higher Education Division. Australian Government Printing Service.

Chapter XIV

Access Grid

Introduction

Videoconference has been used for interactions between students and teachers in distance education for many years. The newer technology, video chat, a computer-based technology that has evolved from instant messaging, appears to be displacing videoconference due to its low cost and ease of use. Access Grid is a similar technology in that like the other two it is based on two-way audio and video communications. Since its inception in the mid-1990s, the Access Grid has been used by researchers and it is not surprising that usage levels in teaching and learning are increasing as many researchers are teachers and see its potential to bring media-rich interactions to e-learning.

Definition

The Access Grid is a computer-based, high-bandwidth video and audio communications technology. It is differentiated from videoconference and video chat by several features. Firstly, the media richness of the environment, which is produced by multi-projector displays of multiple video and data streams. Secondly, multiple cameras capture multiple images of the local participants for transmission. Thirdly, integrated with the Access Grid software are a number of other software modules designed for application and file sharing. If it is assumed that online learning technologies are evolving in a similar direction to other online technologies, then it is reasonable to expect that interactions will increase and that the preferred media for them will change. It is expected that they will move from the solely text-based technologies of e-mail, chat, and discussion forums to media-rich technologies similar to video chat. Of course the text-based communications technologies will remain, just as most superseded technologies usually remain. Often they are used for different purposes and often the usage levels change. It is expected that video chat and Access Grid will both be used in distance education and e-learning for media-rich communications and interactions.

Description of the Access Grid

The Access Grid Experience

There are two basically different types of installation of the Access Grid, room-based nodes, and personal interfaces to the grid or PIGs. To experience the Access Grid in a room-based node is to sit in a room with other participants (perhaps one or two or up to 50). The lighting in the room will have been configured to light the participants without spilling to a large degree onto the large screen that runs the length of the front wall. Usually three projectors are used to create a wall of video on this screen with many windows. The windows may contain images of participants at other room-based nodes, shared files, and shared applications. Cameras are located around the room. Generally mounted to the walls or ceiling there can be three or four cameras to capture images of the participants in the room and perhaps a document camera. An example of a room layout is shown in Figure 14.1. The voices of the participants at other nodes on the Access Grid can be heard clearly through the loudspeakers in the room and microphones on the tables or desks in the room capture the voices of local participants. Echo canceling and noise filtering technology is located in the equipment rack to ensure the high quality of the audio transmitted and received. Also in the rack is the computer (or computers) that form the basis of the node. To experience the Access Grid in a room-based node is to experience the full multimedia potential of the Access Grid. However, if a room-based node is not available or not affordable, an alternative is to use a PIG.

A PIG, typically consists of a computer (either desktop or laptop), a Web camera, and a headset consisting of headphones and microphone (see Figure 14.2). PIGs do not need to be limited to this hardware configuration and a level of flexibility of nodes on the Access Grid exists. For example, adding a second screen and an echo-canceling microphone can convert a PIG into an expended personal access grid interface, suitable for two or three participants.

Unlike videoconference and similar to video chat the Access Grid is software based. The software is available for several computer platforms and perhaps the most attractive technological aspect of the Access Grid is that the software is open source and available for free simply by downloading it from the Web.

Software

The software for the Access Grid is open source and hence publicly available for download. At the time of writing versions exist for the Windows XP, Linux, and Mac OSX operating systems. The software has been written primarily in the python language and hence requires some python applications to be installed. These applications are also freely available from the Access Grid Web site. As the software is

Figure 14.1. Access grid room-based node: Layout

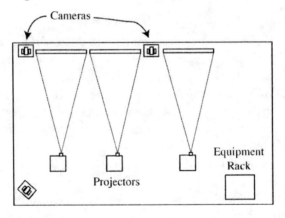

Figure 14.2. Personal and expanded interfaces to the grid

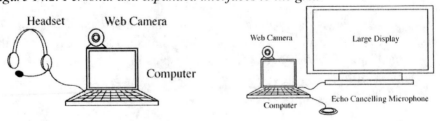

open source, development is constant and ongoing. Like most open source products the development is slower than a commercial product of equivalent complexity. However, as the developers are users, each version of the software performs more closely to the desires of users.

The software uses the metaphor of rooms or venues to which Access Grid nodes connect by clicking on an icon or entering the URL in the Venue Client. The Venue Client, as shown in Figure 14.3 is part of the graphic user interface of the Access Grid. The Venue Client is the window used to connect the node to a virtual venue. This navigation can be accomplished by inputting a URL or by clicking on the desired venue in a list on the left hand side. The Venue Client also contains a list of participants and links to some of the sharable software modules. A text chat area is located in the Venue Client and is often used during the connecting process or if network problems render the audio and video channel unusable.

The virtual rooms or venues are located on Access Grid servers and several popular servers are located around the world. The two most well known in the USA are at the National Center for Supercomputing Applications (NCSA) at the University of Illinois at Urbana Champagne and Argonne National Laboratory attached to the University of Chicago. The graphic user interface also includes windows for the audio controls, called robust audio tool (RAT) and the video controls called video conferencing tool (VIC). The RAT is an audioconference tool that contains the audio level controls and meters as well as indicating the connection status of participating nodes, as shown in Figure 14.4.

The VIC links multiple sites with multiple video streams and allows users to select the size of the displayed video. The images displayed in the VIC are thumbnails

Figure 14.3. The venue client

Figure 14.4. The RAT

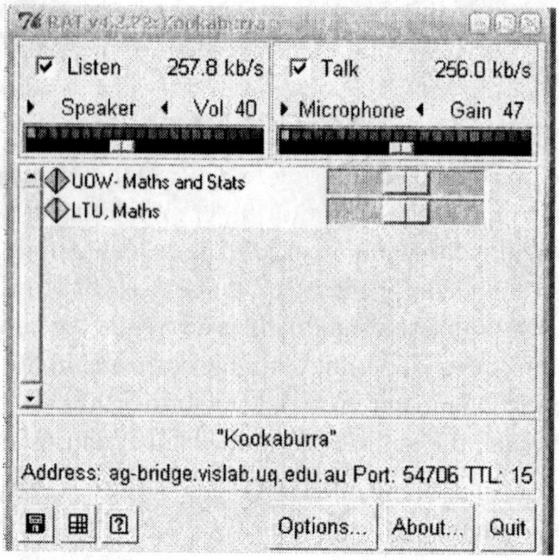

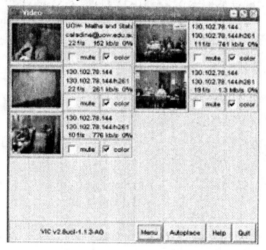

Figure 14.5 The VIC (Videoconference tool)

of the video streams being received. Clicking on a thumbnail produces a medium-sized window of that video stream. The window can be resized by highlighting the window and typing an *s* for small, *m* for medium, or *l* for large.

Multicast and Unicast

The Access Grid takes advantage of the Internet's multicast standard, thus keeping bandwidth to a minimum. Multicast enables servers and Internet routers to receive a single stream and forward it to multiple recipient routers or nodes. A simple analogy is sending an e-mail message to a list rather than to each recipient. With Access Grid multicast is used to allow several video streams to be sent to many receivers while minimizing the bandwidth used (as shown in Figure 14.6). Hence for the Access Grid to operate as efficiently as possible, multicast needs to be enabled on the network. This makes Access Grid more affordable and increases its suitability to academic and research networks.

A Comparison of Videoconference, Video Chat, and Access Grid

While Access Grid, video chat, and videoconference are similar in that they all facilitate the two-way exchange of video and audio, Access Grid can be differentiated by the ability to send and receive multiple video streams from each endpoint or *node* and the number of additional software modules that increase the functionality of the Access Grid. These modules include, shared presentation, shared browser, shared eWhiteboard, true application sharing, and many more. They are described in more detail later in this chapter. Some commercial products that claim to offer application sharing in fact use the term to describe a facility that allows files to be transferred between participants. True application sharing allows participants to work on the same file at the same time. The comparison of the three technologies is summarized in Table 14.1.

Figure 14.6. Multicast and unicast

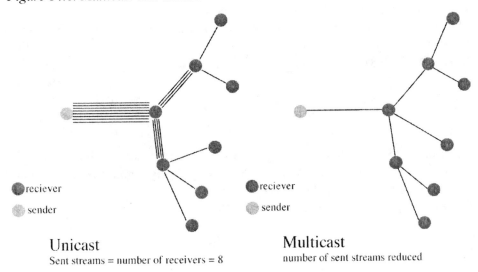

reciever

sender

reciever

sender

Unicast
Sent streams = number of receivers = 8

Multicast
number of sent streams reduced

Table 14.1. A comparison of some aspects of access grid, videoconference, and video chat

	Access Grid	Videoconference	Video Chat
Video	Multiple concurrent channels from each location	Single switchable channel from each location	Single channel from each location
Control of video position and size on display	Controlled by operator or students	Preset or controlled by operator	Fixed
Control of other location's cameras	Possible	Possible	No
True application sharing	Yes as part of the software	Requires parallel application	Requires parallel application

Equipment and Configurations

As mentioned, there are two basic configurations of nodes on the Access Grid, room-based nodes and PIGs. Room-based nodes take full advantage of the technology through multiple cameras and multiple projectors and PIGs provide a low cost alternative.

Room-Based Nodes

While there are no fixed rules regarding size, most room-based nodes on the Access Grid are designed to seat in the vicinity of 20 to 50 participants. The capacity of the room depends largely on the planned usage. If the room is to be mainly used for giving or receiving presentations then a larger capacity probably represents a better return on investment. However, smaller groups of users can take advantage of the collaborative elements of the Access Grid in a more equitable manner with all getting a chance for hands on, in a smaller capacity room. Most room-based nodes use three projectors to create a display wall, and a fourth screen for the operator. However, the flexibility of the installation generally allows the operational elements of the graphic user interface to be placed on any screen. For example, when students are operating, the control items are placed where all can see and interact with them.

The cameras to capture the local participants are generally located on the front wall of the room and are operated by remote control. Typically they are set to auto focus and auto exposure, leaving the pan, zoom, and tilt controls available to the operator or the participants. Also, often a camera is located to one side or in a back corner of the room. This camera when left in a wide shot (or zoomed out) provides video of the whole room so that participants at other locations can see the layout of the room. A document camera can also be used to provide video of documents or small objects.

The use of the document camera differs little from its use in videoconference. See Chapter XIII for a discussion of the use of the document camera.

With video and data projection, and cameras in the same room, some attention needs to be paid to the lighting. The participants need to be sufficiently lit to provide the cameras with a good image yet too much light directly or reflected onto the screens will dilute the images of the projected video and data. Aesthetics can be important as well. For example, a plain background will create images of participants where the viewers' attention is less distracted by something in the background.

Additional Software Modules for the Access Grid

These software modules can add another layer of activity to teaching and learning interactions. Examples of the software modules include:

- Shared browser
- Shared presentation
- Use of pen stroke capture
- Shared eWhiteboard
- Shared desktop
- Shared movie viewer
- Camera controller

The Shared Browser

The shared browser is included with the Access Grid software and can be opened by clicking on the appropriate menu and dragging down to the shared browser item. This creates an item in the main window of the Venue Client under the Applications Sessions button. The item will be called Shared Browser followed by the date and time. Participants right click and drag down to Open in the pop up menu to open the shared browser. This opens a browser widow that can be accessed by each party connected to the Access Grid venue at that time.

The Shared Presentation

The shared presentation tool can be operated in a similar fashion to the Shared Browser. When users right click on the item under the Application Session button and select Open the presentation will be displayed. Any participant can take control of the presentation.

Pen Stroke Capture and Shared eWhiteboard

The eWhiteboard is a projected image of a computer-hosted whiteboard that can be shared just as desktops and applications are shared. The pen-stroke capture technology can be of the sensitive whiteboard type or the stylus and receiver type. The sensitive whiteboard system is a pressure sensitive whiteboard that conveys electronic impulses to the connected computer to indicate where the pen (or finger as pressure is all that is required) is on the board. The stylus and receiver technology relies on a transmitting device fitted to a stylus or whiteboard marker that sends a signal to a receiver, generally attached to the side or corner of the whiteboard. The receiver is connected to a computer and sends the location of the pen or stylus to it. When the eWhiteboard software is shared between connected nodes of the Access Grid, and if each node has pen stroke capture or sensitive whiteboard technology then participants at any connected node can *write* on the board with the stylus and the image will be seen by all. In this way the eWhiteboard can be used as a collaborative electronic canvas.

Shared Desktop

The shared desktop allows any participant, with the appropriate permissions, in the Access Grid session to take control of the desktop of any other connected partici-

Figure 14.7. The Control panel for shared desktop

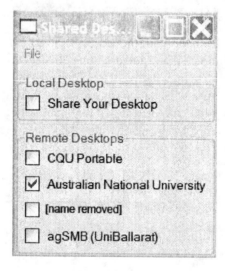

pant. For example, in a computer programming class the teacher can take control of a student's computer desktop (at another location) and show it to the rest of the connected participants and comment on or perhaps correct the code. The on-screen control panel for the shared desktop is shown in Figure 14.7.

Camera Controller

With a software module called AG device control, participants at one location may take control of the cameras at another connected node. In this way they can optimize the video images they receive.

The Role of the Operator

As mentioned earlier, the Access Grid software is open source and hence free to download from the Web. It was also mentioned that the development curve for open source software is often flatter than that of equivalent commercial products. Combining with the flatness of the development curve with the complexity of the Access Grid software, has resulted in many installations of room-based nodes having an operator on hand to optimize the experience and to ensure minimal down time. The operator has a number of duties that include, starting the computer and equipment in the node, making the connection to the desired virtual venue, monitoring connections and audio levels, and troubleshooting. The operator can also set up shots of the local participants with the remote control for the cameras in the room and they can organize the size and position of the images of the remote parties on the projected display.

In some situations the effectiveness of learning with the Access Grid can be enhanced if students can control the cameras and the displays. By controlling the cameras they control the images they send from the node to the virtual venue. For example, they may choose a close shot of a presenter and a wider shot of the other participants. They should be encouraged to change shot sizes during the Access Grid session to reflect the changing activities. If students are in control of the display they can position and size the video and data windows to optimize their learning experience. For example, they may select a medium-sized shot of a remote participant working on a whiteboard and position it adjacent to the images from the pen-stroke capturing whiteboard. In this way they can see the body language of the person writing in the board in the video window and see what's being written next to it. Figure 14.8 shows a possible arrangement of the display elements. On the left hand side is the shared eWhiteboard, in the center is a shared file, and the images of the participants are on the right hand side. Medium size has been selected for the images from the remote

Figure 14.8. Access grid display: E-whieboard, shared file, and participants

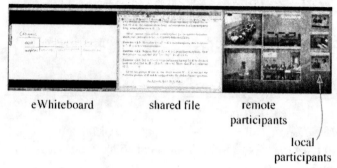

eWhiteboard   shared file   remote
                                          participants

                                              local
                                          participants

Figure 14.9. Access grid display: Document camera and participants

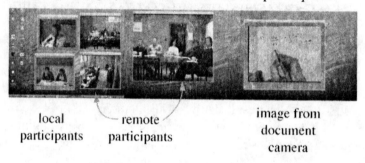

local   remote   image from
participants   participants   document
                                    camera

site and small has been selected for the local participants. Figure 14.9 shows the arrangement of the display elements for a different Access Grid session in which a local participant is teaching using a document camera.

Teaching with Access Grid

The Access Grid has only been used sparingly in teaching and learning and hence it is too early in its history for significant literature, if any to have developed. This makes it more difficult to classify the technology by the learning technology model (LTM). However, as the Access Grid is similar to videoconference in functionality, a comparison of the technologies can be used as a starting point for its classification. A full comparison of Access Grid, videoconference, and video chat is provided in Chapter XV. The comparison provides the rationale for installations that use combinations of Access Grid, video chat, and videoconference as different learning technologies for different teaching and learning tasks. It is recommended that the technologies serve three slightly different pedagogical purposes. Access Grid is a high-end technology and is designed for use primarily in room-based nodes in which students use the additional software modules to participate in media-rich collaborations. On the other hand video chat is a low cost, simple technology that is flexible enough to be installed on students' laptops and used from home, work, or on campus. As the technology of video chat is simpler it is suggested that it be used predominantly for collaborative-dialogic interactions and that Access Grid be used more for collaborative-productive interactions. The productive learning activities facilitated by the Access Grid are largely made possible through the software modules described in the previous section.

Access Grid and the Learning Technologies Model

The Access Grid is based on two-way audio and video communications and as mentioned previously can be used as a collaborative-productive learning technology of level three capabilities. Clearly it is a synchronous technology as all parties are connected at the same time. While there is technology available to record Access Grid sessions, its primary use is synchronous. Like videoconference the Access Grid can introduce a degree of flexibility in place, location, or where students learn. As mentioned earlier the use of the Access Grid in teaching and learning does not have sufficient history to have generated sufficient literature to inform usage as categorized in the learning activities model (LAM). However, as a collaborative-productive or collaborative-dialogic technology it obviously supports the categories, *interactions between learners* (IL) and *interactions with the facilitator* (IF) of learning. Furthermore when students are immersed into an Access Grid teaching and learning environment with multiple video windows and sharable applications such as eWhiteboard, it is suggested that limited presentations probably can be effective teaching and learning activities. Hence the *provision of materials* (PM) and *interaction with materials* (IM) have been added to the LAM for the Access Grid. The Access Grid as represented in the LTM is shown in Table 14.2.

In the previous chapter teaching with videoconference and video chat were discussed. Access Grid is functionally similar to videoconference and video chat, as all three technologies support two-way video and audio communications. Hence it would be reasonable to expect that the activities and approaches mentioned in the last chapter will, in the main, successfully transfer to Access Grid. However, there are many aspects and features of Access Grid that differentiate it from videoconference and video chat, and these aspects impact on teaching and learning with it. Firstly,

Table 14.2. The LTM: Access Grid

Access Grid
Collaborative-productive, level 3
Synchronous
Flexibility-place (some)
Learning activities model (LAM) Suitable categories: Interaction between learners (IL) Interaction with facilitator (IF) Provision of materials (PM) Interaction with materials (IM)

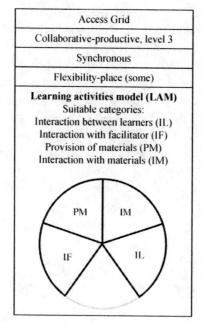

room-based nodes on the Access Grid transmit up to four (or more) video streams thus providing up to at least four times the visual information of a videoconference or video chat. A further differentiation then occurs when the controls of the Access Grid node are placed into the hands of the students. They can move the incoming video windows around the video display wall and resize them to optimize the visual message. Further, as mentioned, there are a number of software modules that can be added to an Access Grid node.

Another differentiation is that additional software modules can facilitate true application sharing. Some commercially available products claim they support application or file sharing when in reality they have a file transfer mechanism built in. In true application sharing students at each node connected to the Access Grid session can work on the one document, spreadsheet, image, or file in real time. Some of the software modules include a control device so that participants can hand control of the application between themselves just as when working on the same computer students will hand over the keyboard and the mouse.

Teaching and Learning Activities

The activities mentioned in the last chapter as being suited to videoconference and video chat are all likely to be suitable for teaching and learning with the Access Grid. In many of the activities, the multiple streams available with the Access Grid will add an extra dimension of richness and variety to the experience. The activities include, but are not limited to:

- Expert presentation
- Experts
- Buzz groups
- Brainstorming
- Case studies
- Role plays
- Debate

Just as planning for the videoconference was emphasized, planning for Access Grid is essential to ensure effective learning. An agenda of activities, complete with names of participants and presenters will help to keep the session on track and on time. While the technical similarities between videoconference, video chat, and Access Grid have been identified and thus indicate their suitability for similar teaching and learning activities, there are activities possible with Access Grid that are difficult or impossible with the other two technologies. Most of these involve the additional software modules mentioned earlier.

Using the Additional Software Modules in Teaching and Learning

Probably the simplest of the additional software modules is the shared desktop. While simple it has a plethora of uses. As mentioned previously it can be used to share the teacher's or a student's desktop with the rest of the group. In this way a dynamic demonstration can be delivered to students from the teacher's desktop accompanied by the teacher's voice and image. Alternatively, the teacher can take control of a student's desktop and use it to demonstrate a learning point, or students could use the shared desktop to show project works to the rest of the class. Sharing desktops also can be used for collaboration on the construction of content. Students can use any software suitable for the platform to create reports, spreadsheets, images, media, and so on. The content is constructed in real time with collaboration from all connected parties by video and audio. In order to mange the collaboration a protocol similar to handing over the keyboard and mouse needs to be adopted.

Perhaps one of the more useful teaching and learning activities made possible by the Access Grid comes about when shared eWhiteboards are used. When pen stroke capture or sensitive whiteboard technology is combined with the shared eWhiteboard software, a very powerful teaching and learning application of the Access Grid is created. Students and/or the teacher can write on the eWhiteboard at any location connected to the Access Grid venue and the drawn information will appear at all connected sites. In this way a teacher at one location can write notes that are seen at all connected locations. They can then invite a student at any of the locations to write on the eWhiteboard which again will be seen by all. In this way the eWhiteboard can become a collaborative electronic canvas.

A Hierarchy of Appropriate Activities for Teaching and Learning with the Access Grid

A hierarchy of activities that are suitable for teaching and learning with the Access Grid is shown in Figure 14.10. The hierarchy is based on a similar relationship between teaching and learning activities and videoconference or video chat. However, due to the increased media-richness of Access Grid it is suggested that a higher degree of presentation or one-way activities can be undertaken with Access Grid

Figure 14.10. A hierarchy of appropriate activities (adapted from Cole et al 2004)

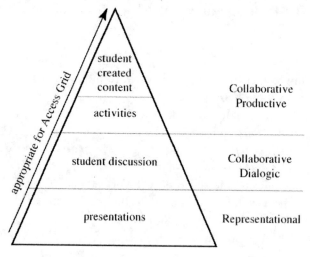

and still result in effective learning. This is reflected the base layer of the hierarchy being thicker than that for videoconference and video chat.

In Chapter XI the hypothetical concept of a continuum of learning activities was introduced. The pole at one end of the continuum represents a learning event that consists of solely one-way learning activities and at the other end, two-way learning activities. At some location along the continuum the threshold for effective learning with a learning technology can be located. It is suggested that below the threshold the effectiveness of learning diminishes due to lack of two-way activities such as interaction between learners and interaction with the facilitator of learning. For the reasons described previously, media-richness, student control, and additional software modules, it is reasonable to assume that the threshold for Access Grid will be lower on the continuum than that for videoconference and video chat. That is the threshold will be closer to the one-way end of the continuum.

Setting Up a Room-Based Node on the Access Grid: A Case Study

In early 2005 a funding opportunity was provided to use the Access Grid in teaching and learning. The opportunity was offered by the Australian government through an Australian professional body and was to meet the problem of small student numbers in postgraduate mathematics and statistics subjects. The following case study details the establishment of a room-based node on the Access Grid and its use for teaching and learning.

Background

Most, if not all, of the 40 universities in Australia offer studies in mathematics at the honors and postgraduate levels. However, student numbers attracted to these subjects are sufficiently small to render them inefficient to run. At one Australian university class sizes of one or two were not uncommon and apparently the numbers at the other Australian universities were similar. With numbers this low the courses faced extinction unless another teaching and learning rationale could be found.

Technology was seen as a solution if it could be used to connect students at different universities and thereby increase the numbers in each class. If the technology was two-way, academics at any of the participating universities could teach classes of students from their own university and students at a number of others. Also if the courses were organized for reciprocity then the teaching load would be reduced. For example, a teacher at university A, teaches subject X to students at universities A, B, and C and teachers at

Figure 14.11. Teaching across institutions

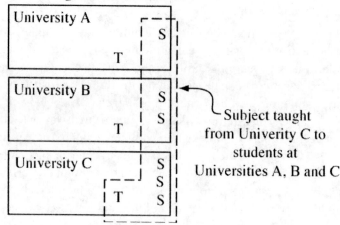

universities B and C teach subjects Y and Z to students at the three universities. In this way one academic at each university is teaching only one subject, yet three subjects are being offered at each university. Figure 14.11 is a graphic representation of a subject taught at university C to students at universities A, B, and C. With cross-institution teaching, student numbers in honors subjects have more than doubled.

Of course the reciprocity is not limited to three collaborators but at the time of writing the project was in its first semester and only three universities were participating. Plans are in place for this number to increase in subsequent semesters. There would be other benefits to this approach to cross-institution teaching and learning. For example, students could audit subjects at other universities while deciding on their own postgraduate studies program. Another benefit of the project is the provision of opportunities for mathematicians and statisticians at different universities to use the technology to collaborate on research. Overall the goals of the project were to:

- Increase efficiency of teaching and learning in higher education.
- Maintain (or increase) the diversity of subjects taught.
- Develop a nexus between research and teaching/learning.
- Enrich research through providing opportunities for collaboration.

The application for funding was successful and the project for inter-institutional teaching and learning of mathematics and statistics with the Access Grid commenced.

The Funding Application

The funding application was in three parts, an outline of the proposed physical resources, an outline of the proposed academic program including proposed subjects, and an equipment list with budget.

The physical resources centered around a room in the Department of Mathematics and Statistics. It is approximately 7.5 meters long and 5 meters wide. The room has an abundance of general power outlets and network points. The room comfortably accommodates up to 15 participants when used as an Access Grid room. One of the long walls was used for the projection screens. The walls are of brick, the ceiling suspended and the floor carpeted. The existing furniture consisted of floating desks and student chairs. These will be evaluated for use in the Access Grid room activities. The original lighting was fluorescent. Low voltage, quartz-halogen, down-lights were installed to provide an area of adequate light levels for the capture of good video images, while minimizing spill and reflection onto the screens The light from the windows along the south wall was regulated by Venetian blinds. Curtains were installed to further control the light and to reduce acoustic distortion and noise. The room is air conditioned. The air conditioning unit produces low levels of noise that can be adequately treated by the noise filter in the echo-cancellation hardware.

Originally there was a large whiteboard on one end wall. Three additional screens were purchased and installed one of which was a matte finished whiteboard. The whiteboard surface is necessary to cater to the stylus used in the shared eWhiteboard. And a matte finish minimized the reflection from the projector.

Figure 14.12. The layout of the access grid room

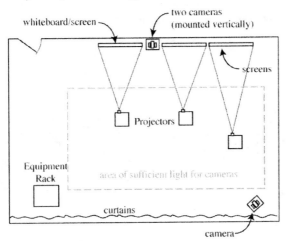

Figure 14.13. Cross section of the access grid room

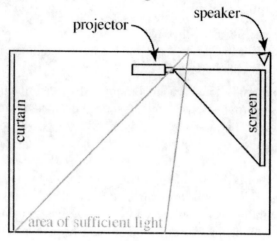

Equipment

A room-based node on the Access Grid contains audio visual and computing equipment. The audio visual equipment captures the sounds and images of local participants and displays the sounds and images of the remote participants. It also captures images of documents and displays computer images. The computer at the heart of the Access Grid contains the software and hardware to operate the room-based node. A full equipment list is provided in Table 14.3.

Cameras

Three Sony EDI-100 cameras were installed to capture video of local participants. Two were mounted vertically between the screens as shown in Figure 14.12 The third was mounted at the rear of the room to capture a wide-angle view of the room or alternatively, the image of a presenter. The cameras were installed on custom built brackets and operated with the supplied remote control. The remote control features a camera selection function that enables the selection of individual cameras. The cameras are used in auto-focus and auto-exposure modes. The operator or the participants can use the remote control to pan, tilt, and zoom the cameras. Also, an Elmo document camera is used to capture video of work on documents and small items. Composite video cables connect the four cameras to the video capture card in the Access Grid computer.

Projectors

Three, ceiling-mounted projectors were installed. The projectors are used to display:

- Participants at the local and other Access Grid nodes.
- High resolution images including shared applications.
- Medium resolution images for example projected whiteboard.

The projectors were controlled by a touch screen controller that communicates to the projectors using the RS-232 protocol. VGA cables connect the projectors to the two, graphics cards contained in the Access Grid computer.

Pen-Stroke Capture and eWhiteboard

A Mimio device was purchased and used to capture work on the projected eWhiteboard. To date the Mimio and eWhiteboard have been used as a shared eWhiteboard between participating nodes. The Mimio communicates with the Access Grid computer via a wireless connection.

Audio Equipment

Four Beyer dynamic microphones capture the audio of the participants. The microphones are of the boundary type and have adequate sensitivity to capture participants' voices up to several meters distant. The audio from the microphones is mixed and echo cancellation provided by a ClearOne XAP400. The output from this is then input to the sound card of the Access Grid computer. A pair of Genelec 1029A speakers was installed to project audio of far end participants. Far-end audio amplification is provided by the ClearOne XAP 400, which is also connected to the output of the audio card in the Access Grid computer.

Network

The building and the room are equipped with 100Mbps network to the desktop and the university's information technology personnel were contacted to enable multicast.

Computer

A custom built, rack-mountable, computer was purchased and installed. The computer was designed for high performance and low noise. For example, heat pipes rather than fans were used to cool the 3.2GHz central processing unit. The computer uses the Windows XP operating system and several versions of the Access Grid software have been installed. Other software includes:

- Mimio pen stroke capture
- Microsoft Office
- G Ware—controls for the ClearOne
- Virtual network computing (client and server)
- Python

The computer was mounted in the equipment rack in the Access Grid room. A second, similar computer was purchased as back-up.

Finding Out About the Access Grid

As the Access Grid was a new technology to the university, technical staff downloaded and installed copies of the software on several computers so that testing and familiarization could be conducted. Before purchasing equipment several PIGs were established, enabling exploration of the software. The technical personnel also subscribed to two email discussion lists about the Access Grid, one on technical matters and one on general topics. A number of Internet searches was undertaken to determine what work had been conducted on the use of the Access Grid in teaching and learning. While there were isolated instances of the Access Grid being used for teaching and learning, its major use was for collaborative research. As there was very little literature to inform the practice of teaching and learning with the Access Grid, one staff member joined an international group working on the use of the Access Grid in education. This group provided a double benefit as not only did they provide access to a discussion on Access Grid in education but as well met via the Access Grid thus providing the staff member with further experience. Technical personnel also attended one of the annual Access Grid retreats. The Access Grid retreat is an annual event, usually held in the United States of America and hosted by a university computer department or a computing facility. It is an opportunity for developers and users to meet face-to-face. The retreat has two streams of presentations and discussions, one for developers of the Access Grid software and another for users. The retreat is also used to post challenges to the Access Grid community

Table 14.3. Access grid equipment list

Item	Details	Use/Justification	Quantity
Computer	Window XP		2
LCD screens	Dell Ultra Sharp 17"	Operator screens	2
Projector	NEC HT1100 - video	Display of far-end participants	1
Projector	Hitachi CP-SX5600 - Hi Resolution	Display of hi resolution images including application sharing	1
Projector	NEC LT245 - data	Display of lower resolution images, e.g., shared whiteboard	1
Projector mounts		Ceiling installation	3
Projector screen			3
Cameras	Sony EDI-100	Video capture from the AGR	3
Document Camera	Elmo 5600XG	Video capture of documents, small items	1
Presentation Laptop	Dell PC	presentation	1
Audio Canceling	ClearOne (Gentner) XAP400	Echo cancellation and audio mixing as recommended	1
Microphones	Beyerdynamic MPC66	Audio capture from AGR	4
Speakers	Genelec 1029A	Far end audio	1pr
Equipment rack	45 unit	Equipment storage	2
Mimio	Xi plus wireless module	Pen capture from whiteboard	1
Lighting		Current fluorescent room lighting is not suitable	
Cables	Cables and management—patching etc.		

and welcomes attendance of beginners as well as those who are very experienced. The Access Grid retreat also provides an opportunity to meet with developers and users of the Access Grid from around the world and to gain an understanding of current practices.

The Installation

The equipment was procured and installed and the university's information technology personnel were brought into the project to ensure that multicast was enabled from the network points in the Access Grid room. The IT personnel also helped monitor and later manage the bandwidth requirements. Testing was undertaken in several ways. Initial testing was carried out between a laboratory in another pert of the university and the Access Grid room. A PIG was set up in the laboratory and when it and the Access Grid room connected to a virtual room on a server testing of audio and video performance and quality were undertaken. A specialist technician was brought in to configure the ClearOne echo-canceling device. The technical staff from the university's audio visual department installed and configured the rest of the equipment.

Current Use: Mathematics Subjects

In the first semester the Access Grid room at the university is being used for three mathematics subjects. The subjects are all at the honors or postgraduate level. The subjects are taught between three universities and have student numbers at the local university of one, two, and two. These numbers are clearly too small for the subjects to be offered at that university alone. One is taught from the local university and the others are taught from the other two participating universities. In the next semester as well as subjects, the Access Grid will be used to share research seminars between the three participating universities.

Projected Use of the Access Grid

Several deans of other faculties and heads of other departments have expressed interest in the use of the Access Grid for teaching and for collaborative research in their own areas. Several PIGs have been set up in other faculties at the local university to further explore the potential of this technology.

One school that has shown a great deal of interest is the School of Medicine. Technologists from the school are keen to use the capacity of the Access Grid to transmit and receive high definition video between two of the school's campuses. High definition video is the emerging standard for video production and a growing percentage of television broadcasts are in the HD format. As the name suggests HD video captures and replays images with increased the definition or clarity. The increased definition is achieved through increasing the number of pixels (or picture elements) that make up the image. Standard digital TV images are made up of about 200,000 pixels. HD images are made up of about 2,000,000, which produces an obvious increase in clarity. In addition, another change that leads to better quality is the change from interlaced pictures to progressively scanned ones. Television and video monitors build pictures by assembling horizontal rows or lines of pixels. A clearer picture can be obtained by scanning all lines in a progressive manner. Hence we see video signals, televisions, and monitors rated at a number and the letter i or p to designate interlaced or progressive scan.

To date the Access Grid has used standard definition video. However, a recently developed interface to the Access Grid makes possible the transmission of HD video pictures. The interface uses MPEG-4/h.264 compression to reduce the bandwidth to levels that make possible the transmission of HD images across broadband Internet connections. The HD pictures consist of more pixels and use progressive scan.

The experience gained in the installation and development of the room-based node in the Department of Mathematics and Applied Statistics will benefit the application of the Access Grid to learning and teaching in the School of Medicine. It is proposed that HD video and the Access Grid could be used to facilitate synchronous and asynchronous learning events.

Synchronous Learning

The proposal is to create two types of HD video nodes on the Access Grid: room-based and portable. The portable nodes could be used in any location to capture relevant images and sounds. For example:

- medical imaging facility,
- operating theater,
- general practice surgery,
- laboratory,
- and so forth.

A camera operator at the portable node would gather images and sounds that would be transmitted live to:

- students in the room-based nodes at two of campuses of the medical school,
- students at other locations using portable nodes (e.g., regional practices),
- and so forth.

Also, the images and sounds would be recorded for later, asynchronous use.

An academic at the portable node could:

- provide commentary on the procedure being captured by the video camera,
- interview the practitioners, patients, and so forth,
- answer questions from students,
- and so forth.

Students would:

- see the images from the HD camera,
- see images of other students,
- discuss with the academic and other students the material being captured, and
- talk with interviewees.

Asynchronous Learning

During the synchronous Access Grid session the images and sounds captured by the HD camera will be recorded to either videodisc or hard disk drive in the camera. Also the pictures of the students and the academic along with the audio of their interactions will be recoded to a separate device.

After the Access Grid session the HD material would be edited, chapter marks included, meta-tagged, and placed in a content management system (CMS). This will allow it to be retrieved in part or whole without duplicating the resource.

Students could interact independently or collaboratively with:

- The recording of the AG session for review purposes
- The recording of the AG session via the learning management system (LMS).
- Part or whole of the HD material through the LMS.

Conclusion: Future of Access Grid

The future of the Access Grid in online and distance education appears to be very positive. The sending and receiving multiple video streams can be harnessed for a wide range of rich teaching and learning activities that can lead to effective learning. When this media richness is coupled with the additional software modules of the Access Grid the opportunities presented to the teacher and/or designer of distance education and e-learning far exceed those available with videoconference and video chat.

The current version of the Access Grid (version 3.1 at the time of writing) still requires medium to high levels of technical support. These levels render Access Grid too labor intensive for immediate, widespread use in e-learning and distance learning. However, the Access Grid software is open source and continually being developed. It is anticipated that future versions of the software will be more user friendly and hence require less technical support, thus making Access Grid an affordable technology in terms of support. Other developments on the horizon for the Access Grid include refinement of the AGVCR, a recording software for Access Grid sessions and the use of HD video streams through compression standards such as h.264.

Room-based nodes will always be an expensive installation by virtue of the multiple, screens, projectors, and cameras as well as the computing power required to handle them. It is likely that the number of room-based nodes will increase but probably not exceed the level of several per institution. On the other hand it could reasonably be expected that more use of PIGs will be made in distance education and e-learning as the prices of computers, Web cameras, echo-canceling microphones, and second screens decreases. This will create more opportunities to increase the flexibility

Figure 14.14. Possible future integration of the access grid with other online learning elements

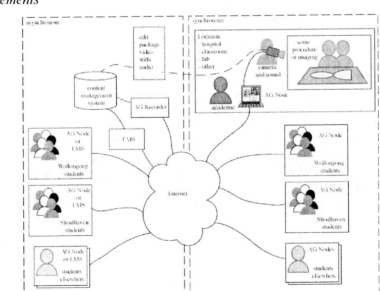

of where students study, as they will be able to use a PIG from any connection of sufficient bandwidth.

While there are immediate difficulties with the Access Grid in e-learning, in the longer term as the software is developed and refined it has the potential to be a very powerful technology for e-learning. In the next chapter the Access Grid is compared with other communications technologies and in the last chapter the concept of the integration of the Access Grid with LMSs is discussed. This integration will increase the seamlessness of the learning experience for students and provide easy connections between resources and interactions. When this integration takes place students will be able to share the environments and tools of the LMS thus facilitating collaborative construction of new resources and knowledge by students in a social, media-rich environment. And they will be able to do this from a convenient location.

Reference

Cole, C., Ray, K., & Zanetis, J. (2004). *Videoconference for K-12 classrooms: A program development guide*. ISTE: Washington.

Chapter XV

The Future of Real Time Communications Technologies in E-Learning

Introduction

In the previous chapters three real time communications technologies (RTCs) have been discussed. Videoconferences have been used for real time communications in distance learning for many years. In recent years many institutions have used videoconferences in addition to the text-based communications tools in learning management systems: discussion forums and chat. Video chat is a new technology. It is computer based and inexpensive after the purchase of the computer as software is often free and the basic audio and video equipment is inexpensive. Video chat facilitates two-way video and audio communications and thus it is likely to displace videoconference from its place in the market. The Access Grid is also gaining use in education as a teaching tool due to the richness of the experience of multiple video streams, and additional tools that allow true collaboration. How these technologies are used in educational settings has a direct impact on the effectiveness and efficiency of the educational experience and theoretical guides to their use have been discussed earlier in this book. One of the early theoretical approaches was that put forward by Michael Moore.

In the 1970s Moore introduced the *theory of transactional distance* (Moore & Kearsley, 1996). Transactional distance is measured by the degree of structure and the amount of dialogue in a distance education course and a low transactional distance is characterized by frequent and meaningful dialogue between students and faculty. Moore (1972) suggests that communications between faculty and students in distance education "must be facilitated by print, electronic, mechanical or other devices" (p. 76). In distance education and increasingly in e-learning, RTCs are used to facilitate audio and video communications between faculty and students and between students.

The RTCs include videoconference, videoconference plus virtual network computing (VNC), Access Grid, and video chat. While these technologies are similar, a comparison of them within the context of e-learning and distance education and within a three to five year time frame will provide probable directions for their future use that are cost effective and appropriate to the participants, the content, the learning objectives, and the infrastructure. In addition a forecast of the future roles of these technologies will provide faculty, instructional designers, and managers of distance education and e-learning with information that is useful in the planning of RTC implementations.

RTCs and the Taxonomy of Learning Technologies

Learning technologies have been categorized as *representational* or *collaborative* in the *taxonomy of learning technologies* (Caladine, 2006). The taxonomy has been derived from the LTM which was discussed in Chapter VII, and it borrows from the terminology derived for the LTM. The term representational is used to describe technologies that facilitate the one-way representation of material. The term collaborative is used to describe technologies that facilitate two-way communications. This category is divided into the sub-categories of *dialogic* and *productive*. Dialogic learning technologies are defined as those that are confined to the support of dialogue alone: for example, the telephone. Productive learning technologies combine two-way communications with the facilitation of the creation of products. Within each of these categories individual technologies can be further described by their synchronicity or asynchronicity. A graphic representation of the taxonomy is given in Figure 15.1.

When technologies are described by the taxonomy their appropriate use is signified in general terms by their classification. A videoconference is classified as collaborative, dialogic, and synchronous, which clearly indicates that it is a two-way technology

Figure 15.1. The taxonomy of learning technologies

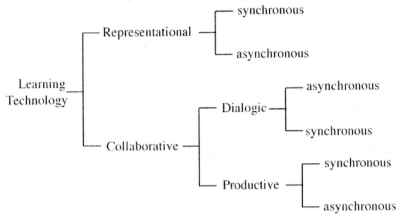

and is intended to host a dialogue in which all participants are present at the same time. This contrasts to Access Grid when it is used as the host for collaboratively, synchronously produced materials, in which case it is a two-way technology intended to host a dialogue in which all participants are present at the same time and produce something. These technologies are available to faculty, designers, and managers of online learning and a comparative description of them will help to further differentiate between them.

RTCs

A comparison of RTCs will assist managers in the decision-making process and lead to the appropriate use of RTCs by faculty and designers in e-learning through clearly differentiating between their functions and features.

Videoconference

One of the earliest technologies to significantly reduce transactional distance was videoconference. Videoconference is defined here as a technology that allows two-way video and audio communications between remote parties. In videoconference parlance the parties or locations are referred to as *points* or *endpoints*. In essence videoconference has been around for as long as television, as videoconference can be thought of as two parallel, counter-directional, closed circuit, television systems.

However, it was not until the 1980s that dedicated videoconference technology appeared on the market that could take advantage of the then new digital telecommunications networks such as integrated, services digital network (ISDN). At this time videoconference use in distance education took a decided upturn. Today the majority of videoconferences use the Internet rather than ISDN lines.

Videoconference plus VNC

Videoconference is by no means a new technology for teaching and learning. However, there are some limitations to its use. Videoconference typically provides video and audio communications of the participants and the sharing of computer images such as PowerPoint presentation. While this is suitable for many teaching and learning events, for others in which students interact with display technology it is not adequate. For example, mathematics subjects are often taught with a high degree of student participation. In a classroom this participation would generally take the form of writing on a whiteboard (or blackboard). To emulate this participation in distance learning videoconference can be run in parallel with VNC. VNC is a remote display system that allows a computer desktop to be viewed by other computers. The host computer runs the VNC server and the clients all connect by running a VNC viewer. Most VNC software is open source and can be configured to facilitate client control of the serving computer. VNC has traditionally been used by information technology support staff in the remote maintenance and upgrading of computers. In teaching and learning VNC can be used to share learning environments. If the shared computer screen is projected onto a touch sensitive electronic whiteboard, when used in conjunction with videoconference, VNC can host a shared eWhiteboard session in which students and faculty write on a shared electronic canvas. The combination of videoconference and VNC thus provides the class with video and audio of all participants by videoconference, images of PowerPoint slides (or other computer files) by videoconference, and a shared virtual or eWhiteboard through VNC.

Web Conference

Since Microsoft launched Netmeetings in the 1990s, other Web conference applications have been developed and are now commercially available for use in distance education and e-learning. Typically Web conference applications are defined as a combination of synchronous video and/or audio communications with a shared computer application or presentation. Examples of Web conference applications include: Webex, Adobe Connect (which was Macromedia Breeze), Elluminate, and Live Classroom by Horizon Wimba.

Video Chat

In the late 1990s and early 2000s the technology of text-based instant messaging gained wide acceptance by computer users. A similar technology, Internet chat applications have been in use for many years but the ease and accessibility of Web-based instant messaging has led to its widespread acceptance. Instant messaging applications were first limited to text interchanges and were generally free of charge. They evolved quickly by adding facilities to communicate with voice and the voice over Internet protocol (VoIP) applications such as Skype (in 2007, Skype was probably the most popular of the Internet-based voice and video communications) have been very widely adopted. After voice, video was a natural development and video chat applications such as iChatAV, AIM Triton, MSN Messenger, Windows Live, and others were launched. Video chat is defined as an application of computer technology that allows two-way audio and video communications between remote parties. Thus video chat can be thought of as videoconference on a computer. Applications like Apple's iChat AV can be seen as a prediction of the future direction or evolutionary outcome of video chat as a multipoint video communications tool with integrated file exchange and sharing. For the purposes of this book this is referred to as *enhanced video chat*. iChatAV is supplied at no extra cost with the Apple operating system.

Video chat is rather simple and inexpensive to set up as all that is needed is the generally free software, a computer, a Web camera, and a headset. Of course the Internet connection will need to be of sufficient bandwidth to support video chat and most broadband connections are ample for this. If video chat is to replace videoconference a few additions to the basic configuration mentioned previously will need to be made as video chat has been designed mainly for isolated individual users. To cater for more than one person at an endpoint a larger screen may be needed so all local participants can see and some audio equipment will be needed to enable all to hear and be heard. A more detailed description of this technology is provided in Chapter XII.

The Access Grid

Researchers have used the Access Grid as a communications and collaboration technology since its development in the mid-1990s. The Access Grid takes advantage of the Internet's multicast ability to receive one and send multiple video and audio streams thus keeping bandwidth to a minimum. Multicast is an Internet protocol whereby a server can send a single message to multiple recipients. A simple analogy is sending am e-mail message to a list rather than to each recipient.

While Access Grid, video chat, videoconference, and videoconference plus VNC are similar in that they all facilitate the two-way exchange of video and audio, Access

Grid can be differentiated by the multiple video streams sent and received from each endpoint or *node* and the number of additional software modules that increase the functionality of the Access Grid. These modules include, shared presentation, shared browser, shared eWhiteboard true application sharing, and many more. Some commercial products that claim to offer application sharing in fact use the term to describe a facility that allows files to be transferred between participants. True application sharing allows participants to work on the same file at the same time. While room-based nodes on the Access Grid usually contain a wall of projected video images, (see Chapter XIV), smaller installations are possible. These are referred to as personal interfaces to the Grid or PIGs, and require similar technology to video chat, that is, a networked computer, Web camera, and headset. Halfway between room-based nodes and the PIG is a configuration of technology suitable for two to three concurrent users.

Comparing Videoconference, Access Grid, Web Conference, Video Chat, and Enhanced Videoconference.

The role of videoconference in distance education is quite clear, as it has been used for the past fifteen to twenty years for communications between students and between students and faculty. Access Grid and video chat are newer technologies and are yet to become established and associated with particular teaching and learning activities. However, due to the low costs of video chat and the enhanced functionality of Access Grid, both technologies have the potential to play effective and efficient roles in distance education and e-learning. A comparison of the technologies on the criteria of functions and costs will help to determine the future of these technologies in distance education and e-learning.

The difference in functionality between the Access Grid, videoconference, video chat, and videoconference plus VNC can be conceptualized, one way as the different numbers of available video and data streams. Room-based nodes on the Access Grid are generally capable of sending three or four video streams and at least one data stream. Videoconference generally sends a single video stream and a single data stream. These may be sent serially or in parallel. Videoconference plus VNC sends single video and data streams as well as the two-way VNC data connection. Video chat is generally confined to one stream of audio and video from each participant. To users these differences are apparent as the following:

- In a room-based Access Grid node the participants can see multiple video streams from other rooms as well as the data stream of a presentation, application, or interaction. They heard the audio of all participants.

- In a videoconference participants generally see one image that can switch between the video of the participants and data. If a continuous presence function is available small images of all participating sites will be visible. However, at any given time, only one video stream is sent from each endpoint. Participants can generally hear the audio from all participants.

- In videoconference plus VNC participants generally see one image that can switch between the video of the participants and data and another interactive image. Participants generally hear the audio from all participants.

- In video chat participants see the image and hear the sounds of the other participant(s).

While the technologies are all similar, they differ in the type and level of functions they facilitate. Videoconference and video chat are characterized by two-way video and audio. By comparison Web conference in many cases cannot fully support two-way video as well as deliver images from a participant's computer. Access Grid with add-on products can be configured to do both and video chat is based firmly on two-way video and audio. Table 15.1 provides a comparison of the functionality of the technologies and includes the predicted enhanced video chat.

The equipment required for the technologies ranges from the simple to the complex, and hence the cost of the technology ranges from low to high. However, the initial cost of the technology is only one part of the costs criterion. Other elements of using the technologies that cause costs to be incurred are the software, the personnel to support the technology, and the costs of the network traffic created by the use of the technology.

It is assumed that in three to five years time Access Grid software will have developed and require less operational support. Also within the same time frame, compression algorithms will change to provide more efficient use of bandwidth and the general trend towards higher bandwidth connections is expected to continue.

In terms of technical functionality, the Access Grid is superior to videoconference and Web conference applications as it can provide multiple video streams and audio of all participants as well as shared desktop, applications, and eWhiteboard. As Access Grid uses multicast bandwidth, costs are limited and no local, expensive bridging technology is required hence making Access Grid more cost effective than videoconference. The downside of Access Grid is the high levels of technical support required. Perhaps this is the single greatest barrier to the wide adoption of access grid for teaching and learning for the present. For this reason the some institutions and organizations have investigated and implemented the use of videoconference plus VNC rather than Access Grid.

Videoconference technology has been used in teaching and learning for quite some time and the technology has improved in reliability, quality of pictures, and of sound. Perhaps the change that has had the greatest impact on the way in which videoconference is used and organized is the change from ISDN to the Internet. The

Table 15.1. A generalized comparison of functionality (adapted from Caladine & Aminifar 2007)

	Video-conference	Web Conference	Access Grid	Video chat	Enhanced video chat	Video-conference plus VNC
Functions	Video and audio of participants	Audio (and video in some cases) of presenter—some have capacity for audio of participants	Video (multi-streams) and audio of all participants	Video and audio of participants	Video and audio of participants	Video and audio of participants
	Presentation of computer images (e.g., PowerPoint) by participants	Presentation of computer images (e.g., PowerPoint) by one participant	Presentation and sharing of computer images (e.g., PowerPoint) by participants		Presentation of computer images (e.g., PowerPoint) by participants	Presentation of computer images (e.g., PowerPoint) by participants
			Control of computer images by any participant			Control of computer images by any participant
		Document or presentation transfer	True application sharing (e.g., spreadsheets, documents, movie viewers, and others)			True application sharing (e.g., spreadsheets, documents, movie viewers, and others)
		eWhiteboard sharing	eWhiteboard sharing		eWhiteboard sharing	eWhiteboard sharing
			Computer desktop sharing.			
Hardware costs	Endpoint—medium Bridge—high	Server—medium	Room-based node—medium Personal interface to the Access Grid—low	Low	Low	Endpoint—medium Bridge—high
Software costs	Included—firmware	License—medium/high	Open source (free)	free	free	Included—firmware VNC—open source
Support costs	Technician—low	Technician—low (server support)	Technician—medium	none	none	Technician—low
Bandwidth required	Medium	Medium	Medium—high	Medium	Medium	Medium

Internet has increased the number of possible points of connection in an organization and has reduced the need for designated videoconference studios that required participants to relocate to an environment which may not always have been relevant to the subject matter of the conference. The change to Internet protocol is certainly a great opportunity to initiate new practices that enhance the way videoconferences are conducted. For example, videoconference can now be easily installed in mock clinics, mock surgeries, moot courts, and laboratories. The trade off between Access Grid and videoconference plus VNC is that the benefits of the multiple video streams of Access Grid are offset by the lower technical support required by videoconference plus VNC.

Video chat is gaining acceptance as a video communications application and it is developing into enhanced video chat. It is clear that enhanced video chat could pose a threat to the market traditionally held by videoconference technology suppliers. Perhaps, for this reason several videoconference hardware manufacturers have recently initiated strategies to reposition themselves in the marketplace. Two of the largest videoconference hardware suppliers are now aggressively marketing products other than standard videoconference hardware. The products include high definition videoconference and Telepresence. In addition, both Polycom and Tandberg are offering video chat or video telephony solutions (Polycom, 2007; Tandberg, 2006).

Given that videoconference endpoint technology is expensive, it is reasonable to predict that its use will contract to specialist areas such as high definition uses for medical imaging, microscopy and motional analysis, and high level board-meeting-style, immersive videoconferences. On the other hand video chat developed as an enhancement of instant messaging and is expected to become as ubiquitous as its text forebear. As students are used to video chat technology and as there are great cost savings to be had, it is reasonable to predict that the use of video chat in distance education and e-learning will grow and maybe eventually eclipse videoconference. Perhaps one of the greatest advantages of video chat over videoconference is the flexibility of place. The technology is relatively cheap and if students have sufficient bandwidth they can connect from home, the workplace, or on campus. As enhanced video chat has the functionality of Web conference applications, without the expensive price tag it is reasonable to suggest that these will be displaced by enhanced video chat. Unfortunately for the vendors of Web conference software, to date, a place to which they could reposition themselves in the market has not become evident.

In terms of its basic functions, video chat is the same as videoconference. Both provide two-way audio and two-way video communications. Cost alone is enough of a driver to see institutions replace expensive endpoint equipment with the cheaper video chat. The additional benefit of being computer-based and hence able to be located at any networked computer can be seen as another driving force for this change. In addition, the enhancements of file sharing and using video chat in conjunction with shared applications will see video chat develop into a collaborative–productive, synchronous learning technology. This will allow students, no matter where they are located, to undertake a range of collaborative tasks that go beyond discussion, such as building resources, compiling reports, debating issues, brainstorming ideas, and more. In the medium term, technology that enables videoconference and video chat endpoints to connect to the same conference is available for some applications if they comply to one of the standards such as h.323. This will allow videoconference and video chat endpoints to participate in multipoint conferences thus connecting large lecture theatres, small and medium classrooms, and students at home or in the workplace.

Conclusion

The rich multimedia experience of room-based nodes on the Access Grid, coupled with true application sharing differentiates Access Grid from video chat. While Access Grid has been used for some years in research collaboration, its potential for learning is only now becoming evident. Due to the multiple video streams sent and received, the Access Grid learning experience is visually much richer than videoconference. When Access Grid takes advantage of software modules that allow participating students to control the size of the received video windows and to control the cameras at other endpoints, the experience can be tailored to suit participants on a level far beyond that of videoconference and video chat. Access Grid also has software modules that facilitate true sharing of files and applications and hence can be described as collaborative-productive making it more attractive to distance education and e-learning than videoconference. In some institutions Access Grid has a role in distance education and e-learning through initiatives that share the teaching of small classes across institutions and link research collaborations to teaching. While the technology necessary for a room-based node on the Access Grid can be a cost issue, the software is open source and hence free. Being open source the development curve of the software is probably flatter than an equivalent commercial product and hence the current version of Access Grid requires higher levels of technical support than videoconference plus VNC, videoconference, or video chat. The development of the Access Grid software is a collaborative effort and is ongoing. In three to five years it is quite likely that a robust version will be available and require little technical support. In the meantime it is likely that institutions and organizations will use a mixture of technologies that will need to be used in ways that facilitate easy interactions and thus render the technology transparent, while maintaining sustainable levels of costs for support and implementation. The next chapter discusses the slightly longer-term future for RTCs and for other rich media technologies that can enhance e-learning.

References

Caladine, R. (2006). A taxonomy of learning technologies: Simplifying online learning for learners, professors and designers. In M. Khosrow-Pour (Ed.), *Emerging trends and challenges in information technology management.* Hershey, PA: Idea Group.

Moore, M. (1972). Learner autonomy: The second dimension of independent learning. *Convergence, 5*(2), 76-88.

Moore, M., & Kearsley, G. (1996). *Distance education a systems view.* Belmont, CA: Wadsworth.

Polycom. (2006). *Real presence experience (RPX).* Retrieved September 25, 2006, from http://www.polycom.com/solutions/0,1694,pw-15772-15773,00.html

Tandberg. (2006a). *HD videoconferencing at your desktop.* Retrieved September 25, 2006, from http://www.tandberg.net/

Tandberg. (2006b). *Videoconferencing standards. D10740 Rev 2.3.* Retrieved September 25, 2006, from http://www.tandberg.net/collateral/documentation/White_Papers/Whitepaper_Video-Conferencing_Standards.pdf

Chapter XVI

The Future of Rich Media, Learning Management Systems, and Content Management Systems

Introduction

In a world of increasing bandwidth it is no surprise that the content of the Web is changing. A trend away from text richness towards media richness is evident. The rise and popularity of video sites such as YouTube and media–rich, social software are further examples of this trend and it is reasonable to expect a future that will be rich in online media. When rich media are integral components of online social and leisure experiences, it is reasonable that students will expect video and other examples of media richness in their online learning experiences rather than a pre-ponderance of text as is the current experience in many institutions. Rich media have for years played the role of adjuncts to teaching and learning. For example, for many years assessment by video, in some classes, has been an option although one that has been slow to be adopted. Perhaps the time is now ripe for this and other online uses of video and audio as the tools for production are becoming simpler and cheaper. In the past, sharing video was limited to the physical distribution of the tape or disc. Today one preferred method of sharing of video is by uploading to purpose-built, public Web sites.

Learning management systems (LMSs) have played a significant role in learning for the past six to eight years. To date they have usually been text-rich in both content and interactions. The content, generally written by academics, has been dominated by text. This is not surprising as writing in their discipline is a large part of academic work. However, for the reasons mentioned previously, manufacturers of LMSs must be feeling the need to include media-rich content. Further, many institutions are moving to couple content management systems (CMSs) with LMSs. CMSs are repositories for digital learning objects that can be conveniently tagged, stored, and reused. There are many benefits that can be achieved with CMSs. Faculty who invest large amounts of time in the production of rich media resources can see greater returns on their investments when they are reused and reuse can be maximized through CMSs. Publishers are extending their traditional markets, selling digital learning objects to accompany textbooks, these too can be stored on CMSs to not only maximize reuse but also to track copyright provisions. There is a role for student-created content to be stored in CMSs and used as resources by subsequent classes, as often student perspective can provide appropriate perspectives. These are all ways in which the levels of rich media content in e-learning will increase. However, the change from text-rich to media-rich is not limited to content. The past few years have seen the birth and growth of instant messaging and its evolution into voice messaging, Voice over Internet protocol (VoIP), and video instant messaging. Videoconference has for some years been used for interactions in teaching and learning and as the communication tools become widely distributed it is expected to increase.

Clearly rich media have roles in the content and interactions of online learning. The challenge then to those who design learning events is to take these new applications of the technology and design events that are appropriate to the subject material and the participants, their preferred way of learning, the context, and the budget. This challenge is made more complex due to the changing technological environment. The Web is changing to Web 2.0 and e-learning is changing to e-learning 2.0.

Web 2.0 and E-Learning 2.0

Web 2.0 and e-learning 2.0 were mentioned in the first chapter of this book. Those writing about e-learning 2.0 suggest that it will represent a major paradigm shift from e-learning 1.0, or text-rich e-learning. However, technological changes of this magnitude generally do not happen overnight. Rather the changes are gradual and graduated with the newer technology operating in parallel with the older for a period of time. O'Hear (2006) suggests that e-learning 2.0 will be a loose connection of different applications such as blogs, wikis, and social software to create ad hoc learning communities. This can lead to learning opportunities that have higher levels of authenticity as they are situated in real online activities. This is also positively biased towards the flexibility of learning. That is providing learning opportunities where and when learners want it. It is not an approach that will readily fit with the practices of institutions that are based on courses, subjects, and awards. Indeed while the functions and scope of LMSs will more than likely change, institutions need a central point of comparison between students so that they can be scored and awarded the credentials they have enrolled to attain. Of course a revolution in the way education takes place could occur and radically change the current approach but in the meantime we need to meet the challenge of student expectations of media richness in their online e-learning experiences. Perhaps the next generation of LMSs will incorporate some Web 2.0 elements, or provide integration pathways or connections to Web 2.0 applications. They will also contain media-rich resources and host media-rich interactions while retaining the central tracking and record keeping functions. One way in which media-rich interactions could be undertaken in e-learning is through multiple user virtual environments (MUVEs) such as Second Life. While a discussion of the use of MUVEs in e-learning is beyond the scope of this book, managers and designers of e-learning need to remain aware of developments in this area as the potential for e-learning is significant. The key information required in order to plan for this next step in the evolution of e-learning includes:

- A list of the technological elements that are possible to include in the LMS.
- A list of technologies that will be connected to, but not part of, the LMS, how they will be integrated.
- A list of other e-learning technologies that are used in the learning event.

Also, a rough time line of their implementation must be determined so that technological changes can be anticipated well before their implementation. The timeline provided in Figure 16.1 is based on the author's work at an Australian university and on joint research with other universities in Australia, North America and Europe.

Putting it all Together:
The Future of Learning Technologies

In the past few years a number of technologies have been debuted in higher education and human resource development. The efficient and appropriate use of these technologies provides challenges for faculty, designers, and managers. Figure 16.1

Figure 16.1. Approximate time lines of learning technology implementation

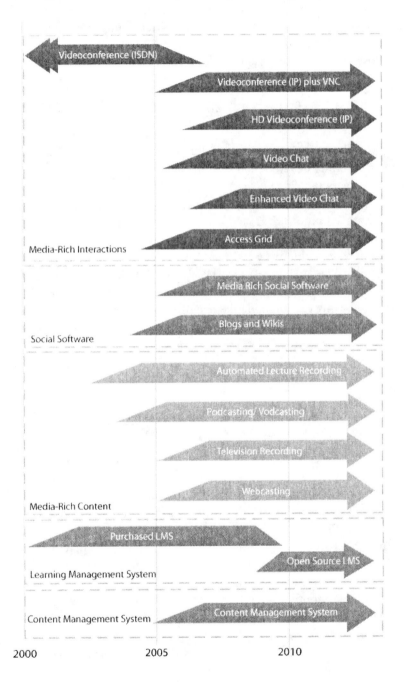

lists the main technologies and provides further information about their projected longevity. In Figure 16.1 the technologies have been grouped in the categories of: media-rich interactions, social software, media-rich content, learning management system, and content management system. The future uses of the technologies in each of these categories are discussed hereafter.

The Future of Media-Rich Interaction Technologies

For the past 15 or more years videoconference has been used in higher education and human resource development as a means to connect students and faculty. In the past few years the change from telco supplied ISDN lines to the Internet has been marked. This change has enabled higher bandwidth connections at lower costs and hence high definition (HD) videoconferences have gained a growing portion of the market. It is expected that HD videoconference will replace the equipment at many existing videoconference endpoints, with others being replaced by video chat, enhanced video chat, and Access Grid. While Access Grid has the potential to offer the richest, media-rich interactions in education, it requires high levels of technical support. For this reason alone the use of Access Grid in teaching and learning in several institutions is growing slowly and in some cases videoconference plus virtual network computing (VNC) has been used as an alternative.

Content Management and Rich Media

CMSs have been used for some time to manage the vast amounts of files and data behind large Web sites. However, in recent years they have been introduced to online learning. CMSs in education play a different role to that played in Web site management. In education, CMSs are used as repositories for learning objects. The learning objects can range from text documents to Web pages to rich media files. All content files are tagged with metadata that indicate to other potential users of the files a number of criteria including who created the file, any restrictions on its use, where it has been used before, and ways in which it has been used. While CMSs are not new their adoption in higher education has been slower than expected by many. Standards have been prepared for the metadata so that learning objects can easily be transferred between CMSs. Among the most popular standards are sharable content object reference model (SCORM), instructional management system (IMS), and learning object metadata (LOM).

CMSs foster the sharing of resources across faculty boundaries and potentially facilitate the sharing of files between institutions and organizations. Of course there are organizational issues that need to be addressed before the majority faculty or designers will place the content they have created into a CMS and make it freely available to other faculty and designers. The range of rich media that could be placed on a CMS is wide and could include:

- Professionally produced video
- Student produced video
- Faculty produced video
- Podcasts recorded from presentations by teachers or students
- Specially prepared podcasts
- Recordings of rich media interactions
- Others

A further development of CMSs could be the use of chapter marks in rich media files as a way to increase the use of them. In this way designers of online learning could insert a link to one or more chapters of a rich media file rather than the whole thing. This can be extended to linking to several chapters in different rich media files and organizing the playback to be seamless. While managing rich media content will be a large part of the future of e-learning, the organization of rich media interactions may be even larger.

Integration of Rich Media and LMSs

Rich media interactions are part of our networked world. However, for the past six to eight years communications between students and with faculty, when inside an LMS, have been limited to text. Students could use the LMS e-mail system to send a message to faculty or other students. They could engage in a text chat session or send a message to a text-based forum. In a world where video chat is fast displacing text as the preferred medium for instant messaging, it can be expected that video chat style communications will be integrated with LMSs in the near future. The benefits of such integration are much more than just convenience. If video communications are integrated with LMSs, templates for their use and secondary applications can elevate simple video communications to rich learning events. Two examples of such events are online brainstorming and online debating.

Rich Media in Online Brainstorming

Brainstorming has been used in classroom education for many years and can transfer to e-learning easily if media-rich communications are integrated with the LMS. To brainstorm online an eWhiteboard can be used in conjunction with video chat or videoconference. In this way geographically dispersed students can collaborate. A student working at home can use a tablet computer or a graphics tablet to *write* on the eWhiteboard. Students in classrooms at different campuses can write on the same eWhiteboard if it is projected onto a touch sensitive electronic whiteboard. In this way all local class members will be able to see what all students have written. Students in the classrooms will be able to communicate with students at home and at the other campuses via the video chat or videoconference. As the eWhiteboard is integrated with the LMS it can be recorded and made accessible afterwards to students via the LMS. Further if the technology to record the video chat or video-conference interactions is available, a recording of the complete session is possible. Also, the student input to the online brainstorm can be connected with the grade book, which is also located in the LMS, thus streamlining the grading of student contributions to the brainstorm.

Online Debating with Rich Media

Rich media can be used to facilitate debates between geographically dispersed students. A debating team could consist of class members from different locations and the debate could be held in a virtual space on the LMS. The benefits of integrating the online debate with the LMS are similar to those mentioned previously.

While concentrating on media-rich communications it is easy to assume that in the future, there will be no use of text-based communications. It is not suggested that this will be the case. E-mail is a deeply entrenched communications technology that is expected to be in use for many years. Often text is preferred due to its simplicity and convenience for synchronous and asynchronous communications.

Commercial or Open Source LMSs

Further benefits would arise if videoconference, video chat, and the Access Grid software could be integrated with the LMS. Such integrations would allow the flexibility to use room-based and personal interfaces in the same learning event. In this way it would be possible to have a small group of learners at a regional center, a larger group at a campus and individuals at home or work all collaborating on the same project or undertaking the same learning activity. At the time of writing the most popular LMS is a commercial product. However, open source LMSs are increasing in popularity. By their very nature open source systems are simpler to integrate and thus it is suggested that the integration of Access Grid (incidentally also open source) with an open source LMS could be imminent. Further in the future the integration of other rich media communications applications could follow in the same vein.

Open source products have advantages and disadvantages. They are generally cheaper to acquire, implement, and use. They are generally customizable. On the other hand they can take longer to develop. Figure 16.2 compares hypothetical development curves for commercial and open source products. For the commercial product the investment levels during the development phase are higher than that for the open source product. This leads to a shorter development time, steeper development curves, and shorter time to market. In Figure 16.2 the commercial product reaches the market at Time A, before the open source reaches the same level of development at Time B. Open source applications are often continuously developed, as shown by the open source curve reaching level E. In this way the open source product can be a closer fit with the needs of users.

Figure 16.2. Hypothetical curves of open source and commercial product development

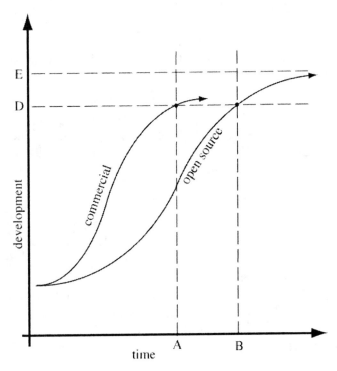

Conclusion

This book argues that if e-learning is to be effective and efficient, rich media will feature significantly in the content and in the interactions contained within it. The book has investigated the literature from a number of fields and has found a shortage of theories that guide the design of e-learning. In particular the literature was found to be characterized by an abundance of case studies and a paucity of theories that can guide designers in the appropriate application of technology to e-learning. In the central section three theoretical tools were developed. These are the learning activities model, the learning technologies model, and the technology selection method. The basic principle behind the technology selection method is that of matching categories of learning activities to technologies that are innately suited to them. In this way guidance is provided for instructional designers and for faculty who are also designers. The models and method are simple enough to be put into use quickly and effectively by faculty designers with little training in technology selection. They are also sufficiently robust to be used successfully in a wide variety of contexts and disciplines.

In the third section of the book a number of technologies or technological elements of LMSs have been described and examples of their appropriate use provided. While the technologies may change, the principles for their use in education will remain fundamentally the same. For example, HD videoconference has displaced standard definition products from the market place. The higher quality of sound and pictures does improve the communicative potential of the technology but does not alter the fact that it is essentially a two-way technology and no matter how clear the picture may be, a boring presentation delivered by videoconference will still be boring and faculty will still be asking, "Why do they go to sleep in my videoconferences?"

Obviously the future will see further changes to technology in addition to those mentioned here. This coupled with the shortage of guiding theories for the field creates a challenge for those who research in the area of educational technology; that is, to further investigate the use of the technologies in effective and efficient learning, seek generalities, and build theories that can be used by the future designers of e-learning.

References

Caladine, R. (2006). A taxonomy of learning technologies: Simplifying online learning for learners, professors and designers, In M. Khosrow-Pour (Ed.), *Emerging trends and challenges in information technology management*. Proceedings of the 2006 Information Resources Management Association, International Conference, Washington, D.C., Idea Group: Hershey.

Caladine, R. & Aminifar, E. (2007). The future of real time communications technology in online learning. In *Proceedings of the 18th Information Management Resources Association Conference, Canada.*

O'Hear, S. (2006). *E-learning 2.0—How Web technologies are shaping education.* Retrieved April 2, 2007, from http://www.readwriteweb.com/archives/e-learning_20.php

Appendix I

A Glossary of Terms, Initials, and Acronyms

Access Grid	The Access Grid is a computer-based, high-end video and audio communications technology. It is differentiated from videoconference and video chat by several features. Firstly, the media richness of the environment, which is produced by multi-projector displays of multiple video and data streams. Secondly, multiple cameras capture multiple images of the local participants for transmission. Thirdly, integrated with the Access Grid software are a number of software modules designed for application and file sharing. The software for Access Grid is open source.
Asymmetric Digital Subscriber Line (ADSL)	ADSL is a standard for the delivery of broadband connections to the Internet as well as voice telephony over standard telephone wires. The asymmetry refers to different speeds for receiving and transmitting. DSL is the symmetrical equivalent of ADSL. ADSL2 and ADSL2+ are extensions to the ADSL standard that offer higher bandwidth.
Aspect Ratio	The aspect ratio refers to the dimensions of a cinema, television, computer, or other screen or image. It is the ratio of the horizontal dimension to the vertical. Standard definition television is 4:3 and wide screen television is 16:9.

Audioconference	Audioconference is the technology that allows two-way audio communications between remote parties. By this definition a person-to-person phone call is an audioconference so to differentiate, audioconferences are defined as the technology that allows two-way communications between at least three remote parties, also known as conference calls.
Blended Learning	Blended learning refers to an approach to the structure of intentional learning that combines the convenience of the flexibility of online learning with the rich interactions possible in face-to-face learning.
Blog	Blog is short for Weblog which is an online journal designed for public consumption. Often a scripting software is used that publishes entries to the blog directly to a Web site.
Blu-ray	Blu-ray is one of the two formats that represent the second generation of DVD technology. The other is HD DVD. At the time of writing neither has emerged as the preferred standard.
Categorization	A way of grouping similar objects or concepts according to the role they play.
Classification	A way of grouping similar objects or concepts according to similar or like characteristics.
Collaborative Technology	The learning technologies model (LTM) divides learning technologies into two broad groups: collaborative and representational. Collaborative technologies facilitate interactions between students and between students and facilitators. They can be thought of as two-way. Representational technologies are those that provide materials to learners and can be thought of as one-way.
Constructivism	An approach to, and underlying philosophy of, learning in which students construct their own knowledge through connecting their own experiences and thoughts with the learning environment. Constructivism is about building personal knowledge rather than absorbing *facts* (contrast to instructivism).
Content Management System (CMS)	While most definitions of CMSs refer to the management of content of Web sites, in education CMSs are used to store digital learning objects. In addition to storing the objects the CMS allows metadata about each object to be attached to it (see metadata).
Distance Learning	(Also known as distance education.) Learning or education in which learners are separated from facilitators or faculty.

DVD	Originally DVD stood for digital video disc but as the use of DVD expanded to include storage of other types of data the name changed to digital versatile disc. Today they are generally referred to simply as DVDs. DVDs are the same size as CDs but can store up to seven times the data on a single layer and side.
Education	A structured program of Intentional learning from an institution. It is more specific than learning which can be intentional or unintentional.
E-learning	E-learning generally refers to a structured educational program that uses electronic technologies such as computers, Internet, CD-ROMs, Television, PDAs, or others.
E-learning 1.0 and 2.0	Just as software version numbers indicate generational changes so is the difference between e-learning 1.0 and e-learning 2.0. E-learning 2.0 represents the harnessing of those characteristics that are specific to Web 2.0, such as social software, sharing of flies, and the exchanges of student data between the institution's learning management system and student owned software.
Electronic Canvas	Electronic canvas refers to the digital equivalent of an artist's canvas, that is, it is a space on a computer on which users can use pen and brush tools as well as paste text and objects.
eWhiteboard	eWhiteboards are typically used in two different ways. The simplest use is to capture the pen strokes of a whiteboard marker and thus create a record of what was written on the whiteboard. The second use of eWhiteboads is what some suppliers refer to as *projection mode*. In this mode a computer image is projected onto the whiteboard and a stylus is used as a mouse. eWhiteboards can be of the receiver and stylus type or of the touch sensitive screen type.
Facilitator	(Also known as facilitator of learning.) The facilitator is the person who has prime or shared responsibility for the facilitation of learning. It is used as a general term rather than instructor, faculty, teacher, trainer, or developer.
Flexible Learning	Flexible learning is an approach to learning in which the time, place, and pace of learning may be determined or altered by learners. In some cases other aspects of flexibility may be present; these can be entry time, exit time, curriculum, assessment, and others.
Hard Disc Drive (HDD)	An HDD is a computer storage device that stores data on rotating magnetic surfaces. Hard refers to the metallic material of the disc or discs in the drive as compared to the floppy materials in floppy disks. HDDs are generally supplied as internal components of computers. However, external HDDs are available to provide additional storage space. HDDs are replacing videotape in several video recording applications (e.g., video cameras and personal video recorders).

High Definition (HD)	HD is a television standard that contains more data than standard definition television in, both the audio and video. While there is some disagreement about the exact dimensions of HD, particularly by retailers of Plasma and LCD screens. It is generally recognised that an HD picture in the NTSC format consists of 1920 x 1080 pixels. This compares with the standard definition of 640 x 480. The aspect ratio in standard definition is 4:3 and the aspect ratio in HD is 16:9.
Higher Education	Intentional learning in universities and colleges.
Human Resource Development (HRD)	HRD is intentional learning in organizations. It can include training that is generally specific to the learner's job and development, which is more general.
Instructional Design	The process of instructional design is concerned with the planning, design, development, implementation, and evaluation of instructional activities or events. The purpose of the discipline of instructional design is to build theoretical frameworks and knowledge about the steps in the development of instruction.
Instructivism	An approach to, and underlying philosophy of, education that is characterized by delivery of knowledge from the teacher to the students (contrast to constructivism).
Interaction	Interaction is defined in a number of ways. It is the reciprocal actions between humans or between a human and an object including a computer or other electronic device that allows a two-way flow of information between it and a user responding immediately to the latter's input.
Just-In-Time Training (JIT)	JIT training is usually on-the-job and can provide gains due to the training being received precisely when it is required to perform a new task. Also, there is reduced disruption to working hours. If the training materials are encapsulated in, and delivered by, a learning technology, as they can be available for reinforcement when and where it is needed. However, due to the absence of the instructor or trainer, to immediately interact with learners, the technology must be able to facilitate the complete learning experience or at least provide direction to the location of answers to learners' queries. JIT training is often a form of e-learning.
Learner	Learner is a generic term to describe the person learning, rather than the more specific terms such as *trainee* and *student*.

Learning	An umbrella term to include training, development, and education, where training is learning that pertains to the job, development is learning for the growth of the individual that is not related to a specific job and education is learning to prepare the individual but not related to a specific job. Learning is often subdivided as intentional and unintentional. Intentional learning refers to classes or programs that a student intentionally attends. Unintentional learning often happens by accident.
Learning Activities	The things learners and facilitators do, within learning events that are intended to bring about the desired learning outcomes.
Learning Event	A session of structured learning such as classes, subjects, courses, and training programs.
Learning Management System (LMS)	(Also known as virtual learning environment, course management system, and managed learning environment.) A Web-based system for the implementation, assessment and tracking of learners through learning events. Typically, LMSs consist of a number of components including, content, interaction applications, and a record of student assessment and progress.
Learning Technologies	Technologies that are used in the process of learning to provide material to learners, to allow learners to interact with it, to host dialogues, and to facilitate the collaborative production of content by and between learners and between learners and facilitators.
Metadata	Data that describe other data. More broadly metadata is information about a particular object (or data set) that may describe details of how it was created and used (see content management systems). Popular standards of metadata are sharable content object reference model (SCORM), instructional management system (IMS), and learning object metadata (LOM).
MP3	Literally, MPEG-1 audio layer-3, this is a standard for compressing audio. It is capable of reducing files sizes by up to a factor of ten. MP3 files have become a popular means of distributing and sharing music files over the Internet.
Multicast	Multicast is an Internet transmission protocol or method whereby a server can send one stream to multiple recipients, rather than individual streams to each recipient. In this way multicast can save on bandwidth and thus transmission costs of streams.
Multipoint	Multipoint is a videoconference term that refers to conferences to which more than two endpoints are connected. Multipoint conferences require a bridging device (often referred to as a multiple conference unit [MCU]) to allow all users to see and hear each other.
Online Learning	Flexible or distance learning containing a component that is accessed via the World Wide Web, often used interchangeably with e-learning.

Open Learning	An approach to intentional learning in which one or more degrees of openness may be offered to students. Open entry refers to the absence of prior qualifications needed to enroll. Openness of entry time and exit time means students can commence and complete courses at times of their choosing. Other aspects of openness are place, time, pace, and other.
Podcast	Podcasting and vodcasting (video podcasting) are systems that use software on a user's computer to automatically download media files. For example, for a student to subscribe to a podcast of lectures for a subject, they copy a URL from the recording Web site to their podcasting software (e.g., iTunes, iPodder, etc.). When they next connect to the Internet the software automatically interrogates the server and downloads any new files. The software they may alert the user. In this way podcasting (or vodcasting) is an automated downloading of media files.
Preproduction, Production, Postproduction	Preproduction refers collectively to those activities in the process of creating video, film, or television programs that occur before production. Production refers to all the activities in the same process that are required to collect the raw footage. Postproduction refers to all the activities that convert the raw footage into the finished product and may include distribution.
Representational Technology	The learning technologies model (LTM) divides learning technologies into two broad groups: representational and collaborative. Representational technologies are those that provide materials to learners and can be thought of as one-way. Collaborative technologies facilitate interactions between students and between students and facilitators. They can be thought of as two-way.
Semantic Web	A project of the World Wide Web Consortium (W3C) and has as a goal the provision of "a common framework that allows data to be shared and reused across application, enterprise and community boundaries." The Semantic Web is about connecting data from different places.
Streaming	Streaming is the playing of video or audio files as they are downloaded from the Internet. Most computers are sold today with software that will play audio and video streams. Apple computers use QuickTime and Windows computers use Windows Media Player. Downloaded files that are of the appropriate format can be played on these as well. For example, MP3 audio and MP4 video can generally be played on Windows Media Player and on QuickTime.
Video Chat Video Telephony	Video chat or video telephony is defined as an application of computer technology that allows two-way audio and video communications between remote parties. Perhaps an appropriate name for this technology is personal computer videoconference (PCVC). Thus video chat can be thought of as videoconference on a computer. Previously referred to as *Web cam* as small Web cameras are generally used.

Videoconference	Videoconference (vcf), sometimes referred to as video-teleconference (vtc) is the technology that allows two-way video and audio communications between remote parties. In videoconference parlance the parties or locations are referred to as *points* or *endpoints*. Videoconference technology is well evolved and often combines two video signals from an endpoint. In this way video of participants can be combined with a presentation such as Power-Point.
Virtual Network Computing (VNC)	VNC is a remote display system that allows a computer desktop to be viewed by other computers. The host computer runs the VNC server and the clients all connect by running a VNC viewer. The software is open source and can facilitate client control of the serving computer. VNC can be used to share computer desktops and hence applications in e-learning.
Web 2.0	There are a number of different descriptions of Web 2.0. Some refer to Web 2.0 as the Web you write to as well as read from. Others refer to Web 2.0 as the Web that serves applications to end users. Perhaps if Web 2.0 is an indication of the direction in which the Web is evolving it is both and maybe more.
Webcasting	Streaming can be of prerecorded materials or of live events. Often recorded lectures are not streamed live due to the increase in technology and expertise required. However, sometimes circumstances warrant live streaming. The occasion might be media worthy or perhaps is a visit by an important subject expert. Streaming of live events is called Webcasting.
Wiki	A Wiki is a Web page that allows users to add and/or edit content on a Web page. Wiki also refers to the software that makes this possible. A popular use of this application is the Wikipedia is an online encyclopedia that allows users to add and edit content.

Appendix II

Bits, Bytes, Definition, and the Measurement of Bandwidth and Storage

Introduction

The advent and spread of computers in our world has changed the way many of us work and play. Computers have had a significant impact on language with many technical terms added to everyday speech on a continuing basis. Thirty years ago very few would have heard and understood terms like hard disc drive, floppy disc, mouse (the device), laptop, and many more. With these changes to language there has been a rising awareness of the computer elements that are measured numerically. From the time of the first personal computers, users have spoken about the size of the computer's memory and since the first connections to the Internet they have spoken of the speed of the connection. Both memory and speed are two criteria that continue to increase as computer power grows. They are measured as the quantity of data stored in the case of memory, and the quantity of data delivered, received, or exchanged in a given amount of time for the case of speed. Both are concerned with data in digital environments.

What are Data?

For computers and other digital devices the simplest form of data is digital, that is, zeros and ones. These are the only digits that make up binary or base-2 arithmetic. Historically, a one could represent a switch turned on and a zero a switch turned off. Today on digital discs such as CDs and DVDs a one or zero can be indicated by a reflection being detected by a sensor. In Figure A1, a greatly magnified cross section of an optical disc (CD or DVD) is shown. In A the laser beam passes through the transparent polycarbonate layer, is reflected by the aluminum and is not detected by the sensor. In B in Figure A1 the laser is detected by the sensor. The *lands* and *pits* that cause the difference in reflection are the way in which information is encoded on a DVD or CD.

The electronics in the DVD or CD player interpret these changes in reflection into one and zeros.

The simplest data are ones and zeros and are referred to as bits, which is a contraction of binary digit. A group of eight bits is used to make up a character, such as a letter of the alphabet and is called a byte. The amount of data in a device is measured in bits and bytes and the speed of transfer of data between devices is measured in bits per second.

Definitions

Bandwidth

Bandwidth is a measure of the volume of data arriving, leaving, or being transferred in a given period of time. Bandwidth is often referred to as speed as slow loading times of files such as Web pages are often the result of low bandwidth and hence *slow* connections. Bandwidth is defined as the number of bits that can be delivered to a device or received from a device in a unit of time. It is normally measured in bits per second (bps or b/s), thousands of bits per second (kilobits per second, kbps, or kb/s), millions of bits per second (megabits per second, Mbps, Mb/s) or trillions of bits per second (gigabits per second, Gbps, Gb/s). No doubt one day bandwidth will be measured in terabits per second or even petabits per second.

Memory

Memory is a measure of the amount of data that can be stored on a device. For some reason, perhaps to indicate the number of characters stored, memory is usually measured in bytes. A kiloByte (KB) is not 1000 bytes but rather 2 to the 10th

Figure A1. Cross section of an optical disc (greatly magnified)

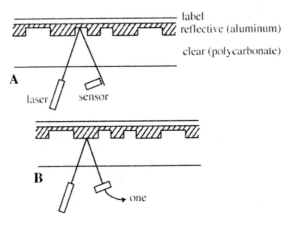

Table A1. Decimal and digital quantifications of memory

Name	Abbrev'n	Amount	Amount
bit	b	1	1
byte	B	8	8
kilo (decimal)	K	10 to the 3rd	1000
kilo (binary)	K	2 to the 10th	1,024
mega (decimal)	M	10 to the 6th	1,000,000
mega (binary)	M	2 to the 20th	1,048,576
giga (decimal)	G	10 to the 9th	1,000,000,000
giga (binary)	G	2 to the 30th	1,073,741,824
tera (decimal)	T	10 to the 12th	1,000,000,000,000
tera (binary)	T	2 to the 40th	1,099,511,627,776
peta (decimal)	P	10 to the 15th	1,000,000,000,000,000
peta (binary)	P	2 to the 50th	1,125,899,906,842,624

power bytes or 1024 bytes. Likewise the mega, giga and tera prefixes refer to 2 to the 20th, 30th, and 40th powers not 10 to the 6th, 9th, and 12th.

Traditionally bits and bytes were both measured using the binary definitions. However, there is some confusion as some manufacturers label storage devices as containing a quantity of gigabytes or terabytes, that when analyzed indicate that the manufacturer has used the decimal interpretation. Table A1 indicates the values and it is only in the higher memory devices that the difference between the decimal and digital definitions of memory exceeds 10%.

Bandwidth Examples

In the early days of the Internet the bandwidth of connections was limited and measured in *baud* which was an indication of the number of times the signal changed in a second, it should not be confused with bits per seconds. Before broadband connections to the Internet were common, dial-up connections were used with designated modem speeds of 14Kbps, 28Kbps, and 56Kbps. Usually, the actual connection speed was lower than the rated speed of the modem.

Today in the age of broadband the connection speed is sometimes asymmetric, that is, the speed with which data are received is different to the speed with which they are transmitted. For example, an asymmetrical digital subscriber line (ADSL) 256/512 connection is rated as having the capability of receiving 512Kbps while being able to transmit only 256Kbps. There are several standards for ADSL and DSL connections and the newer ADSL2 and ADSL2+ promise speeds of up to almost 25Mbps. ADSL and DSL connections have been limited by proximity to the telephone exchange of the provider. Newer technologies have been discussed in the press that extend the reach of conventional DSL and increase the bandwidth up to 250Mbps but at the time of writing the bandwidth decreases quickly as distance from the exchange increases. Of course there are other broadband solutions such as satellite that are available to users in remote or regional areas.

Storage Devices

Storage devices have been around since the first electronic computers and have increased in capacity at an exponential rate for the past 20 years. At the same time they have decreased in physical size. In the 1980s a 3 and ¼" diskette held 1.4 MB of data. In the early years of the 21st century diskettes are all but obsolete and many small devices such as portable hard disc drives (HDD), CD-ROMs, DVDs, USB memory sticks (sometimes called flash memory), and MP3 players such as iPods are used to store data.

HDDs are located in most computers or can be dedicated external devices. Their sizes can range from less than 100 GB to 1 or 2 TB. HDDs are re-writeable. On the other hand CD-ROMs and DVDs can be either re-writeable or write once read many (WORM).

Compact disc read only memory (CD-ROMs) have replaced diskettes as removable storage devices that could store more than the 1.44 MB. Originally the capacity of CD-ROMs was 650 MB, but this has increased up to 800MB with recent technological developments.

USB memory has become a convenient way to move files from one device to another. USB memory is compact and can be used to store up to 5GB of data (at the time of writing). iPods and other MP3 players, like most computer equipment have been increasing in capacity. The first iPods were launched in 2001 and stored 5 or 10GB of MP3 tunes. Later, models could be used as removable storage devices as well as MP3 players, and in early 2007 the top of the range iPods had 80GB capacity.

While DVDs were first introduced as a way to store movies for television at a higher quality than VHS tape they are now used for the storage of computer data as well. Most recent computers contain a DVD drive that allows the reading and writing of data to and from DVDs. Initially DVDs were single layer and single sided. However this limited the quantity of data that could be stored. Double-sided DVDs were released but today they are comparatively rare as there is little room to include disc identification (label). Double layer DVDs provided an answer as they allowed almost double the capacity of single layer DVDs while maintaining one side available for labeling. Of course double sided, double layered DVDs would provide even greater storage space but these are rather rare. Table A2 compares the available storage capacities for the different DVD configurations.

The second generation of DVD has recently arrived and unfortunately there are two competing formats, Blu-ray and HD DVD. Like DVD both of the new formats use the same principles of a laser and reflection. Both formats use smaller lands and pits and spiral tracks that are more tightly wound than on DVD. This is how they can store more information on a disc of the same diameter. However, the finer the information stored the more susceptible the discs may be to damage or dirt. The formats are not compatible as they use different sized lands and pits as well as differently pitched tracks. They are both available as dual layer and there has been some mention of double sided discs. As Blu-ray uses smaller lands and pits and has a tighter spiral track more information can be encoded on it. Table A3 compares the capacities of Blu-ray and HD DVD.

Table A2. DVD configurations and storage capacity

Configuration	Available Storage
Single-sided single layer	4.7GB
Double-sided single layer	9.4GB
Single-sided double layer	8.5GB
Double-sided double layer	17GB

Table A3. Blu-ray and HD-DVD capacities

	Blu-ray	HD-DVD
Single layer	25GB	15GB
Double layer	50GB	30GB

Standard, Low, and High Definition Video

Since its inception one-way video technology has gradually increased in the quality of the pictures and sounds delivered by broadcast or media. The change from VHS tape to DVD saw a major stepping up of quality and the change to HD DVD or Blu-ray is another leap forward in the quality of pictures and sounds. However, in the past the limiting factor was the television standards to which most domestic television and video equipment was designed. New standards for high definition television (HDTV) are emerging although many countries are yet to confirm the details. The advent of HDTV has been made possible by the change from analogue to digital television recording and broadcasting. In HDTV, as well as an increase in the number of picture elements that make up the picture, the aspect ratio has changed from four by three (4:3) to sixteen by nine (16:9), which is closer to the aspect ratios of most modern movies. In Australia the PAL standard dictated that the maximum picture for standard definition television was 720 picture elements (or pixels) wide and 576 high. This upper limit of standard definition picture quality has been removed with the inception of HDTV. While in Australia there appear to be several emerging standards and many different resolution screens available, it appears that the standard for HD will include pictures that are 1920 pixels wide by 1080 pixels high and pictures that are 1024 by 768. Another change that leads to better quality is the change from interlaced pictures to progressively scanned ones. Television and video monitors build pictures by assembling horizontal rows or lines of pixels. Thus most standard definition PAL monitors display approximately 576 lines. In the NTSC standard, video pictures consist of 30 frames per second. Interlaced frames consist of two fields, sequentially displayed, one containing the odd numbered lines and the other the even. In this way the lines contained in two fields are interlaced to form one complete frame. Interlacing can lead to flickering images and poor treatment of hard diagonal lines. A clearer picture can be obtained by scanning all lines in a progressive manner. Hence we see video signals, televisions, and monitors rated at a number of lines and the letter i or p to designate interlaced or progressive scan.

While the trend to HD has seen many households replace their televisions with wide and flat high-resolution screens, there has also been remarkable growth in low definition video. This has occurred as a result of two technologies: mobile phones

Table A4. Examples of low, standard, and HD video

Definition	Low	Standard	High
Typical picture dimensions (pixels)	320 x 240	640 x 480 (NTSC) 720 x 576 (PAL)	1920 x 1080 (HD NTSC) 1280 x 720
Examples	YouTube	Analogue television	HDTV

with inbuilt video cameras and online sharing of video. The standards for these technologies are somewhat flexible but both use small images. For example, at the time of writing, the most popular online video-sharing site is YouTube. YouTube allows users to upload video, which can then be seen by anyone with a networked computer and sufficient bandwidth. YouTube recommends video files with a picture size of 320 by 240 pixels. So at the same time there appears to be divergence in the quality of video towards high definition for viewing off-air and off-media and towards low definition for video viewed off the Internet (see Table A4).

Transmission Methods

Just as there are different ways in which data are stored there are different ways by which they are transferred between devices. The different ways can have different speeds of transfer. Earlier USB memory was discussed. It is called USB memory as it uses a USB connector to plug into a computer.

USB is a common format of connector for modern computers and is often used to connect keyboards, mice, and devices like digital cameras. There are two USB transmission standards and there has been some talk about a possible third. The first USB standard theoretically can transfer data at speeds up to 12Mbps. USB 2.0, completely overhauled the first standard and is capable of transfer speeds of up to 480Mbps. Although the capacity of both standards is far higher, many devices such as keyboards, mice and joysticks communicate with computers via USB 2.0 or USB 1.0 at up to 1.5Mbps.

Firewire is another way in which data can be transferred between devices. Firewire is Apple's name for the IEEE1394 standard and the name has gained a high degree of popular usage. Firewire is a high-speed communications method and has replaced parallel SCSI in many applications. Sony calls this iLink and it is commonly used for connections between video cameras and computers, as it allows control of the camera by the computer as well as a download channel. It has been adopted by High Definition Audio-Video Network Alliance (HANA) as a standard for audio-visual component communications and control and almost all modern video camcorders and many computers are equipped with it.

There are two basic firewire standards:

- Firewire 400 with nominal transfer rates of 100, 200 and 400Mbps, and
- Firewire 800 with transfer speeds of up to 800Mbps.

However the standard also includes a further protocol (IEEE1394b) with transfer speeds of up to 3.2Gbps

While there is much that cannot be predicted with computer technology, it is reasonably certain that, for the same price the next new computer a user buys will have the capacity to store more data and to communicate at a higher speed. The standards that are mentioned here are also in a state of flux with new standards being written as the needs for more storage and speed increases.

About the Editor

Richard Caladine is the manager of Learning Facilities and Technologies at University of Wollongong, Australia. He is responsible for the operation of University of Wollongong's audiovisual and rich media educational systems. These include a videoconference service consisting of 32 endpoints and a 40–port, videoconference bridge that connects the seven New South Wales (NSW) campuses of the university. He is also responsible for the podcasting, Webcasting, and streaming services. He is actively involved with the training of staff in the pedagogically appropriate use of these systems and other educational technologies. Since 1994 he has researched the use of rich media in higher education, has published many papers, book chapters, and books, all on the appropriate pedagogical use of educational technologies. Dr. Caladine's PhD is in the area of educational technology and he supervises postgraduate students in the area of learning, innovation, and future technologies. Dr. Caladine regularly speaks at international conferences, symposia, and forums about the pedagogically appropriate application and future of learning technologies. His other interests include surfing, bushwalking, photography, and he regularly enters paintings and drawings in competitions. He is a foundation member of the Illawarra Ukulele Club.

Index